This excellent publication on sustainability accounting and integrated reporting has been edited by two senior academics in the field. The various chapters provide interesting insights into sustainability accounting and integrated reporting starting from voluntary external disclosure, stakeholder engagement, organizational focus and finally, assurance. The book testifies that the notion of integrated reporting and sustainability accounting is vibrant and offers various perspectives about and to organisations and society to manage and disclose valuable capital, other than just financial capital. This book is a valuable step for anyone who wishes to participate in dialogs about sustainability accounting and integrated reporting theoretically and practically. A must for scholars, students, practitioners and policy makers who are working in these areas.

—Professor James Guthrie, *Distinguished Professor of Accounting, Department of Accounting & Corporate Governance, Macquarie University*

Sustainability Accounting and Integrated Reporting

Sustainability Accounting and Integrated Reporting deals with organizations' assessment, articulation, and disclosure of their social and environmental impact on various groups in society.

There is increasingly an understanding that financial information does not sufficiently discharge organizational accountability to members of society who are demanding an account of the social and environmental impacts of companies' and other organizations' activities. As a result, organizations report ever more social and environmental information, and there are simultaneous movements towards providing the information in an integrated fashion, showing how social and environmental activities influence each other, members of society and the financial aims of the organization.

The book *Sustainability Accounting and Integrated Reporting* provides a broad and comprehensive review of the field, focusing on the interconnection between different elements of these topics, often dealt with in isolation. The book examines the accounting involved in the collection and analysis of data, control processes over the data, how information is reported to external parties, and the assurance of the information being reported. The book thereby provides an overview useful to practitioners (including sustainability managers, consultants, members of the accounting profession, and other assurance providers), academics, and students.

Charl DE VILLIERS is a professor of accounting, Graduate School of Management, The University of Auckland, New Zealand, where his research interests include sustainability accounting and integrated reporting. He is also a professor at the University of Pretoria, an adjunct professor at several other South African universities, and a research fellow at the Centre for Sustainability Management, Leuphana University Lüneburg, Germany. Charl has more than 250 research based publications and presentations, including over 60 articles in refereed journals, including in *Accounting, Organisations and Society; Journal of Management; European Accounting Review; Accounting, Auditing & Accountability Journal; Journal of Accounting and Public Policy; Accounting and Business Research; Accounting & Finance;* and *British Accounting Review*. Charl is the editor-in-chief of *Meditari Accountancy Research* and serves on the editorial board of several other research journals.

Warren MAROUN is a professor at the School of Accountancy, University of the Witwatersrand. His research interests include: corporate reporting, integrated reporting, external audit and corporate governance with a specific focus on the functioning of mechanisms of accountability. Warren has published over 30 journal articles, including in *Accounting, Auditing & Accountability Journal; British Accounting Review; Accounting Forum;* and *International Journal of Auditing*. He has also produced technical and practitioner-focused reports for the Association of Certified Chartered Accountants and the South African Institute of Chartered Accountants. Warren holds a PhD from King's College London.

Finance, Governance and Sustainability: Challenges to Theory and Practice
Series Editor:
Professor Güler Aras, *Yildiz Technical University, Turkey;
Georgetown University, Washington DC, USA*

For a full list of titles in this series, please visit www.routledge.com/Finance-Governance-and-Sustainability/book-series/FINGOVSUST

Focusing on the studies of academicians, researchers, entrepreneurs, policy makers and government officers, this international series aims to contribute to the progress in matters of finance, good governance and sustainability. These multidisciplinary books combine strong conceptual analysis with a wide range of empirical data and a wealth of case materials. They will be of interest to those working in a multitude of fields, across finance, governance, corporate behaviour, regulations, ethics and sustainability.

Sustainable Governance in Hybrid Organizations
An International Case Study of Water Companies
Linne Marie Lauesen

Transforming Governance
New Values, New Systems in the New Business Environment
Edited by Maria Aluchna and Guler Aras

Strategy, Structure and Corporate Governance
Nabyla Daidj

Corporate Behavior and Sustainability
Doing Well by Being Good
Edited by Güler Aras and Coral Ingley

Corporate Social Responsibility and Sustainable Development
Social Capital and Corporate Development in Developing Economies
Risa Bhinekawati

Cosmopolitan Business Ethics
Towards a Global Ethos of Management
Jacob Dahl Rendtorff

Sustainability Accounting and Integrated Reporting
Edited by Charl DE VILLIERS and Warren Maroun

Sustainability Accounting and Integrated Reporting

Edited by Charl DE VILLIERS
and Warren MAROUN

Routledge
Taylor & Francis Group

LONDON AND NEW YORK

First published 2018 by Routledge

2 Park Square, Milton Park, Abingdon, Oxfordshire OX14 4RN
52 Vanderbilt Avenue, New York, NY 10017

Routledge is an imprint of the Taylor & Francis Group, an informa business

First issued in paperback 2019

British Library Cataloguing-in-Publication Data
A catalogue record for this book is available from the British Library

Library of Congress Cataloging-in-Publication Data
Names: De Villiers, Charl, editor. | Maroun, Warren, editor.
Title: Sustainability accounting and integrated reporting / edited by
    Charl de Villiers and Warren Maroun.
Description: 1st Edition. | New York : Routledge, 2018. | Series: Finance,
    governance and sustainability: challenges to theory and practice |
    Includes bibliographical references.
Identifiers: LCCN 2017034778 | ISBN 9781138091412 (hardback) |
    ISBN 9781315108032 (ebook)
Subjects: LCSH: Sustainable development reporting. | Environmental
    management. | Social responsibility of business.
Classification: LCC HD60.3 .S873 2018 | DDC 658.4/083—dc23
LC record available at https://lccn.loc.gov/2017034778

ISBN: 978-1-138-09141-2 (hbk)
ISBN: 978-0-367-88946-3 (pbk)

Typeset in Bembo
by Apex CoVantage, LLC

Contents

Figures

Tables

Contributors

Binh BUI, Victoria University Wellington, New Zealand

Dr Binh Bui has research expertise in the fields of sustainability accounting and climate change.

Muhammad Bilal FAROOQ, Auckland University of Technology, New Zealand

Dr Muhammad Bilal Farooq has research expertise in the fields of sustainability accounting and assurance.

Pei-Chi Kelly HSIAO, The University of Auckland, New Zealand

Kelly Hsiao has research expertise in the field of integrated reporting.

Sumit LODHIA, University of South Australia, Australia

Associate Professor Sumit Lodhia is director of the Centre for Sustainability Governance (CSG), where he leads research focused on sustainability accounting, reporting, and governance.

1 Introduction to sustainability accounting and integrated reporting

Charl DE VILLIERS

The University of Auckland, and University of Pretoria

Warren MAROUN

University of the Witwatersran

Abstract

The practice of sustainability accounting has evolved on a voluntary basis because of a need for information, pressure for more transparent reporting, and a need for companies to explain their business models in more detail. Disclosure frameworks evolved first as industry initiatives to deflect criticism, and later as independent initiatives as pressure groups saw through the often-superficial industry initiatives and demanded broader accountability. The Global Reporting Initiative (GRI) standards are now the most widely used of these independent frameworks. The GRI standards require a process of stakeholder identification, followed by a stakeholder engagement process to identify material social and environmental matters that should be covered in disclosure. Integrated reporting can be seen as the latest development in the reporting of social and environmental matters. A framework and a brief overview of the rest of the book is provided.

Introduction

This book will provide an overview of sustainability accounting and integrated reporting, including its background; what we can learn from different theoretical perspectives that have been applied to this practice, especially around the question of why organizations choose to disclose; the information stakeholders require; what happens to reporting after a crisis; other determinants of disclosure; the consequences of disclosure; disclosures by public sector and not-for-profit organizations; the management control systems that underpin reporting; and the assurance of sustainability and integrated reporting.

For much of the 20th century, reporting and the accounting systems that supports it were explained as a rational technical development driven by the information needs of the capital market (Watts and Zimmerman 1976; Watts and Zimmerman 1978; Hopwood 1987). Changes in social norms during the 1960s and 1970s brought different pressures to bear on companies and other organizations, including demands for greater social and environmental accountability. This led to a broader conceptualization of the nature of accounting, starting in the 1980s. Using theories drawn from sociology, psychology and political science, researchers started to explain accounting as a dynamic social construction and more than just a neutral information processing system (Burchell et al. 1980; Cooper 1980; Hoskin and Macve 1986; Hopwood 1987). Of particular interest for this book is the realization that corporate reporting could provide an 'account' to interested constituents and that the conventional accounting system could be expanded to include more than just reporting on financial matters (Hopwood 1987; Gray et al. 1995). The emergence of different types of non-financial or environmental, social and governance (ESG)[1] reporting can, therefore, be seen as a practice driven by stakeholder demands and pressures, and a need for organizations to respond to these pressures by explaining their social and environmental impacts. These voluntary disclosure initiatives have, in some jurisdictions, led to regulations that mandate social and environmental disclosures.

Theoretical perspectives

The conventional view at the heart of early mainstream accounting research was that a company's goal is to maximize profit for shareholders. This position was challenged and replaced with a more inclusive model, which stresses that a company is accountable to a broad group of stakeholders rather than only its shareholders (Solomon 2010). The result is that companies cannot focus only on generating financial returns for the benefit of debt and equity providers. A company operates according to a social licence which necessitates the management of ESG-related concerns and expectations to ensure stakeholders' continued support and in turn, an organization's ability to continue as a going concern (De Villiers and Barnard 2000; Deegan 2002; Atkins and Maroun 2015).

From this perspective, early forms of ESG reporting and the emergence of codified non-financial reporting standards, can be explained as a product of underlying stakeholder pressures and the desire to gain and maintain organizational legitimacy. As ESG reporting gained prominence from the 1980s onwards, social scientists have argued that its function in the contemporary business practice has increasingly become taken for granted (De Villiers and Alexander 2014). This has contributed to the institutionalization of many codes of best practice dealing with different aspects of non-financial reporting and has provided further impetus for the proliferation of what is now referred to as sustainability and integrated reporting.

A stream of research deals with the economic determinants and consequences of different types of non-financial disclosures. These involve establishing relationships between the levels of non-financial disclosures and: economic performance and firm value (for recent examples, see Cahan et al. 2016; De Klerk and De Villiers 2012; De Klerk et al. 2015; Marcia et al. 2015; De Villiers and Marques 2016); organizational processes (Churet and Eccles 2014); quality of management (Churet and Eccles 2014); and information asymmetry (De Klerk and De Villiers 2012). This body of work is based on the business case for non-financial reporting and agency theory.

A critical reader may note that the term 'sustainability reporting' is used in this book as a synonym or collective term for social and environmental reporting; corporate social responsibility reporting; environmental, social and governance reporting; integrated reporting and other forms of so-called non-financial reporting.

Inconsistent use of terms (and definitions for these types of reporting) suggest that 'sustainability' accounting is often not about enhancing sustainability, but about the disclosure of information that relates to social and environmental sustainability and portrays, for example, enhanced eco-efficiency. The critical perspective that sustainability reporting may have been captured by powerful organizations as a method to deal with stakeholder pressure and that capitalism, a masculine orientation, business competitiveness, and the role of accounting in these processes may actually undermine true sustainability is not explored in depth in this book.

Sustainability reporting

Sustainability reporting has a long history (De Villiers et al. 2014a). For example, Lewis et al. (1984) find evidence of an early form of financial accounting to employees dating to 1917. There are also examples of basic forms of corporate social responsibility (CSR) reporting by an American steel and an Australian mining company in their corporate reports issued in the late 1890s and early 1900s (Hogner 1982; Guthrie and Parker 1989). Increased disclosures often followed stakeholder pressure, which intensified following social or environmental incidents, such as major oil spills (Patten 1992; Summerhays and De Villiers 2012). Stakeholders were not always appeased by the additional disclosures, as they were aware that organizations could use these disclosures to emphasize positive and ignore negative aspects. In order to enhance the credibility of their social and environmental disclosures, companies formed organizations that purported to independently determine what companies within that industry should report. Companies could then subscribe to these 'independent' bodies' disclosure frameworks. Of course, sophisticated stakeholders soon saw through these tactics. Truly independent bodies, each with their own social and environmental disclosure framework, sprang up, providing a broader choice of frameworks for companies. Framework providers vied for a period to be the most relevant and credible. The most widely used framework today is the standards issued by the Global Reporting Initiative (GRI) (KPMG 2015).

Sustainability reporting is now commonplace, with most of the world's largest companies disclosing sustainability information (KPMG 2015; Hughen et al. 2014). Where these companies specify a framework, most mention the GRI (KPMG 2015). Governmental and non-governmental organizations often also disclose sustainability information and use the GRI framework.

The GRI does not define 'sustainability', directly but its guidelines point to a three-dimensional model based on an organization's economic, environmental and social impact (Lamberton 2005). According to the GRI (2016, p. 3), its standards:

> create a common language for organizations and stakeholders, with which the economic, environmental, and social impacts of organizations can be communicated and understood. The Standards are designed to enhance the global comparability and quality of information on these impacts, thereby enabling greater transparency and accountability of organizations.

The GRI's guidelines consist of universal and topic-specific standards. The former provide core reporting principles (GRI 100); recommend general disclosures

designed to provide context about an organization (GRI 102); and provide guidance on how to deal with material issues, which are managed and reported on
using topic-specific standards (GRI 103). These include GRI 200, GRI 300 and
GRI 400, which deal with reporting on an organization's economic, environmental

Table 1.1 Analysis of sustainability accounting and reporting

Attribute, characteristic or theme	*Discussion*
Socially constructed and varied meaning	There is no single definition of 'sustainability' and how the concept should be applied in a corporate reporting and management context (Milne and Patten 2002; Lamberton 2005). The GRI uses a three-dimensional model (as explained above), but academics have also considered sustainability at the ecological level (Jones and Solomon 2013; Mansoor and Maroun 2015), the emancipatory potential of sustainability reporting (Dillard and Reynolds 2008; Atkins et al. 2015) and sustainability as part of a broader integrated business philosophy (Eccles and Krzus 2010; Atkins and Maroun 2015).
Indicator-driven	An organization's sustainability cannot be measured directly (Lamberton 2005). As a result, sustainability reporting requires disclosures on various indicators or metrics which, collectively, and using the GRI's concept of sustainability, provide an account of an organization's economic, environmental and social impact (GRI 2016). Exactly which indicators need to be reported, the emphasis placed on each and how the interconnection between indicators is explained are hotly debated issues (Gray et al. 1995; Lamberton 2005).
Multiple measurement bases	Unlike financial reporting, sustainability reporting is inherently qualitative. Some organizations provide quantified measures of economic, environmental and social outcomes, but this is usually complemented with qualitative disclosures, narrative information and diagrams/images (Thomson and Bebbington 2005; Michelon et al. 2015).
Interdisciplinary practice	Reporting on financial and non-financial metrics requires an interdisciplinary perspective of a firm (Lamberton 2005). In particular, detailed reporting on social and environmental metrics can require specialized knowledge and experience.
Dependent on accounting principles and practices	High-quality reporting will require an organization to identify sustainability indicators, collect data and analyse the data to prepare a sustainability report. This requires effective reporting infrastructure, controls and reporting protocols similar to the conventional financial reporting system (Alrazi et al. 2015; McNally et al. 2017).
Inherently limited	While the GRI represents an important development in the sustainability reporting movement, it is not without limitations (Lamberton 2005). Academics have raised concerns that sustainability reporting often amounts to rhetoric and that the changes needed at the operational and strategic level to ensure long-term sustainability are lacking (Bebbington et al. 2009; Milne et al. 2009; Tregidga et al. 2014).

and social impacts respectively (GRI 2016). The GRI standards require the identification of stakeholders, followed by a stakeholder engagement process to identify
material social and environmental matters that should be covered in disclosure.

Whereas much of the development of non-financial disclosure has been voluntary, changes in stakeholder expectations over time have led to increased regulations. For example, an EU directive requires firms with more than 500 employees
to provide certain social and environmental disclosures, starting in 2017, and the
Johannesburg Stock Exchange requires that South African–listed companies provide an integrated report or explain why they do not (De Villiers et al. 2017).

The prior academic research identifies different attributes or characteristics
of sustainability accounting and reporting and related themes. These are outlined in Table 1.1.

Integrated reporting

Integrated reporting can be seen as the most recent development in sustainability
reporting (De Villiers et al. 2014b; De Villiers et al. 2017). The recently issued framework on integrated reporting is the result of the efforts of the International Integrated Reporting Council (IIRC), the Integrated Reporting Committee of South
Africa (IRCSA), the GRI, the World Business Council for Sustainable Development, the World Resources Institute, the Carbon Disclosure Project and the UN
Global Compact (IRCSA 2011; De Villiers et al. 2014b; Atkins and Maroun 2015).
The IIRC states that the primary purpose of an integrated report is to:

> explain to providers of financial capital how an organization creates value
> over time. An integrated report benefits all stakeholders interested in an
> organization's ability to create value over time, including employees, cus-
> tomers, suppliers, business partners, local communities, legislators, regula-
> tors and policy-makers.
>
> (IIRC 2013, p. 4)

Like sustainability reporting under the GRI, integrated reporting has been subject to criticism. Some are concerned that the emphasis placed on providers of
debt and equity will limit a genuine commitment to social and environmental
responsibility (Flower 2015; Thomson 2015). This is supported by the fact that
while integrated reporting has been associated with an increase in the extent of
ESG-related disclosures, the first sets of integrated reports often contain generic
and repetitive information (Solomon and Maroun 2012; Stent and Dowler 2015;
Raemaekers et al. 2016). Preliminary research – based mainly in Australia –
also challenges the extent to which integrated reporting will result in the
reforms to business processes and strategies necessary to drive real sustainability
(Brown and Dillard 2014; Higgins et al. 2014; Stubbs and Higgins 2014).

Nevertheless, integrated reporting has the potential to become the primary
means for organizations to communicate with stakeholders. The IIRC issued
its integrated reporting framework in 2013, and over 100 companies are already
participating in a global pilot study (in collaboration with different networks of

investors) on the new reporting format (DeVilliers et al. 2014b). In South Africa, the decision has been taken to require listed companies to prepare an integrated report or provide clear reasons for not doing so, with the result that integrated reporting is effectively mandatory for large South African corporations (Atkins and Maroun 2015).While this is not the case in other jurisdictions, many of the principles in the IIRC's framework are already being applied by companies in the USA, the European Union and Australia (Massie 2010; DeVilliers et al. 2014b; Dumay et al. 2017; Guthrie et al. 2017). Research on the state of integrated reporting in South Africa, widely accepted as a pioneer in this area, also suggests that companies are beginning to internalize the provisions of the IIRC's framework and provide higher-quality reporting on sustainability indictors.

For example, Atkins and Maroun (2015) and PwC (2014, 2015) found that South African companies are beginning to understand that their integrated reports are a vehicle for providing stakeholders with a more balanced perspective on how value is being generated. As part of this, the links between ESG metrics, strategy and risk – while still requiring improvement – are starting to become more apparent. There are also signs that systems and processes necessary for ensuring valid and reliable reporting on financial and non-financial performance are beginning to take shape (Maroun 2017). Consequently, while integrated reporting is still in its developmental stage, it has the potential to bolster confidence in the South African capital market (Maroun et al. 2014; Atkins and Maroun 2015; King 2016) and provide value-relevant information for investors and other stakeholders (Zhou et al. 2017).

Framework of sustainability accounting and integrated reporting influences

The framework shown in Figure 1.1 is adapted from Alrazi et al.'s (2015) framework, relating to environmental accounting and reporting to the broader concepts of sustainability accounting and integrated reporting. According to this framework, sustainability and integrated reporting, as well as the assurance of these reports, form part of accountability. Accountability influences an organization's legitimacy (arrow 1). Sustainability and integrated reporting are dependent on the information provided and managed by sustainability accounting, sustainability management control systems and stakeholder engagement (arrow 2). Several other factors, labelled "determinants" in this framework, influence sustainability accounting and integrated reporting (arrow 7). This framework sets the stage for a discussion of the treatment of these concepts in the rest of this book.

Overview of sustainability accounting and integrated reporting as covered in this book

Chapter 1 has introduced the practice of sustainability and integrated reporting, recounting its evolution as a result of stakeholder pressure to disclose more social and environmental information, and the need for organizations to explain their impacts. Disclosure frameworks evolved to enable organizations to claim

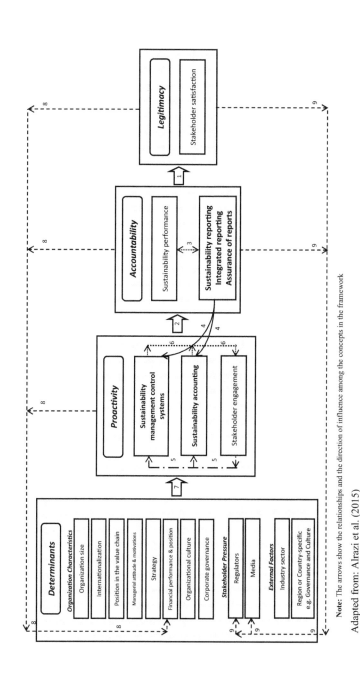

Note: The arrows show the relationships and the direction of influence among the concepts in the framework

Adapted from: Alrazi et al. (2015)

Figure 1.1 Framework of sustainability accounting and integrated reporting influences

that their disclosure complied with best practice, with the Global Reporting Initiative now being the most important player.

Chapter 2 introduces integrated reporting in more depth, originating as a voluntary corporate reporting practice before the IIRC was formed to promote it as a better way of understanding and communication organizations' future value creation plans, while paying particular attention to integrating non-financial information, such as social and environmental disclosures, into financial disclosures.

Chapters 3 to 5 discuss why organizations disclose sustainability information, including the use of integrated reports, using three different theoretical perspectives: legitimacy theory, institutional theory and institutional work and agency theory. Legitimacy theory (Chapter 3) regards voluntary disclosures as a method of maintaining and repairing legitimacy to ensure continued access to resources. Organizations can use disclosures in an attempt to alter values and expectations, manage perceptions or explain how they have adapted and conformed. Institutional theory (Chapter 4) sees voluntary disclosures as a response to the social pressures organizations encounter, and predicts that disclosure solutions are likely to converge over time for organizations that encounter similar pressures. The term 'decoupling' is applied to situations where organizations' actions and disclosures are contradictory. Contrary to institutional theory, the concept of institutional work acknowledges that individuals (especially professionals) have the capacity to create, maintain and disrupt institutions. By taking an agency theory approach, Chapter 5 continues the theme of focusing on managers' motivations for disclosures. Managers (agents) know more about companies' operations than the shareholders (principals), a phenomenon known as information asymmetry. Managers would be reluctant to reveal bad news voluntarily but will have to disclose the reasons for bad news that is already known to the market, or likely to become known. Managers are likely to disclose good news voluntarily to maximize their income.

Chapter 6 explores stakeholder sustainability information needs. Investors need sustainability information in order to fully understand companies' future prospects, including future cash flows and the associated risks. Therefore, the entire investment industry now uses sustainability information. Managers, employees, auditors, customers, pressure groups (for example, environmental groups) and the media have all been shown to demand sustainability information. Stakeholders tend to rely on corporate sustainability and integrated reports for periodic assessments, referring to organizational websites for current information as important matters, such as environmental crises, unfold.

Several environmental and social challenges give rise to threats to legitimacy and prompt companies to adopt different reporting strategies either to maintain or to repair legitimacy. Chapter 7 deals with crises as determinants of voluntary sustainability and integrated reporting, and Chapter 8 deals with other determinants, including: company-specific features such as size, strategic attitude, organizational culture and financial performance; external forces (including industry characteristics and geographical location); and stakeholder pressures. In Chapter 9, the focus shifts to the consequences of sustainability or integrated reporting, including providing more accountability; enhancing legitimacy; improving profitability/performance; reducing information asymmetry; and enhancing governance.

The public and not-for-profit sector form an important part of the global economy, and Chapter 10 discusses the drivers of sustainability and integrated reporting in this sector and deals with the challenges involved. Chapter 11 examines the role played by sustainability management control systems (MCSs) in supporting sustainability reporting and sustainability strategy, proposing a sustainability MCS framework for both formal and informal controls. MCSs can be used for operational and strategic purposes.

Chapter 12 deals with the external assurance of sustainability and integrated reports, which is used as a method to enhance the credibility of the reports among stakeholders. Accounting professionals see assurance as an opportunity to extend their services into new territory.

Chapter 13 concludes the book with a discussion of the likely future of the practice of and research around sustainability accounting and integrated reporting, which of course includes reporting, management control systems and assurance. Many of these practices have become institutionalized and taken for granted as a requirement, leading to renewed interest from the research community. In future, these trends are likely to continue.

Note

1 We use the term non-financial reporting and ESG reporting interchangeably to refer to the different forms of reporting which are not concerned primarily with reporting on financial position and performance.

References

Alrazi, B., De Villiers, C. and van Staden, C. J., 2015. A comprehensive literature review on, and the construction of a framework for, environmental legitimacy, accountability and proactivity. *Journal of Cleaner Production*, 102, 44–57.

Atkins, J., Atkins, B., Thomson, I. and Maroun, W., 2015. 'Good' news from nowhere: imagining utopian sustainable accounting. *Accounting, Auditing & Accountability Journal*, 28 (5), 651–670.

Atkins, J. and Maroun, W., 2015. Integrated reporting in South Africa in 2012: perspectives from South African institutional investors. *Meditari Accountancy Research*, 23 (2), 197–221.

Bebbington, J., Higgins, C. and Frame, B., 2009. Initiating sustainable development reporting: evidence from New Zealand. *Accounting, Auditing & Accountability Journal*, 22 (4), 588–625.

Brown, J. and Dillard, J., 2014. Integrated reporting: on the need for broadening out and opening up. *Accounting, Auditing & Accountability Journal*, 27 (7), 1120–1156.

Burchell, S., Clubb, C., Hopwood, A., Hughes, J. and Nahapiet, J., 1980. The roles of accounting in organizations and society. *Accounting, Organizations and Society*, 5 (1), 5–27.

Cahan, S., De Villiers, C., Jeter, D., Naiker, V. and Van Staden, C., 2016. Are CSR disclosures value relevant? Cross-country evidence. *European Accounting Review*, 25 (3), 579–611.

Churet, C. and Eccles, R. G., 2014. Integrated reporting, quality of management, and financial performance. *Journal of Applied Corporate Finance*, 26 (1), 56–64.

Cooper, D., 1980. Discussion of towards a political economy of accounting. *Accounting, Organizations and Society*, 5 (1), 161–166.

De Klerk, M. and De Villiers, C., 2012. The value relevance of corporate responsibility reporting: South African evidence. *Meditari Accountancy Research*, 20 (1), 21–38.

De Klerk, M., De Villiers, C. and van Staden, C., 2015. The influence of corporate social responsibility disclosure on share prices: evidence from the United Kingdom. *Pacific Accounting Review*, 27 (2), 208–228.

De Villiers, C. and Alexander, D., 2014. The institutionalisation of corporate social responsibility reporting. *The British Accounting Review*, 46 (2), 198–212.

De Villiers, C. J. and Barnard, P., 2000. Environmental reporting in South Africa from 1994 to 1999: a research note. *Meditari Accountancy Research*, 8 (1), 15–23.

De Villiers, C., Low, M. and Samkin, G., 2014a. The institutionalisation of mining company sustainability disclosures. *Journal of Cleaner Production*, 84, 51–58.

De Villiers, C. and Marques, A., 2016. Corporate social responsibility, country-level predispositions, and the consequences of choosing a level of disclosure. *Accounting and Business Research*, 46 (2), 167–195.

De Villiers, C., Rinaldi, L. and Unerman, J., 2014b. Integrated reporting: insights, gaps and an agenda for future research. *Accounting, Auditing & Accountability Journal*, 27 (7), 1042–1067.

De Villiers, C., Venter, E. and Hsiao, P., 2017. Integrated reporting: background, measurement issues, approaches and an agenda for future research. *Accounting & Finance*.

Deegan, C., 2002. Introduction: the legitimising effect of social and environmental disclosures – a theoretical foundation. *Accounting, Auditing & Accountability Journal*, 15 (3), 282–311.

Dillard, J. and Reynolds, M., 2008. Green Owl and the Corn Maiden. *Accounting, Auditing & Accountability Journal*, 21 (4), 556–579.

Dumay, J., Guthrie, J. and La Torre, M., 2017. Barriers to implementing the international integrated reporting framework: a contemporary academic perspective. *Meditari Accountancy Research*, 25 (4).

Eccles, R. G. and Krzus, M. P., 2010. *One report: integrated reporting for a sustainable strategy*. Hoboken, NJ: Wiley. Published online October 2015, doi:10.1002/9789199960.

Flower, J., 2015. The international integrated reporting council: a story of failure. *Critical Perspectives on Accounting*, 27, 1–17.

Gray, R., Kouhy, R. and Lavers, S., 1995. Corporate social and environmental reporting: a review of the literature and a longitudinal study of UK disclosure. *Accounting, Auditing & Accountability Journal*, 8 (2), 47–77.

GRI, 2016. *Consolidated set of GRI sustainability reporting standards (2016)*. Available: www.globalreporting.org/standards/gri-standards-download-center/?g=ae2e23b8-4958-455c-a9df-ac372d6ed9a8 www.globalreporting.org/reporting/g4/Pages/default.aspx [Accessed 10 February 2017].

Guthrie, J., Manes-Rossi, F. and Orelli, R. L., 2017. Integrated reporting and integrated thinking in Italian public sector organisations. *Meditari Accountancy Research*, 25 (4).

Guthrie, J. and Parker, L. D., 1989. Corporate social reporting: a rebuttal of legitimacy theory. *Accounting and Business Research*, 19 (76), 343–352.

Higgins, C., Stubbs, W. and Love, T., 2014. Walking the talk(s): organisational narratives of integrated reporting. *Accounting, Auditing & Accountability Journal*, 27 (7), 1090–1119.

Hogner, R. H., 1982. Corporate social reporting: eight decades of development at US Steel. *Research in Corporate Performance and Policy*, 4 (1), 243–250.

Hopwood, A. G., 1987. The archaeology of accounting systems. *Accounting, Organizations and Society*, 12 (3), 207–234.

Hoskin, K. W. and Macve, R. H., 1986. Accounting and the examination: a genealogy of disciplinary power. *Accounting, Organizations and Society*, 11 (2), 105–136.

Hughen, L., Lulseged, A. and Upton, D., 2014. Improving stakeholder value through sustainability and integrated reporting. *CPA Journal*, March, 57–61.

IIRC, 2013. *The international framework: integrated reporting.* Available: www.theiirc.org/wp-content/uploads/2013/12/13-12-08-THE-INTERNATIONAL-IR-FRAMEWORK-2-1.pdf [Accessed 1 October 2013].

IRCSA, 2011. *Framework for integrated reporting and the integrated report.* Available: www.sustainabilitysa.org [Accessed 5 June 2012].

Jones, M. J. and Solomon, J. F., 2013. Problematising accounting for biodiversity. *Accounting, Auditing & Accountability Journal*, 26 (5), 668–687.

King, M., 2016. Comments on: *integrated reporting, GARI Conference.* Henley on Thames, UK, 23 October.

KPMG, 2015. *The KPMG survey of corporate responsibility reporting 2015.* Available: https://home.kpmg.com/xx/en/home/insights/2015/11/kpmg-international-survey-of-corporate-responsibility-reporting-2015.html [Accessed 17 May 2017].

Lamberton, G., 2005. Sustainability accounting – a brief history and conceptual framework. *Accounting Forum*, 29 (1), 7–26.

Lewis, N. R., Parker, L. D. and Sutcliffe, P., 1984. Financial reporting to employees: the pattern of development 1919 to 1979. *Accounting, Organizations and Society*, 9 (3–4), 275–289.

Mansoor, H. and Maroun, W., 2015. Biodiversity reporting in the South African food and mining sectors. *In:* 27th International Congress on Social and Environmental Accounting Research, 27 August 2015, Egham, United Kingdom. United Kingodm: Centre for Social and Environmental Accounting Research.

Marcia, A., Maroun, W. and Callaghan, C., 2015. Value relevance and corporate responsibility reporting in the South African context: an alternate view post King-III. *South African Journal of Economic and Management Sciences*, 18 (4), 500–518.

Maroun, W., 2017. Assuring the integrated report: insights and recommendations from auditors and preparers. *The British Accounting Review*, 49 (3), 329–346.

Maroun, W., Coldwell, D. and Segal, M., 2014. SOX and the transition from apartheid to democracy: South African auditing developments through the lens of modernity theory. *International Journal of Auditing*, 18 (3), 206–212.

Massie, R. K., 2010. Accounting and accountability: integrated reporting and the purpose of the firm. *In:* R. G. Eccles, B. Cheng and D. Saltzman, eds. *The landscape of integrated reporting: reflections and next steps.* Cambridge, MA: The President and Fellows of Harvard College Cambridge, 2–8.

McNally, M.-A., Cerbone, D. and Maroun, W., 2017. Exploring the challenges of preparing an integrated report. *Meditari Accountancy Research*, 25 (4), Forthcoming.

Michelon, G., Pilonato, S. and Ricceri, F., 2015. CSR reporting practices and the quality of disclosure: an empirical analysis. *Critical Perspectives on Accounting*, 33, 59–78.

Milne, M. J. and Patten, D. M., 2002. Securing organizational legitimacy: an experimental decision case examining the impact of environmental disclosures. *Accounting, Auditing & Accountability Journal*, 15 (3), 372–405.

Milne, M., Tregidga, H. and Walton, S., 2009. Words not actions! The ideological role of sustainable development reporting. *Accounting, Auditing and Accountability Journal*, 22 (8), 1211–1257.

Patten, D. M., 1992. Intra-industry environmental disclosures in response to the Alaskan oil spill: a note on legitimacy theory. *Accounting, Organizations and Society*, 17 (5), 471–475.

PwC, 2014. *Value creation: the journey continues. a survey of JSE Top-40 companies' integrated reports.* Available: www.pwc.co.za/en/assets/pdf/integrated-reporting-survey-2014.pdf [Accessed 7 August 2015].

PwC, 2015. *Integrated reporting where to next?* Available: www.pwc.co.za/en/assets/pdf/integrated-reporting-survey-2015.pdf [Accessed 16 February 2016].

Raemaekers, K., Maroun, W. and Padia, N., 2016. Risk disclosures by South African listed companies post-King III. *South African Journal of Accounting Research*, 30 (1), 41–60.

Solomon, J., 2010. *Corporate governance and accountability*, 3rd ed. Bognor Regis, UK: John Wiley and Sons.

Solomon, J. and Maroun, W., 2012. *Integrated reporting: the new face of social, ethical and environmental reporting in South Africa?* London: The Association of Chartered Certified Accountants (ACCA). Available: www.researchgate.net/publication/236586863

Stent, W. and Dowler, T., 2015. Early assessments of the gap between integrated reporting and current corporate reporting. *Meditari Accountancy Research*, 23 (1), 92–117.

Stubbs, W. and Higgins, C., 2014. Integrated reporting and internal mechanisms of change. *Accounting, Auditing & Accountability Journal*, 27 (7), 1068–1089.

Summerhays, K. and De Villiers, C., 2012. Oil company annual report disclosure responses to the 2010 Gulf of Mexico Oil Spill. *Journal of the Asia-Pacific Centre for Environmental Accountability*, 18 (2), 103–130.

Thomson, I., 2015. 'But does sustainability need capitalism or an integrated report' a commentary on 'The International Integrated Reporting Council: a story of failure' by Flower, J. *Critical Perspectives on Accounting*, 27, 18–22.

Thomson, I. and Bebbington, J., 2005. Social and environmental reporting in the UK: a pedagogic evaluation. *Critical Perspectives on Accounting*, 16 (5), 507–533.

Tregidga, H., Milne, M. and Kearins, K., 2014. (Re)presenting 'sustainable organizations'. *Accounting, Organizations and Society*, 39 (6), 477–494.

Watts, R. L. and Zimmerman, J. L., 1976. *Positive accounting theory*. Upper Saddle River, NJ: Prentice-Hall.

Watts, R. L. and Zimmerman, J. L., 1978. Towards a positive theory of the determination of accounting standards. *The Accounting Review*, 53 (1), 112–134.

Zhou, S., Simnett, R. and Green, W., 2017. Does integrated reporting matter to the capital market? *Abacus*, 53 (1), 94–132.

2 Integrated reporting

Charl DE VILLIERS
The University of Auckland, and University of Pretoria

Pei-Chi Kelly HSIAO
The University of Auckland

Abstract

Integrated reporting centres on the understanding and communication of an organization's value creation plans by linking financial and sustainability information. It encourages integrated thinking as a new way to conceive of corporate success with the aim of ensuring greater capital market stability and sustainable development. This chapter reviews key milestones of the development of integrated reporting, introduces the International Integrated Reporting Framework and discusses the motivation for and deterrents to integrated reporting, its impact on internal operations and its use and consequences from an external user perspective. Integrated reporting is an evolving concept that faces many challenges.

Introduction

Integrated reporting (IR) is the current frontier in corporate reporting, introducing an alternative perspective to the traditional economic notion of profit maximization by encouraging the assessment of corporate success based on an organization's ability to create sustainable value (De Villiers et al. 2017). IR is a process about changing internal systems and external reporting practices. Managers need to assess the interrelationships between their organization and the external environment and the effects their operations have on the resources used. Business models and corporate strategies are to incorporate this new way of thinking to achieve sustainable value creation. An integrated report is a product of the IR process. The report connects financial and non-financial information in a concise manner, centring on the understanding and communication of value creation. The International Integrated Reporting Council (IIRC) released the International Integrated Reporting Framework (IRF) to guide the preparation of integrated reports. Proponents of IR argue that it could facilitate more efficient managerial and investment decision-making that takes into account the potential value created by an organization over the short, medium and long term.

Recurring financial crises have emphasized the risks of viewing corporations from a narrow perspective, providing momentum for a more integrated and holistic approach to corporate reporting (Rowbottom and Locke 2016). The IIRC launched a pilot programme in 2011 to test and put into practice the underlying principles of the IRF. The programme involved more than 75 businesses and 25 investor organizations, from 23 countries. While IR is gaining momentum on the global scene, it may take several years for organizations to produce a full integrated report due to the complexity of the process (IIRC 2012). Eccles et al. (2015) consider it promising for IR to become a universal practice as there has been a positive trend in the release of sustainability reports, a small but growing number of integrated reports, and the contents of annual reports are becoming more connected and are considerate of value creation (see also: Stent and Dowler 2015; Adams et al. 2016). There has also been a gradual consensus among investors regarding the financial nature of social and environmental issues, increasing the demand for private information on the risks and opportunities of sustainability issues (Atkins et al. 2015).

While IR has been gaining global momentum, future developments and the prospects of the IRF remain unclear. KPMG's (2015) survey shows no significant growth rate in the adoption of the IRF amongst the largest 4500 companies in the world. Furthermore, an increasingly high rate of corporate responsibility disclosures does not necessarily equate to high rates of IR. EY's (2014) international survey evidences that managers face the need to update their reporting infrastructure following growing business complexity, business growth, regulatory and accounting requirements, as well as various demands from external stakeholders. The idea of IR is valuable as it enables greater alignment between management processes and information reported to external stakeholders, allowing the provision of information that improves decision-making and investment efficiency. However, the initial hurdles to implementing IR is to have in place adequate information technology systems that improves data availability and accuracy. Managers prioritize overcoming these hurdles above the adoption of the IRF. Research on IR has been emerging, providing initial insights into IR from theoretical and practical perspectives; however, there needs to be further empirical research on its application and impacts (De Villiers et al. 2014; De Villiers et al. 2017; Dumay et al. 2016).

The aim of this chapter is to provide the reader with a broad overview of IR. The following section present a background to the development of IR. Thereafter, details of the official IR framework and its associated concerns are presented. Next, the motivations for managers to engage in IR, or dismiss the idea are outlined. This is followed by discussions on the effects IR has on internal operations, and the external use and consequences of IR. The chapter concludes with reflections on the challenges ahead.

Background to integrated reporting

IR reflects the endeavour to make corporate disclosures a more effective means of communication to improve efficiency in management and investment decision-making. It emerged as a reporting mechanism to address the shortcomings in current accounting systems. Corporations have been producing numerous disconnected reports that are increasing in length and complexity, leading to issues of information overload (IIRC 2013a; Eccles and Krzus 2010). In addition, accounting systems have been criticized for their backward-looking nature, short-term orientation and failure to capture intangible factors that are primary drivers of organizational performance (De Villiers et al. 2014; EY 2016). IR emerged from the need to mitigate sustainability concerns. Social and environmental issues in the forms of diminishing natural resources and ecosystem degradation urge for the development of reporting mechanisms that can support the transition into sustainable economic models (IIRC 2010). IR aims to provide decision-makers with forward-looking and strategic-focused information, presented in terms of a holistic view on corporate operations and performance. It encourages decision-makers to adopt a forward-looking and long-term perspective, which are attributes that support stable capital markets and sustainable societies (IIRC 2013a). IR is applicable to both corporate and governmental organizations (Guthrie et al. 2017). While the emergence of IR is associated with the continuous developments in non-financial measurement systems and reporting frameworks, IR differs from sustainability reporting in terms of its target audience, information contents and focus on disclosing strategic and forward-looking information (De Villiers et al. 2014).

IR is a practice-led initiative that occurred prior to any policy and regulatory requirements. The first integrated reports were produced by the Danish biotech company Novozymes and Brazilian cosmetics manufacturer Natura, in 2002 and 2003, respectively (Eccles and Krzus 2010). Novozymes' (2002) first integrated report combined financial, environmental and social information into a single report. The report contained information their senior managers viewed as the most material to their stakeholders. Novozymes' CEO described the decision to prepare an integrated report as "a natural consequence of business and sustainability moving ever closer together, and of various stakeholders asking for a wider overview of the business" (Novozymes 2002, p. 5). Eccles and Krzus (2010) refer to integrated reports as 'One Report', which is both a tool and a symbolistic representation of organizational commitment to sustainability. IR has the potential to alter corporate operations and investors' mind-set from a short-term orientation towards a long-term orientation. Early advocates envisioned it as a means of communication for all stakeholders, and an opportunity to rebuild the trust between businesses and society (Eccles et al. 2010).

The phrase 'integrated reporting' was formally introduced in the King Code of Corporate Governance Principles (King III) as a part of ongoing corporate governance reforms in South Africa (Haji and Anifowose 2016). The reforms are set to support national objectives of increasing the inflows of foreign direct investments, and to reduce corruption as well as social and economic inequalities in the country. King III encourages managers to connect financial and sustainability information in a single medium of communication. Following the incorporation of King III into the Johannesburg Stock Exchange listing requirements on an 'apply or explain' basis, listed corporations were required to prepare an integrated report, effective from March 2010. This requirement made South Africa the first country, and currently the only country, to mandate the preparation of an integrated report. In the same year, the Prince's Accounting for Sustainability Project and the Global Reporting Initiative jointly formed the IIRC. The IIRC comprises of representatives from the civil society and corporate background. It is a collation of regulators, standard setters, the accounting profession, investors, companies and non-governmental organizations (IIRC 2010). The task entrusted to IIRC was to create a globally acceptable accounting framework that brings together information in a clear, concise, consistent and comparable format, otherwise termed as an 'integrated' format.

Sustainability and accountability to stakeholders were initially strong features of IIRC's initial discussion papers, but later the target audience and focus of IR was refined to emphasize sustainable value creation for capital providers. The IIRC (2013c) and Adams (2015) justified the focus on capital providers based on the complexity and diversity of the notion of value creation. 'Value creation' is a widely used term and represents a variety of meanings to different stakeholder groups. The argument is that capital providers equate value creation with potential future cash flows and sustainable financial returns. This takes into account the different forms of resources and relationships that affect value creation. While investors may not be influenced by all factors that affect value creation, diverse sets of factors do have indirect impacts on financial returns and should therefore be considered in investment decision-making. After a series of amendments and discussions, the IRF was released in December 2013 as the first framework that guides the preparation of an integrated report.

The International Integrated Reporting Framework (IRF)

Core concepts and guidance

The IRF is a voluntary principles-based framework consisting of three core sections. It introduces the concepts that underpins the Framework, the guiding principles that inform the preparation of an integrated report and the content elements that specifies categories of information that are to be included in the disclosure. 'Integrated thinking' builds the foundation of the IR process and results in a report that communicates material interactions relating to value creation and the creation of value over time. Integrated thinking requires the active consideration of the relationships between organizations' operations and departments, and the diverse set of resources and relationships organizations use and affect. The IIRC (2013a) describes an integrated report as a concise and forward-looking communication that details how an organization's strategy, governance, performance and prospects lead to value creation in the short, medium and long term. While the IIRC deems capital providers as the primary target audience of integrated reports, it is expected that the IR process will benefit broader stakeholder groups through greater corporate transparency and encouragement of sustainable operations.

The Framework expresses the IIRC's interpretation of value creation, introduces the concept of the 'six capitals', and explains the 'value creation process'.

The IRF links an organization's ability to create value to the value it creates for others. An organization is influenced by its external environment, which includes economic conditions, technological changes and social and environmental issues. Value is created, changed or destroyed based on a wide range of activities and relationships, which are otherwise termed as 'capitals'. The 'six capitals' are: financial, manufactured, intellectual, social and relationship, human and natural. Financial capital and manufactured capital reflect the traditional factors used in corporate operations pertaining to money and machinery employed in production. Financial capital relates to the pool of funds available to an organization. Manufactured capital are physical objects available for production or the provision of goods and services. In addition to the traditional factors, the IRF identifies other resources and relationships required for an organization's continued success. Intellectual capital reflects knowledge-based intangibles. Human capital relates to qualities of competency and innovative abilities within personnel. Social and relationship capital encompasses relationships and abilities to share information with communities and stakeholder group, and an organization's ability to enhance social well-being. Natural capital includes all renewable and non-renewable environmental resources. The six capitals reflect the inputs and outcomes of the value creation process, and not all capitals are equally applicable across organizations.

The 'value creation process' is dependent on an organization's business model. The business model, expressed as the core of an organization, draws on various capitals as inputs and converts them to outputs and outcomes in terms of products, services and by-products through business activities. The process of using and transforming the capitals to produce outputs and outcomes have both positive and negative effects on the capitals, the organization and its stakeholders. Managers should assess what value is created over different time horizons and to whom the value has been created. Sustainable value creation is unlikely to be achieved through the maximization of a single capital; thereby, organizations need to find an optimal balance and adjust their business model and strategies accordingly.

The IRF provides seven guiding principles and eight content elements. Integrated reports should: (1) be strategic-focused and future-orientated, (2) connect information to reflect a holistic view of how organizations create value over time, (3) provide insight into stakeholder relationships, (4) contain material information, (5) be concise, (6) be reliable and complete by including all material matters in a balanced and unbiased way and (7) be consistent and comparable. Furthermore, the report needs to cover: (1) an overview of the organization and its external environment, (2) governance structure, (3) business model, (4) risks and opportunities, (5) strategy and resource allocation, (6) performance, (7) outlook and (8) basis of presentation on how matters are quantified or evaluated. While the IRF provides an overarching direction, it does not specify key performance indicators or disclosure matrices for adopters to consider. Therefore, reporters should supplement the IRF with other reporting guidelines, such as the Global Reporting Framework and WICI Intangibles Reporting Framework.

Issues and concerns

There are concerns over the IIRC's reinforcement of a business case and the IRF's narrow identification of the target audience for integrated reports. Brown and Dillard (2014) and Milne and Gray (2013) voice concerns over the IRF reinforcing business-as-usual practices rather than encouraging critical reflection and change. Such action may encourage stakeholder management rather than accountability to stakeholders. Additionally, there are views against the IIRC's assumption that shareholder value will generalize into stakeholder value, with arguments that suggest it is improper to assume that the interests of corporations, investors, and society will converge given time without a motivating force or change in mind-sets. Flower (2015) argues that material information to society may require disclosures relating to all six of the capitals, irrespective of their impact on corporate profitability, whereas material information to investors is limited to the capitals related to financial value creation. It is anticipated that the IIRC's leniency towards corporate needs and the level of discretion left to management will have little impact on changing current disclosure practices. Rowbottom and Locke (2016) explain that there are broad philosophical differences between the perspectives of the stakeholder and shareholder, and many individuals view it as impossible to converge the two perspectives given the incongruence between shareholder value maximization, community welfare, resource preservation and labour costs. Van Bommel's (2014) interviews with stakeholder groups in the Netherlands support this argument as it identified varied perspectives held by stakeholder groups regarding what the contents of integrated reports should emphasize and how its success is determined.

The premise that following the guidance of the IRF will lead to substantial changes in corporate operations has been questioned. The IRF privileges financial value creation over stewardship, reflecting the promotion of a weak sustainability paradigm (Stubbs and Higgins 2015). Gray (2010) argues that if the sustainable costs of corporate activity are accounted for properly, such as ensuring all man-made, renewable and critical natural capitals are maintained over an accounting period, there will be few corporations that are actually 'sustainable'. Organizations will not willingly include accounts that threatens their existence, and the resulting sustainability claims that are based on a weak sustainability perspective are largely unsupported and potentially dangerous. Initial sets of integrated reports are viewed as a legitimacy tool as corporations are using sustainability discourses for the purposes of validating their activities and to portray the corporation as trustworthy. Zappettini and Unerman's (2016) analysis of integrated reports found that rather than corporate actions being driven by sustainability, sustainability discourses are embedded in financial and macro-economic propositions, often used to support the pursuit of growth through commercial and financial objectives. Following these issues and concerns, it is uncertain how IR will develop and whether it will make a substantial change in corporate operations.

Engagement in integrated reporting

Emerging research suggest managers engage in IR due to institutional pressures and legitimacy reasons. Higgins et al. (2014) found Australian managers saw a degree of inevitability in IR, irrespective of its value. Top executives face pressure to adhere to the reporting practices of peers, and reporting managers face pressures from both the top and external stakeholder expectations regarding transparency and the disclosure of material and comparable information. Similarly, Lueg et al. (2016) found external pressures driven by demands from shareholders, customers, employees and local authorities to lead to the eventual preparation of integrated disclosures for a manufacturer in Denmark. Potential legitimizing effects of IR is another motivation for managers to prepare an integrated report. IR is often associated with advancements in corporate reputation, improvements in stakeholder relationships and reduction in reputation risk (Steyn 2014; Lodhia 2015). Managers may engage in IR with the intention of manipulating individuals' perceptions about their corporation through selective reporting of favourable information (Melloni et al. 2016).

While there are benefits associated with IR, managers may be deterred from producing integrated reports due to concerns about corporate confidentiality and proprietary costs. The disclosure of forward-looking and strategic information in accordance with the IRF is commonly viewed as an additional reporting burden or is associated with unnecessary exposure to increased litigation risk (Perego et al. 2016). Furthermore, requiring the disclosure of information that is forward-looking poses a significant challenge for reporters. It is a challenge to disclose material information without compromising business confidentiality (Steyn 2014). Due to the difficulty of achieving a balance, integrated reports may contain information that is superficial and merely provided to comply with requirements or external demand (Dumay et al. 2017).

Instability exists concerning the adoption of the IRF, primarily due to alternative reporting mechanisms that overlap with the Framework (Rowbottom and Locke 2016). Concurrent with the development of the IRF, frameworks such as 'Connected Reporting' by Accounting for Sustainability, 'Strategic Report' by the UK Financial Reporting Council, and developments in management commentary guidelines overlap with the IRF's motives and objectives. However, implementation of either of these initiatives suggest managers are moving towards connecting information and are involved in the IR process.

Internal perspectives on integrated reporting

Feedback from the IIRC (2012, 2013b) pilot programme demonstrates growing recognitions of the connections between resources and the relationships that organizations depend on to generate value. IR has led to stronger internal communications by breaking down the barriers between departments and stimulating strategic dialogue between financial and non-financial teams. In addition to strengthening collaboration between units, IR helps clarify the value creation path for each internal function and acts as a tool for a function to present itself to upper level management (Mio et al. 2016). A comprehensive recognition of value creation and communication between departments helps management develop more informed strategies that take into account of sustainability risk and opportunities (Adams 2017; IIRC 2013b).

While there is evidence suggesting that IR leads to the strengthening of internal communications, there is also evidence that suggests IR has little impact on internal operations in its initial stages of adoption. Higgins et al. (2014) and Stubbs and Higgins (2014) found early adopters in Australia consider IR practices an extension of sustainability reporting. Integrated reports are more about story-telling and meeting institutional expectations, and it does not stimulate radical changes or innovations in reporting processes. A case study by Dumay and Dai (2017) supports this proposition. It concludes that the IRF is used to reinforce the existing responsible culture of the company and does not radically change practices. Rather, it reinforces business-as-usual practices. There is evidence suggesting the production of an integrated report is driving IR, which is contrarily to its purpose. Adams (2017) found that there are directors who are sceptical of the changes that IR possibly brings to organizational operations as there are instances of fake integrated reports. Corporations may fail to engage in the IR process and still label their report as 'integrated' even when it contains disintegrated information. This issue is reflected in McNally et al. (2017), which found the production of a report was driving the IR process. Systems are put in place to produce the figures necessary for compliance purposes, and managers are still subject to pressures of generating short-term financial returns.

Adopting the IR process requires managers to develop new ways of measuring, managing, and disclosing information. There are instances where managers find it difficult to make non-financial teams more quantitative based, face difficulties in measuring and identifying trade-offs between capitals and consider it a challenge to balance multiple stakeholder interests and both financial and sustainability considerations (IIRC 2012; IIRC 2013b; Parrot and Tierney 2012; Dumay et al. 2017). Despite the challenges, Parrot and Tierney (2012) found that managers consider IR practices and stakeholder engagement to be fundamental to a company's success, viewing the maximization of long-term value to require addressing ethical and relational concerns.

External use and consequences of integrated reporting

There have been general criticisms on the quality and content of the integrated reports available. Institutional investors require more risk-oriented information, greater explanation of the materiality determination process, more balanced representation of corporate performance and disclosure of material information rather than simply more information (IIRC 2013b). Similarly, while South African institutional investors view integrated reports as an improvement from traditional annual reports, reports are often too lengthy, contain excessive repetition and follow a box-ticking approach (Atkins and Maroun 2015). Managers need to integrate information rather than restricting social and environmental information to certain sections of their reports (Du Toit et al. 2017). Haji and Anifowose (2016) argue that IR, in South Africa, is more ceremonial than substantive, where IR has not brought about major changes in how corporations connect financial and non-financial information. However, the study did find corporations are disclosing more information that is unfavourable and are recognizing interrelationships between capitals. Furthermore, there are problems with comparability across reporting organizations as there is a wide diversity in the type and quality of information disclosed (Doni et al. 2016).

In terms of the consequences of IR, a growing number of archival studies investigate the relationship between IR and market reactions. Knauer and Serafeim (2014) and Serafeim (2015) evidence that integrated thinking and reporting practices change the investor base of a case company. The findings suggest increases in corporate transparency and initiatives that enhance sustainability performance attract long-term investors. The growth in long-term investor base subsequently contributes to stronger economic performance. Barth et al. (2017) found the release of higher-quality integrated reports is associated with lower bid-ask spreads, higher firm value and greater expected cash flows. These findings are supported by Lee and Yeo (2016), who identify organizational complexity and external financing needs to strengthen this relationship. Similarly, Zhou et al. (2017) found that a higher level of alignment between reports and the IRF is associated with lower analyst forecast error. This improvement in alignment leads to a subsequent reduction in cost of equity capital and greater market returns.

Challenges ahead and conclusion

IR encourages the alignment of corporate operations with long-term sustainability and the provision of information for the purposes of improving management and investment efficiency. The situation with IR is rapidly changing as evidenced by its development history and emerging literature. Organizations around the world are getting involved in the IR movement, and this momentum is expected to continue. While the IRF faces criticisms relating to its reinforcement of a business case and focus on financial value creation, the Framework establishes a starting point for managers to think about and initiate IR. Multiple considerations factor into the decision to engage in IR, and for those who have engaged in this process, initial evidence have suggested it results in stronger internal management, corporate performance and communication efficiency. However, there is contrary evidence that suggests the IRF does not stimulate changes in internal operations and instead encourages business-as-usual practices.

There are many challenges ahead for IR to become a widespread reporting tool and fully implemented within corporations. Apart from addressing issues with disclosure contents, quality and comparability (IIRC 2013b; Atkins and Maroun 2015; Doni et al. 2016), there needs to be progress in addressing the complexity and litigation risks associated with integrated report assurance (Burke and Clark 2016; Lodhia 2015). Furthermore, advancements in accounting are needed to support proper measurement of different sources of capitals and the transformation of capitals (Adams 2015). Another challenge lies in addressing the acceptance and use of integrated reports. There are concerns that the short termism of the investment community and their focus on financial information will act as a barrier to IR (IIRC 2012; Adams 2017; McNally et al. 2017). IR is an initiative that requires a genuine change in thinking and mind-sets. It is uncertain what changes will materialize as the idea matures and organizations progress through the stages of implementation.

References

Adams, C. A., 2015. The international integrated reporting council: a call to action. *Critical Perspectives on Accounting*, 27, 23–28.

Adams, C. A., 2017. Conceptualising the contemporary corporate value creation process. *Accounting, Auditing & Accountability Journal*, 30 (4), 906–931.

Adams, C. A., Potter, B., Singh, P. J. and York, J., 2016. Exploring the implications of integrated reporting for social investment (disclosures). *The British Accounting Review*, 48 (3), 283–296.

Atkins, J. and Maroun, W., 2015. Integrated reporting in South Africa in 2012: perspectives from South African institutional investors. *Meditari Accountancy Research*, 23 (2), 197–221.

Atkins, J. F., Solomon, A., Norton, S. and Joseph, N. L., 2015. The emergence of integrated private reporting. *Meditari Accountancy Research*, 23 (1), 28–61.

Barth, M. E., Cahan, S. F., Chen, L. and Venter, E. R., 2017. *The economic consequences associated with integrated report quality: early evidence from a mandatory setting*. Available: https://ssrn.com/abstract=2699409

Brown, J. and Dillard, J., 2014. Integrated reporting: on the need for broadening out and opening up. *Accounting, Auditing & Accountability Journal*, 27 (7), 1120–1156.

Burke, J. J. and Clark, C. E., 2016. The business case for integrated reporting: insights from leading practitioners, regulators, and academics. *Business Horizons*, 59 (3), 273–283.

De Villiers, C., Rinaldi, L. and Unerman, J., 2014. Integrated reporting: insights, gaps and an agenda for future research. *Accounting, Auditing & Accountability Journal*, 27 (7), 1042–1067.

De Villiers, C., Venter, E. R. and Hsiao, P.-C. K., 2017. Integrated reporting: background, measurement issues, approaches and an agenda for future research. *Accounting & Finance*, advance online publication. doi:10.1111/acfi.12246.

Doni, F., Gasperini, A. and Pavone, P., 2016. Early adopters of integrated reporting: the case of the mining industry in South Africa. *African Journal of Business Management*, 10 (9), 187–208.

Du Toit, E., Van Zyl, R. and Schutte, G., 2017. Integrated reporting by South African companies: a case study. *Meditari Accountancy Research*, 25 (4).

Dumay, J., Bernardi, C., Guthrie, J. and Demartini, P., 2016. Integrated reporting: a structured literature review. *Accounting Forum*, 40 (3), 166–185.

Dumay, J. and Dai, T., 2017. Integrated thinking as a cultural control? *Meditari Accountancy Research*, 25 (4).

Dumay, J., Guthrie, J. and La Torre, M., 2017. Barriers to implementing the international integrated reporting framework: a contemporary academic perspective. *Meditari Accountancy Research*, 25 (4).

Eccles, R. G., Cheng, B. and Saltzman, D., 2010. *The landscape of integrated reporting: reflections and next steps*. Cambridge, MA: Harvard Business School.

Eccles, R. G. and Krzus, M., 2010. *One report: integrated reporting for a sustainable strategy*. Hoboken, NJ: John Wiley & Sons.

Eccles, R. G., Krzus, M. P. and Ribot, S., 2015. Meaning and momentum in the integrated reporting movement. *Journal of Applied Corporate Finance*, 27 (2), 8–17.

EY, 2014. *Connected reporting: responding to complexity and rising stakeholder demands*. Available: www.ey.com/Publication/vwLUAssets/ey-assurance-faas-connected-reporting/$FILE/ey-assurance-faas-connected-reporting.pdf [Accessed 17 May 2017].

EY, 2016. *Accounting and reporting for long term value*. Available: ey.com/longtermvalue [Accessed 23 January 2017].

Flower, J., 2015. The international integrated reporting council: a story of failure. *Critical Perspectives on Accounting*, 27, 1–17.

Gray, R., 2010. Is accounting for sustainability actually accounting for sustainability . . . and how would we know? An exploration of narratives of organisations and the planet. *Accounting, Organizations and Society*, 35 (1), 47–62.

Guthrie, J., Manes-Rossi, F. and Orelli, R. L., 2017. Integrated reporting and integrated thinking in Italian public seotor Organisations. *Meditari Accountancy Research*, 25 (4).

Haji, A. A. and Anifowose, M., 2016. The trend of integrated reporting practice in South Africa: ceremonial or substantive? *Sustainability Accounting, Management and Policy Journal*, 7 (2), 190–224.

Higgins, C., Stubbs, W. and Love, T., 2014. Walking the talk(s): organisational narratives of integrated reporting. *Accounting, Auditing & Accountability Journal*, 27 (7), 1090–1119.

IIRC, 2010. *Formation of the International Integrated Reporting Committee (IIRC)*. Available: http://integratedreporting.org/wp-content/uploads/2011/03/Press-Release1.pdf [Accessed 28 May 2017].

IIRC, 2012. *The Pilot programme 2012 yearbook*. The International Integrated Reporting Council. Available: http://integratedreporting.org/resource/2012-yearbook/ [Accessed 17 May 2017].

IIRC, 2013a. *The international <IR> framework*. Available: http://integratedreporting.org/resource/international-ir-framework/ [Accessed 17 May 2017].

IIRC, 2013b. *The Pilot programme 2013 yearbook*. Available: http://integratedreporting.org/resource/iirc-pilot-programme-yearbook-2013-business-and-investors-explore-the-sustainability-perspective/ [Accessed 17 May 2017].

IIRC, 2013c. *Value creation background paper*. Available: www.theiirc.org/wp-content/uploads/2013/08/Background-Paper-Value-Creation.pdf [Accessed 17 May 2017].

Knauer, A. and Serafeim, G., 2014. Attracting long-term investors through integrated thinking and reporting: a clinical study of a biopharmaceutical company. *Journal of Applied Corporate Finance*, 26 (2), 57–64.

KPMG, 2015. *The KPMG survey of corporate responsibility reporting 2015*. Available: https://home.kpmg.com/xx/en/home/insights/2015/11/kpmg-international-survey-of-corporate-responsibility-reporting-2015.html [Accessed 17 May 2017].

Lee, K.-W. and Yeo, G. H.-H., 2016. The association between integrated reporting and firm valuation. *Review of Quantitative Finance and Accounting*, 47 (4), 1221–1250.

Lodhia, S., 2015. Exploring the transition to integrated reporting through a practice lens: an Australian customer owned bank perspective. *Journal of Business Ethics*, 129 (3), 585–598.

Lueg, K., Lueg, R. L., Andersen, K. and Dancianu, V., 2016. Integrated reporting with CSR practices: a pragmatic constructivist case study in a Danish cultural setting. *Corporate Communications: An International Journal*, 21 (1), 20–35.

McNally, M.-A., Cerbone, D. and Maroun, W., 2017. Exploring the challenges of preparing an integrated report. *Meditari Accountancy Research*, 25 (4).

Melloni, G., Stacchezzini, R. and Lai, A., 2016. The tone of business model disclosure: an impression management analysis of the integrated reports. *Journal of Management & Governance*, 20 (2), 295–320.

Milne, M. J. and Gray, R., 2013. W(h)ither ecology? The triple bottom line, the global reporting initiative, and corporate sustainability reporting. *Journal of Business Ethics*, 118 (1), 13–29.

Mio, C., Marco, F. and Pauluzzo, R., 2016. Internal application of IR principles: generali's internal integrated reporting. *Journal of Cleaner Production*, 139, 204–218.

Novozymes, 2002. *The Novozymes report 2002*. Available: https://investors.novozymes.com/investors/financial-reports/annual-reports/default.aspx. [Accessed 7 July 2016].

Parrot, K. W. and Tierney, B. X., 2012. Integrated reporting, stakeholder engagement, and balanced investing at American Electric Power. *Journal of Applied Corporate Finance*, 24 (2), 27–37.

Perego, P., Kennedy, S. and Whiteman, G., 2016. A lot of icing but little cake? Taking integrated reporting forward. *Journal of Cleaner Production*, 136, Part A, 53–64.

Rowbottom, N. and Locke, J., 2016. The emergence of <IR>. *Accounting and Business Research*, 46 (1), 83–115.

Serafeim, G., 2015. Integrated reporting and investor clientele. *Journal of Applied Corporate Finance*, 27 (2), 34–51.

Stent, W. and Dowler, T., 2015. Early assessments of the gap between integrated reporting and current corporate reporting. *Meditari Accountancy Research*, 23 (1), 92–117.

Steyn, M., 2014. Organisational benefits and implementation challenges of mandatory integrated reporting: perspectives of senior executives at South African listed companies. *Sustainability Accounting, Management and Policy Journal*, 5 (4), 476–503.

Stubbs, W. and Higgins, C., 2014. Integrated reporting and internal mechanisms of change. *Accounting, Auditing & Accountability Journal*, 27 (7), 1068–1089.

Stubbs, W. and Higgins, C., 2015. Stakeholders' perspectives on the role of regulatory reform in integrated reporting. *Journal of Business Ethics*, online publication. doi: 10.1007/s10551-015-2954-0.

van Bommel, K., 2014. Towards a legitimate compromise? An exploration of integrated reporting in the Netherlands. *Accounting, Auditing & Accountability Journal*, 27 (7), 1157–1189.

Zappettini, F. and Unerman, J., 2016. 'Mixing' and 'Bending': the recontextualisation of discourses of sustainability in integrated reporting. *Discourse & Communication*, 10 (5), 521–542.

Zhou, S., Simnett, R. and Green, W., 2017. Does integrated reporting matter to the capital market? *Abacus*, 53 (1), 94–132.

3 Why organizations voluntarily report – legitimacy theory

Warren MAROUN
University of the Witwatersrand

Abstract

This chapter provides a brief outline of legitimacy theory. It draws a distinction between an institutional and strategic perspective on organizational legitimacy. The latter is used to examine how companies rely on their sustainability or integrated reports to maintain and repair legitimacy. Four broad strategies are used for this purpose: avoidance, altering values and expectations, managing perceptions and adaption and conformance. Companies may rely on one or more of these strategies to manage their legitimacy depending on whether they are trying to gain, maintain or repair legitimacy and the significance of legitimacy for securing stakeholders' support.

Introduction

Early management theories presented the firm as a rational system designed to ensure the efficient conversion of inputs into outputs (Ouchi 1979). During the 1960s, this view was complemented by an institutional perspective which argues that the dynamics of modern businesses are not only the result of economic imperatives and technological developments but also complex symbolism, ceremonial displays and cultural heuristics (Meyer and Rowan 1977; DiMaggio and Powell 1983; Suchman 1995). At the heart of this socially constructed environment is the concept of organizational legitimacy.

A brief explanation of legitimacy theory

There are many definitions of 'legitimacy', but the one used by Suchman (1995, p. 574) is frequently cited in the academic literature:

> Legitimacy is a generalized perception or assumption that the actions of an entity are desirable, proper, or appropriate within some socially constructed system of norms, values, beliefs, and definitions.

The prior literature often presents organizations as operating under a 'social contract' in terms of which they are expected to adhere to society's conventions,

Table 3.1 Legitimacy typology

Focus	Type	Sub-set	Details
Increasing institutional focus	Pragmatic legitimacy	Exchange legitimacy	An organization is supported by constituents based on the perceived value which it provides to them.
		Influence legitimacy	Legitimacy is the result of the organization being responsive to stakeholders' needs. This can include the provision of favourable exchanges (exchange legitimacy) but also involves the organization including constituents in its decision-making processes or adopting their standards/expectations as its own.
		Dispositional legitimacy	Constituents personify and support the organization if they perceive that its interests are aligned with theirs and that it has a 'good character'.
	Moral legitimacy	Consequential legitimacy	The organization is evaluated according to its accomplishments. In some cases, outcomes can be easily defined and measured but in a complex social setting, an organization's accomplishments can be difficult to evaluate and are judged according to subjective and varying social norms.
		Procedural legitimacy	In addition to producing socially valued outcomes, the organization must ensure that it uses appropriate/generally accepted methods, techniques or processes.
		Structural legitimacy	An organization is worthy of support because of the charisma of its leaders (sometimes referred to as personal legitimacy) and its overall structural characteristics. These characteristics are in addition to the specific routines or processes which give rise to procedural legitimacy. The organization's structure signals its capacity for performing specific tasks or types of work and that, collectively, the organization is capable of producing desired outcomes.
	Cognitive legitimacy	Comprehensibility	An organization may be accepted as legitimate because it can be understood according to the day-to-day experiences and expectations of its stakeholders.
		Taken-for-granted-ness	An organization may come to be seen as such an integral part of society that its role or existence is seen as inevitable and accepted as a natural part of daily life.

(adapted from Suchman 1995)

rules or traditions. To the extent that there is congruence between the goals, values, ideals and norms of an organization and the larger social system of which it is a part, organizational legitimacy results (Dowling and Pfeffer 1975; Ashton 1992; Suchman 1995). It is in an organization's best interest either to establish itself as a legitimate part of society or to maintain its legitimacy in order to ensure support from important stakeholders and secure its continued existence (Meyer and Rowan 1977; Suchman 1995).

The literature making use of legitimacy theory can be categorized as either institutional or strategic. An institutional account presents legitimacy as the product of deeply held beliefs, value systems and the operation of external institutions which define what is an accepted or a taken-for-granted part of the social system (Meyer and Rowan 1977; DiMaggio and Powell 1983). As a result, legitimacy cannot be 'extracted' by specific actions or displays (as is the case with the strategic perspective of legitimacy). Legitimacy results from aligning or integrating the business with entire fields of contemporary society and the belief sets of stakeholders. An institutional perspective of legitimacy is discussed in more detail in Chapter 4.

A strategic perspective of legitimacy can be seen as an extension of stakeholder theory in that legitimacy is interpreted as an operational resource which is used to manage relations with stakeholders (O'Donovan 2002; De Villiers and Van Staden 2006). Management is assumed to have some control over the legitimization process and can rely on different methods, techniques or actions to influence organizational legitimacy (Suchman 1995). Corporate reporting is an essential part of this process. If an entity changes its activities or wishes to alter stakeholders' assessment of those activities or other expectations, appropriate disclosures are needed to inform stakeholders of management's position on the relevant facts or circumstances (O'Donovan 2002; Laine 2009; Brennan and Merkl-Davies 2014). In some cases, this can become an impression management exercise (Atkins et al. 2015). Management can use different types of disclosures to gain, maintain or repair legitimacy, resulting in potential conflict with constituents who prefer substantive action (Dowling and Pfeffer 1975; Meyer and Rowan 1977).

As modern organizations face a combination of strategic/operational and institutional pressures, it is 'important to incorporate [both perspectives of legitimacy] into a larger picture which highlights both the ways in which legitimacy acts like a manipulable resource and the ways in which it acts like a taken-for-granted belief system' (Suchman 1995, p. 577). To this end, different subsets of legitimacy are identified by the prior literature. These are summarized in Table 3.1 and draw on either a strategic or an institutional perspective of legitimacy.

This chapter concentrates on how corporate reporting is used to appeal to different subsets of legitimacy. It draws on a strategic perspective of legitimacy because organizations are seen as reacting to events and circumstances by changing what they include in their annual, sustainability or integrated reports and the extent of reporting on different sustainability-related issues.

Establishing the relationship between sustainability reporting and legitimacy theory

Organizations disclose information in their annual, integrated or sustainability reports to send a message to important stakeholders about their social, environmental or governance performance (Milne and Patten 2002; O'Donovan 2002; Cho 2009; Solomon and Maroun 2012; Brennan and Merkl-Davies 2014). The benefits of doing this include: aligning the organization with prevailing social values; responding to emerging ESG issues; avoiding criticism following a negative event; informing the debate on pressing social or environmental issues and building the organization's reputation (see also Ashforth and Gibbs 1990; Suchman 1995).

Early studies on non-financial reporting used quantitative methods to test for a relationship between environmental performance and disclosure (Deegan 2002; Guidry and Patten 2012). The results revealed weak statistical correlations and challenged a socio-political perspective of corporate reporting which held that companies used information in their annual or sustainability reports as part of a process of managing organizational legitimacy (Guthrie and Parker 1989; De Villiers and Van Staden 2006). A number of more recent papers, dealing mainly with environmental disclosures, have challenged this position. These are discussed below.

After controlling for company size and industry type and relying on more refined disclosure scores, Patten (2002) finds a positive relationship between the extent of environmental reporting and adverse environmental performance (measured by the quantity of released pollutants). The results suggest that larger companies with a high environmental impact face increased public scrutiny. The actual or perceived threat to legitimacy is addressed by providing more environmental disclosures. This is consistent with a second study which shows a statistically significant increase in the extent of environmental disclosures by petroleum companies following the *Exxon Valdez* oil spill in 1989 (see Chapter 7 for additional details). Consistent with legitimacy theory, companies directly affected by the disaster react by increasing information on their environmental performance and remedial plans in order to allay concerns, mitigate criticism and ensure key stakeholders' continued support. Importantly, as the oil spill resulted in increased societal awareness of the importance of environmental management, even companies not implicated directly in the *Exxon Valdez* disaster reacted by providing the public with more information on environmental issues (Patten 1992).

The positive relationship between ESG disclosures, organizational legitimacy and public scrutiny is reaffirmed by, for example, Brown and Deegan (1998), Deegan et al. (2002), Deegan and Blomquist (2006) and Cho and Patten (2007). They find that a poor environmental track record, increased media coverage on environmental issues or lobbying by important environmental action groups leads to an increase in public concern and as a result, additional disclosure. In other words, as society places more emphasis on environmental issues, companies react by providing additional environmental disclosure to justify themselves.

In some cases, however, a company may decrease the extent of reporting as part of its legitimization strategy. Reasons for reducing disclosures include the following:

- When initial concerns or suspicions reduce or an event/circumstance which originally threatened legitimacy becomes less serious;
- If the power/influence of stakeholders requiring specific disclosures diminishes or is reassessed;
- If an organization is able to provide less information or only generic disclosures, such as when it has already gained legitimacy or does not need to work actively to repair damaged legitimacy;
- When managers feel that disclosures are not useful for maintaining or repairing legitimacy; or
- When managers shift the focus of their reporting to cover more recent issues, popular developments or areas in which their organization have performed better.

(Suchman 1995; De Villiers and Van Staden 2006, p. 767)

In addition to the above points, it is possible for additional disclosure in corporate reports to give rise to added scrutiny which, paradoxically, undermines claims to pragmatic or moral legitimacy (see Dowling and Pfeffer 1975; Suchman 1995). De Villiers and Van Staden (2006) illustrate this by examining environmental reporting by the South African mining industry which, in the absence of a specific environmental issue, decreases its environmental disclosures over time. In addition, the sector relies on generic disclosures to provide at least some environmental information to stakeholders but avoids dealing with specific environmental considerations which may draw negative attention (see also Raemaekers et al. 2016; Dube and Maroun 2017). This finding is not unique to developing economies. In a study on corporate social disclosures by Irish companies, for example, O'Dwyer (2002, p. 426) finds that 'attempts at legitimization, especially through environmental disclosure, have been greeted with increased scepticism and heightened public demands for action regarding environmental issues'. The result is the reduction in this type of reporting.

Managing threats to legitimacy

Legitimacy is not constant. A legitimacy 'gap' can result because of changes in an organization's function or operation (Suchman 1995), involvement in negative events (such as environmental or social disasters) (Deegan 2002) and changing societal expectations and related public pressures (O'Donovan 2002). As noted by Alrazi et al. (2016, p. 671):

the implications of a legitimacy gap could be enormous, leading to potential product boycotts by customers, withdrawals of investments by shareholders, and difficulties in securing loans from banks, while increased lobbying activities by the public which could lead to increased regulation, and difficulties in hiring qualified staff.

(see also Dowling and Pfeffer 1975; Brennan and Merkl-Davies 2014)

Consequently, from a strategic legitimacy perspective, organizations must devote considerable effort to managing their legitimacy. The tactics used to gain, maintain or repair legitimacy vary (Dowling and Pfeffer 1975; Suchman 1995). For example, in order to gain legitimacy, an organization needs to be proactive and overcome uncertainty associated with being new (Ashforth and Gibbs 1990). It is likely to comply with pre-existing rules or conventions which are already generally accepted and can be adopted to gain legitimacy (Suchman 1995). Maintaining legitimacy is usually easier. Having already been accepted as credible, the organization needs to remain alert about changing stakeholder expectations and emerging challenges. The aim is to protect past accomplishments and react to specific events or circumstances which may threaten legitimacy (ibid). Strategies used to maintain or gain legitimacy can also be used to repair legitimacy. This usually involves reacting to a perceived threat to the organization's standing by limiting its impact, presenting it as an extraordinary issue and ensuring continued stakeholder support (Ashforth and Gibbs 1990; Suchman 1995).

The amount of effort needed to maintain or repair legitimacy depends on the importance of legitimacy for the organization's continued existence. A company with low levels of legitimacy and pressure from stakeholders has less need to invest in maintaining or rebuilding legitimacy. Conversely, organizations which depend significantly on public support differentiate themselves by being 'good corporate citizens' or face material pressures form powerful stakeholders need to be more proactive in managing existing levels of legitimacy (Suchman 1995; O'Donovan 2002; Clarkson et al. 2008). At the same time, the more significant the threat to legitimacy posed by a given set of events or circumstances, the more effort the organization needs to take to convince important stakeholders not to withdraw their support (Ashforth and Gibbs 1990; Suchman 1995; O'Donovan 2002). Possible legitimization tactics are summarized in Table 3.2.

The prior literature provides several examples of these legitimization strategies. Deegan and Blomquist (2006) and Atkins et al. (2016) argue that the activities of environmental lobby groups and the scientific community can lead to heightened awareness of material environmental issues. An adaptation and conformance strategy leads to changes to business processes, and corporate reporting reflects a genuine commitment to align the organization with prevailing social values which stress the importance of environmental responsibility (see also Gray et al. 1995).

Brennan and Merkl-Davies (2014) examine the reaction of firms in the sportswear/fashion industry to Greenpeace's exposure of harmful environmental practices and provide a more critical analysis of an adaptation and conformance strategy. They find that companies' rhetoric is designed to inform stakeholders about the complexity of the problem in an effort to alter values and expectations partially. The strategy is characterized by some level of

Table 3.2 Strategies for managing threats to legitimacy

Avoidance/denial	• Avoid entering the debate on the ESG issue which may weaken credibility • Deny the relevance of the ESG for the organization • Do not report potentially negative ESG information
Alter values and expectations	• Inform stakeholders about the business environment, including benefits and risks • Offer a normalizing account of the adverse event to present it as an unfortunate but inevitable part of the business environment/prevailing circumstances • Attempt to reframe stakeholders' views on what constitutes acceptable or unacceptable processes and outcomes
Manage perceptions	• Emphasize accomplishments/successes • Present the adverse event as an isolated occurrence • Distance the organization from negative publicity • Manage expectations for reform by highlighting inherent limitations/practical challenges
Adaptation and conformance	• Accept responsibility for negative outcomes • Agree to abide by industry standards, codes of best practice or generally accepted norms • Implement required reforms

(adapted from Suchman 1995; O'Donovan 2002; Bebbington et al. 2008)

conformance but the companies also attempt to negate the need for significant reform by presenting material environmental issues as something which is beyond their control and which can only be addressed by the group of affected stakeholders, including the state (see also Malsch 2013; Cho et al. 2015).

Managing perceptions can also be used to negate the need for change by using sustainability reporting to create the appearance that the company is aligned with prevailing social norms (Ashforth and Gibbs 1990). According to Merkl-Davies and Brennan (2007), for example, companies can use concealment as an impression management technique. This involves emphasizing positive information by increasing the quantity of disclosure and using a positive tone to suggest that the organization is making a good faith effort to ensure sustainability, even if specific plans and actions are not provided (see also Cho et al. 2012; Solomon et al. 2013; Cho et al. 2015). This is complemented with careful selection of narrative and images designed to portray the entity as a good corporate citizen and the omission or obfuscation of negative accounts of environmental or social performance (Merkl-Davies and Brennan 2007; Cho et al. 2010).

Related closely to this is 'attribution', a process which Merkl-Davies and Brennan (2007. p. 126) define as a defensive legitimization tactic based on deflecting blame. Managers seek to attribute positive outcomes to the internal processes while negative events are described as the result of factors beyond the organization's control (see also Suchman 1995). There are a number of examples of this. According to Malsch (2013) and Cho et al. (2015), the tone and temporal focus of sustainability disclosures are often used to present significant environmental or social matters as something which can only be resolved with time (see also

Maroun 2016). Similarly, Tregidga et al. (2014) explains how sustainability report-ing is often 'blended' with financial rhetoric designed to reframe serious environ-mental or social issues as monetary considerations (see also Samkin et al. 2014; Atkins et al. 2015). The aim is to resist far-reaching changes to the organization's business by acknowledging some responsibility for society and the environment but confirming that the organization's primary responsibility is the generation of returns for providers of financial capital (Higgins and Walker 2012; Tregidga et al. 2014; Cho et al. 2015). In doing so, companies are able to retain the appearance of being a responsible corporate citizen although their sustainability initiatives are limited by financial and practical considerations (ibid).

This type of impression management can also be used to inform the debate on the scope of the organization's social or environmental responsibilities. An image of a rational organization trying to balance the expectations of environ-mentalists and the capital market is presented. Concurrently, plausible explana-tions are given for why some issues are beyond the organization's control or are an unfortunate but inevitable outcome of the business process. The purpose is not only to deal with a current threat to legitimacy but to manage expectations and pre-empt future challenges to the organization's standing (O'Donovan 2002; Bebbington et al. 2008; Atkins and Maroun 2014; Tregidga et al. 2014; Atkins et al. 2015; Cho et al. 2015; McNally et al. 2017).

Finally, when stakeholder activism is lacking and the organization is not under scrutiny for a specific issue, it may be possible to exclude details from the sustain-ability or integrated report or avoid a detailed analysis of otherwise material envi-ronmental and social considerations. This can be used to create the impression that material ESG issues are under control and to avoid difficult-to-answer ques-tions about non-financial performance (De Villiers and Van Staden 2006; Maroun 2016). In some cases, it may even be possible for an organization to explicitly reject accountability for a negative outcome or to deny the relevance or existence of an environmental, social or governance challenge (Suchman 1995; Cho 2009).

The matrix developed by O'Donovan (2002, p. 363) is useful for showing how a company's sustainability reporting gives effect to different legitimization

Table 3.3 Legitimization tactics

Purpose and nature		Legitimization tactic			
Purpose	Significance of event	Avoid	Alter perceptions	Alter values	Conform
Gain	High	Likely	Very likely	Likely	Very unlikely
	Not high	Likely	Unlikely	Possible	Possible
Maintain – High	High	Very unlikely	Very likely	Likely	Very likely
	Not high	Unlikely	Possible	Likely	Possible
Maintain – low	High	Likely	Possible	Very likely	Very unlikely
	Not high	Very likely	Inconclusive	Likely	Unlikely
Repair	High	Very unlikely	Unlikely	Very likely	Very likely
	Not high	Unlikely	Unlikely	Very likely	Likely

strategies based on the aim of either gaining, maintaining or repairing legitimacy. The exact legitimization tactics are likely to vary considerably among organizations and will be affected by multiple factors including, for example, management's understanding of the significance of the event, the entity's position in society and the organization's relationship with its stakeholders. Nevertheless, the table presented below is useful for showing how sustainability reporting is dynamic and is influenced by underlying legitimacy considerations.

Summary and conclusion

- The firm's structure, design and processes are not only the result of economic forces and available technologies but also of powerful social and cultural pressures. Legitimacy is a key part of this socially constructed environment and can be framed according to an institutional or strategic perspective.
- This chapter focuses on legitimacy as a strategic resource which is conferred by society. In other words, an organization manages its legitimacy according to a type of social contract it has with society. The aim is to ensure that it meets the expectations of powerful stakeholders in order to ensure its continued existence.
- From a strategic perspective, legitimacy is dynamic and can be influenced by an organization's actions. In particular, organizations can use different types of communication to signal their allegiance to prevailing social norms. This has formed the basis of a large body of research which examines how corporations change the extent of sustainability reporting in response to underlying social or environmental concerns. (Chapter 7 deals with this aspect of sustainability reporting in more detail)
- The prior research also identifies various legitimization strategies. Examples include adaptation and conformance, managing expectations and altering perceptions. There is considerable variation in how companies make use of these strategies in order to gain, maintain and repair legitimacy. As a result, while some research has been carried out to explain how companies vary their legitimization tactics, there is no single approach for how organizations manage legitimacy as a strategic resource in the context of sustainability performance and reporting.
- Legitimacy can also be framed according to an institutional perspective. This focuses on how underlying social and cultural forces shape notions of legitimacy in a way which transcends a single firm.
- The prior research dealing with an institutional view of sustainability reporting is discussed in Chapter 4.

References

Alrazi, B., De Villiers, C. and Van Staden, C. J., 2016. The environmental disclosures of the electricity generation industry: a global perspective. *Accounting and Business Research*, 46 (6), 665–701.

Ashforth, B. E. and Gibbs, B. W., 1990. The double-edge of organisational legitimation. *Organization Science*, 1 (2), 177–194.

Ashton, R. H., 1992. Effects of justification and a mechanical aid on judgment performance. *Organizational Behavior and Human Decision Processes*, 52 (2), 292–306.

Atkins, J., Barone, E., Maroun, W. and Atkins, B., 2016. Bee accounting and accountability in the UK. *In:* K. Atkins and B. Atkins, eds. *The business of bees: an integrated approach to bee decline and corporate responsibility*. Sheffield, UK: Greenleaf Publishers.

Atkins, J. and Maroun, W., 2014. *South African institutional investors' perceptions of integrated reporting*. London: The Association of Chartered Certified Accountants.

Atkins, J. F., Solomon, A., Norton, S. and Joseph, N. L., 2015. The emergence of integrated private reporting. *Meditari Accountancy Research*, 23 (1), 28–61.

Bebbington, J., Larrinaga, C. and Moneva, J. M., 2008. Corporate social reporting and reputation risk management. *Accounting, Auditing & Accountability Journal*, 21 (3), 337–361.

Brennan, N. and Merkl-Davies, D., 2014. Rhetoric and argument in social and environmental reporting: the Dirty Laundry case. *Accounting, Auditing & Accountability Journal*, 27 (4), 602–633.

Brown, N. and Deegan, C., 1998. The public disclosure of environmental performance information – a dual test of media agenda setting theory and legitimacy theory. *Accounting and Business Research*, 29 (1), 21–41.

Cho, C. H., 2009. Legitimation strategies used in response to environmental disaster: a French case study of total SA's Erika and AZF incidents. *European Accounting Review*, 18 (1), 33–62.

Cho, C. H., Guidry, R. P., Hageman, A. M. and Patten, D. M., 2012. Do actions speak louder than words? An empirical investigation of corporate environmental reputation. *Accounting, Organizations and Society*, 37 (1), 14–25.

Cho, C. H., Laine, M., Roberts, R. W. and Rodrigue, M., 2015. Organized hypocrisy, organizational façades, and sustainability reporting. *Accounting, Organizations and Society*, 40 (0), 78–94.

Cho, C. H. and Patten, D. M., 2007. The role of environmental disclosures as tools of legitimacy: a research note. *Accounting, Organizations and Society*, 32 (7–8), 639–647.

Cho, C. H., Roberts, R. W. and Patten, D. M., 2010. The language of US corporate environmental disclosure. *Accounting, Organizations and Society*, 35 (4), 431–443.

Clarkson, P. M., Li, Y., Richardson, G. D. and Vasvari, F. P., 2008. Revisiting the relation between environmental performance and environmental disclosure: an empirical analysis. *Accounting, Organizations and Society*, 33 (4–5), 303–327.

De Villiers, C. and Van Staden, C. J., 2006. Can less environmental disclosure have a legitimising effect? Evidence from Africa. *Accounting, Organizations and Society*, 31 (8), 763–781.

Deegan, C., 2002. Introduction: the legitimising effect of social and environmental disclosures – a theoretical foundation. *Accounting, Auditing & Accountability Journal*, 15 (3), 282–311.

Deegan, C. and Blomquist, C., 2006. Stakeholder influence on corporate reporting: an exploration of the interaction between WWF-Australia and the Australian minerals industry. *Accounting, Organizations and Society*, 31 (4–5), 343–372.

Deegan, C., Rankin, M. and Tobin, J., 2002. An examination of the corporate social and environmental disclosures of BHP from 1983–1997. *Accounting, Auditing & Accountability Journal*, 15 (3), 312–343.

DiMaggio, P. and Powell, W., 1983. The Iron Cage revisited: institutional isomorphism and collective rationality in organizational fields. *American Sociology Review*, 48 (2), 147–160.

Dowling, J. and Pfeffer, J., 1975. Organizational legitimacy: social values and organizational behavior. *The Pacific Sociological Review*, 18 (1), 122–136.

Dube, S. and Maroun, W., 2017. Corporate social responsibility reporting by South African mining companies: evidence of legitimacy theory. *South African Journal of Business Management*, 48 (1), 23–34.

Gray, R., Walters, D., Bebbington, J. and Thompson, I., 1995. The greening of enterprise: an exploration of the (NON) role of environmental accounting and environmental accountants in organizational change. *Critical Perspectives on Accounting*, 6 (3), 211–239.

Guidry, R. P. and Patten, D. M., 2012. Voluntary disclosure theory and financial control variables: an assessment of recent environmental disclosure research. *Accounting Forum*, 36 (2), 81–90.

Guthrie, J. and Parker, L. D., 1989. Corporate social reporting: a rebuttal of legitimacy theory. *Accounting and Business Research*, 19 (76), 343–352.

Higgins, C. and Walker, R., 2012. Ethos, logos, pathos: strategies of persuasion in social/environmental reports. *Accounting Forum*, 36 (3), 194–208.

Laine, M., 2009. Towards sustaining the status quo: business talk of sustainability in Finnish corporate disclosures 1987–2005. *European Accounting Review*, 19 (2), 247–274.

Malsch, B., 2013. Politicizing the expertise of the accounting industry in the realm of corporate social responsibility. *Accounting, Organizations and Society*, 38 (2), 149–168.

Maroun, W., 2016. No bees in their bonnet: on the absence of bee reporting by South African listed companies. *In:* K. Atkins and B. Atkins, eds. *The business of bees: an integrated approach to bee decline and corporate responsibility*. Sheffield, UK: Greenleaf Publishers.

McNally, M.-A., Cerbone, D. and Maroun, W., 2017. Exploring the challenges of preparing an integrated report. *Meditari Accountancy Research*, 25 (4).

Merkl-Davies, D. M. and Brennan, N. M., 2007. Discretionary disclosure strategies in corporate narratives: incremental information or impression management? *Journal of Accounting Literature*, 26, 116–194.

Meyer, J. W. and Rowan, B., 1977. Institutionalized organizations: formal structure as myth and ceremony. *American Journal of Sociology*, 83 (2), 340–363.

Milne, M. J. and Patten, D. M., 2002. Securing organizational legitimacy: an experimental decision case examining the impact of environmental disclosures. *Accounting, Auditing & Accountability Journal*, 15 (3), 372–405.

O' Dwyer, B., 2002. Managerial perceptions of corporate social disclosure: an Irish story. *Accounting, Auditing & Accountability Journal*, 15 (3), 406–436.

O'Donovan, G., 2002. Environmental disclosures in the annual report. *Accounting, Auditing & Accountability Journal*, 15 (3), 344–371.

Ouchi, W., 1979. A conceptual framework for the design of organizational control mechanisms. *Management Science 1979*, 25 (9), 833–848.

Patten, D. M., 1992. Intra-industry environmental disclosures in response to the Alaskan oil spill: a note on legitimacy theory. *Accounting, Organizations and Society*, 17 (5), 471–475.

Patten, D. M., 2002. The relation between environmental performance and environmental disclosure: a research note. *Accounting, Organizations and Society*, 27 (8), 763–773.

Raemaekers, K., Maroun, W. and Padia, N., 2016. Risk disclosures by South African listed companies post-King III. *South African Journal of Accounting Research*, 30 (1), 41–60.

Samkin, G., Schneider, A. and Tappin, D., 2014. Developing a reporting and evaluation framework for biodiversity. *Accounting, Auditing & Accountability Journal*, 27 (3), 527–562.

Solomon, J. and Maroun, W., 2012. *Integrated reporting: the new face of social, ethical and environmental reporting in South Africa?* London: The Association of Chartered Certified Accountants.

Solomon, J. F., Solomon, A., Joseph, N. L. and Norton, S. D., 2013. Impression management, myth creation and fabrication in private social and environmental reporting: insights from Erving Goffman. *Accounting, Organizations and Society*, 38 (3), 195–213.

Suchman, M. C., 1995. Managing legitimacy: strategic and institutional approaches. *The Academy of Management Review*, 20 (3), 571–610.

Tregidga, H., Milne, M. and Kearins, K., 2014. (Re)presenting 'sustainable organizations'. *Accounting, Organizations and Society*, 39 (6), 477–494.

4 Why organizations voluntarily report – institutional theory and institutional work

Muhammad Bilal FAROOQ
Auckland University of Technology

Warren MAROUN
University of the Witwatersrand

Abstract

This chapter discusses institutional theory and its application to sustainability accounting. The chapter is divided into two main sections. The first explores the concept of institutional pressures and how these pressures influence the behaviour of organizations, often resulting in similar procedures being adopted by organizations under similar pressures, for example publishing sustainability and integrated reports that adopt common structures and disclose similar information. The second section discusses the concept of institutional work, which acknowledges that social actors (for example managers and professionals) are able to create new institutions, and maintain or disrupt existing institutions.

Institutional theory

Institutional theory was established in response to the view that all organizational behaviour can be attributed to simple rational and predictable decisions motivated by management's desire to maximize organizational efficiency and effectiveness (Carruthers 1995; Lounsbury 2008; Meyer and Rowan 1977; Meyer et al. 1981; Sharma, Lawrence et al. 2014; Zucker 1977). Instead institutional researchers contended that organizational structures, processes and practices were created and adopted as a result of institutional pressures. These institutions constituted acceptable and expected ways of doing things (Venter and De Villiers 2013). Burns and Scapens (2000) and Greenwood and Suddaby (2006) describe institutions as taken-for-granted assumptions and rationalized myths. These institutions create pressures (referred to as isomorphic pressures) on social actors (both individuals and organizations) which operate within their area of influence, forcing social actors to adopt similar structures, processes and practices (De Villiers and Alexander 2014; De Villiers et al. 2014a; DiMaggio and Powell 1983). As a result, organizational practice, structure or process is not necessarily the result of a calculated managerial decision aimed at improving profits but rather on the need to conform to institutional pressures (DiMaggio 1983; Lounsbury 2008; Powell 1988).

Consequently, early institutionalists focused on identifying institutions and institutional pressures and explaining institutional impacts on organizational life (Greenwood et al. 2008). A similar approach has been adopted by researchers in the field of sustainability reporting and sustainability assurance. Sustainability reporting is not only a rational exercise in providing useful information to investors and other stakeholders (see De Klerk and De Villiers 2012; De Villiers and Marques 2016) or managing legitimacy as a strategic resource (see O'Donovan 2002; Patten 2002; Brennan and Merkl-Davies 2014) as discussed in Chapters 3 and 7. The development of sustainability reporting reflects the operation of powerful social and institutional forces. This is illustrated by examining the relevance of isomorphism, decoupling and the role of the institutional financial reporting systems on sustainability and integrated reporting trends.

Isomorphic pressures

DiMaggio and Powell (1983) identify three types of isomorphic pressures which institutions may exert and which impact the workings of an organizations. These include coercive, normative and mimetic pressures. The first is usually the result of laws, regulations or societal pressures which drive compliance with the respective prescriptions. Normative isomorphism is evident when companies feel compelled to adhere to codes of best practice, ethical standards, industry norms or generally accepted practices in order to secure or maintain legitimacy. Finally, mimetic isomorphism describes a situation where a company seeks legitimacy by replicating the actions or behaviour of the most prominent or successful entities which have already attainted a state of cognitive legitimacy (see also Meyer and Rowan 1977; Suchman 1995).

These theoretical insights have been applied to the field of sustainability accounting (including sustainability reporting, sustainability assurance and integrated reporting). For example, De Villiers et al. (2014) used institutional theory to explain how isomorphic pressures encouraged the institutionalization of sustainability reporting practices amongst mining companies in South African context. The study finds that smaller mining companies mimicked the disclosure practices of larger operators and undertook to disclose the same amount of environmental information and in a broadly similar format.

A similar approach was adopted by De Villiers and Alexander (2014), who compare the sustainabiltiy reporting practices of minining companies based in Australia and South Africa. They find similarities in the patterns of sustainability reporting of these mining companies and explain this as the institutionalization of sustainability reporting within the mining industry at a global level. While adherence to reporting guidelines is not mandated in either jurisdiction, the generally accepted relevance of non-financial reporting frameworks, coupled with societal pressures in both jurisdictions to provide adequate disclosures, drives companies to comply with the applicable local and international reporting guidelines (see also De Villiers and Barnard 2000; Laine 2009b; De Villiers and Alexander 2014; De Villiers et al. 2014a). These findings indicate that isomorphic pressures cause companies to adopt similar practices, despite being located in different countries.

A slightly different approach has been adotped by Maroun et al. (2014), who argue that developing economies attempt to secure legitimacy in the eyes of international investors by adopting international reporting standards. Using South Africa as an illustration, the research explains how political isolation and competition for international capital provide an impetus for the development of codes of corporate governance, non-financial reporting guidelines and most recently, the decision to require listed companies either to prepare an integrated report or to provide reasons for not doing so (see also De Villiers et al. 2014b; Atkins and Maroun 2015).

Studies have also attributed the increasing trends to disclose sustaiability-related issues on coercive pressures. For example, Perego and Kolk (2012) argue that the growing popularity of sustainability reporting in some countries (e.g., France and Japan) can be attributed to the introduction of government regulation as well as stock exchange listing requirements which encourage organizations to provide information on this area. With the introduction of regulation mandating sustainability reporting, it is plausible that the assurance of these sustainability reports will also experience an increase.

Isomorphic pressures are also the result of an increased awareness of human impact on the planet and the need to complement financial statements with a more balanced account of how companies generate sustainable returns (see IIRC 2013; Atkins and Maroun 2014). In particular, the last twenty years have seen a proliferation of different types of non-financial reports in multiple jurisdictions (KPMG 2011; Hughen et al. 2014; Stubbs and Higgins 2014). These have become part of a generally accepted corporate reporting process which has attained a state of legitimacy in its own right and reflects a growing expectation for companies to provide detailed disclosures on material ESG issues in addition to financial statements (see O'Donovan 2002; Cho et al. 2010; De Villiers et al. 2014b; Higgins et al. 2014). As a result, even though most non-financial reporting is not mandated by statute, companies are under significant coercive and mimetic isomorphic pressure to provide at least some ESG disclosures in their annual, integrated or sustainability reports (see IIRC 2013; Atkins et al. 2015a).

Normative pressures have been introduced through the development of sustainability standards and guidelines (e.g., the GRI, IIRC, AA1000AS and ISAE3000). At the same time, non-financial reporting practices have been formalized as part of codes of good governance, industry standards or recommended best practice. These have become a codified set of widely applied reporting practices with which organizations must comply with in order to secure legitimacy. Even if unintended, guidance provided by (for example) the GRI or IIRC has become a source of normative isomorphic pressure as companies seek to signal the quality and credibility of their sustainability or integrated reports by demonstrating compliance with these frameworks (see DiMaggio and Powell 1983). As industry leaders adopt recommended best practices and apply these in their corporate reports, normative isomorphic pressure is reinforced by the mimetic replication of disclosures by less-prominent industry members also seeking legitimacy (consider Laine 2009a; De Villiers et al. 2014a; Maroun and van Zijl 2016).

Decoupling in institutionalized environments

According to Meyer and Rowan (1977, pp. 340–341), the formal structure of modern organizations is often explained using economic theories on transaction costs, economies of scale and marginal benefit. These provide a rational technical basis for determining how companies should be organized and how complex processes and interactions between different parts of an organization should be coordinated, understood and managed. Over time, these conceptions of the firm became institutionalized as a readily accepted or a taken-for-granted way of explaining the modern corporation (see also DiMaggio and Powell 1983; Suchman 1995).

Rationalized institutions are, however, not only dependent on operational efficiency but also on the extent to which an entity is able to align itself with societal norms and expectations. In some cases, adherence to these social rules or conventions is necessary to achieve legitimacy, even if they do not result in improved control and efficiency (Dowling and Pfeffer 1975; Meyer and Rowan 1977). In order to balance operational considerations with conformity to institutionalized rules, organizations 'buffer their formal structures from the uncertainties of technical activities by becoming loosely coupled, building gaps between their formal structures and actual work activities' (Meyer and Rowan 1977, p. 357). Indicators of organizational decoupling include the following:

- Professionals are used to execute activities – the firm relies on the assumption that, because suitably qualified experts exercising due care have performed the assigned task, the outcome is correct even if the technical processes cannot be defined and clearly understood.
- Goals, targets and performance indicators are defined ambiguously or in general terms. The entity refrains from drawing a clear connection between processes and outcomes and data on technical performance is avoided.
- The interconnection between different aspects of the organization is not made explicit. This often allows the organization to secure legitimacy based on stakeholders' assumption that the entity is working to achieve positive outcomes, even if these (and the underlying technical processes) are not entirely aligned and understood.

(see Meyer and Rowan 1977; Suchman 1995)

Evidence of decoupling is evident in the sustainability reporting literature. For example, studies on biodiversity reporting confirm that companies acknowledge the risks posed by issues such as climate change, habitat destruction and extinction of species and the relevance of these metrics for their business models (Intergovernmental Panel on Climate Change 2013; Jones and Solomon 2013; Atkins et al. 2016; Jonäll and Rimmel 2016). At the same time, biodiversity disclosures are generic. Few companies define biodiversity directly and explain clearly their biodiversity management plan (van Liempd and Busch 2013; Romi and Longing 2016). Details on specific initiatives to mitigate biodiversity risks, time frames and key performance indicators are seldom provided, and biodiversity is often framed as a complex issue best left to technical experts than business managers with no scientific expertise (Jones and Solomon 2013; Tregidga 2013; Mansoor and Maroun 2016; Maroun 2016).

More broadly, criticisms of sustainability and integrated reports can also be interpreted as evidence of decoupling. Several technical reports and academic papers question the quality of ESG disclosures, the extent to which corporate reports explain the interconnection between financial and non-financial capital and the value-relevance of sustainability disclosures for stakeholders (see, for example, KPMG 2015; Marcia et al. 2015; Michelon et al. 2015; PwC 2015; Stent and Dowler 2015; Thomson 2015). Consequently, as argued by Solomon and Maroun (2012, p. 14), dealing with the relevance of integrated reporting for the drive for sustainability:

> Although the concept of an integrated report should embed sustainability reporting into the heart of the primary corporate reporting vehicle, the annual report, this does not necessarily imply that the reporting will ful-fil its potential for transforming corporate behaviour or will not produce merely empty rhetoric.

In this context, while the prior research points to significant increases in the amount of non-financial disclosure in annual, sustainability or integrated reports (Solomon and Maroun 2012; KPMG 2015; PwC 2015), critical researchers question the change potential of different types of non-financial reporting (Gray et al. 1995; Gray 2006; Adams and McNicholas 2007; Bebbington et al. 2008). For example, Stubbs and Higgins (2014) examine organizational changes following the introduction of integrated reporting by a sample of Australian firms. The researchers find evidence of some changes to reporting processes and structures. Integrated reporting, which is supposed to be informed by the holistic management of financial and non-financial capital has not, however, resulted in significant reconfiguration of business models (see also Brown and Dillard 2014; Atkins et al. 2015a).

Nevertheless, ambiguous sustainability performance has not undermined the legitimizing potential of the integrated or sustainability report (Tregidga et al. 2014). Language, tone and images included in corporate communications with stakeholders are used to construct an image of a responsible corporate citizen. Stakeholders either overlook the absence of substantive details (Solomon et al. 2013; Atkins et al. 2015b) or operate according to the good faith assumption that the reporting entity is working to ensure sustainable business practices even if the details are unclear (Laine 2009b; Higgins and Walker 2012).

The relevance of the accounting institution

Flower (2015) identifies a number of weaknesses in the IIRC's framework on integrated reporting. These include, *inter alia*, the emphasis on providers of financial capital and the conceptualization of value from the perspective of the firm rather than society (see also Brown and Dillard 2014; Thomson 2015).

These flaws are attributed, in part, to the influence of the accounting fraternity and the concern that existing and emerging non-financial reporting guidelines could undermine the relevance of capitalism and destabilize the accounting profession's dominance of the corporate reporting space. As such, much of the development in non-financial reporting can be thought of as a reaction to the hegemonic challenge posed by the sustainability reporting movement rather than a genuine commitment to changing the status quo (Brown and Dillard 2014; Tregidga et al. 2014).

From a slightly different perspective, the operation of the conventional financial reporting system has a significant socializing effect (see Fogarty 1992; Carruthers 1995) which can constrain alternate perspectives of 'value creation' and how this should be communicated to stakeholders. For example, Malsch (2013, p. 165) explains that institutionalization of accounting and its expansion to include non-financial reporting is not, in itself, problematic but the effects can be questionable:

> the accounting industry plays an important role as a political mediator by regulating the socially responsible practices of organizations based on a rational and instrumental market logic and by side-lining the moral dimension of human values such as altruism and benevolence as a justification for socially responsible action. As a symbol of genuine political power, the mediating role of the accounting industry is conducive to the deployment of an individualistic and instrumental moral rationality, reinforcing the fragmentation of the social body into a multitude of stakeholders and undermining the prospect of a collective agreement on the definition and protection of a common good such as the preservation of natural resources or the maintenance of social protection for the most vulnerable groups in society.

Atkins et al. (2015a), Brown and Dillard (2014) and Dillard and Reynolds (2008) raise similar concerns. They point out that financial reporting models have become institutionalized and generally accepted as the primary means for describing a firm's performance. The result is that sustainability indicators are interpreted as being of secondary importance and the development of innovative management control and reporting frameworks which champion actual sustainability is stifled (see also Gray 2006; Stubbs and Higgins 2014)

Institutional work perspective

It is important to note that institutions are the product of social activity (Jepperson 1991). They depend on the social actors who establish, reproduce and maintain them (Berger and Luckmann 1976). While institutions influence the behaviour of social actors (both individual and organizations), social actors also impact and change institutions (Scott 2008; Lawrence and Suddaby 2006). This phenomenon is captured in the concept of institutional work (Lawrence and

Suddaby 2006; Lawrence et al. 2011; Lounsbury 2008; Suddaby 2010). Lawrence and Suddaby (2006, p. 216) define institutional work as "the broad category of purposive work action aimed at creating, maintaining and disrupting
institutions". In a review of the literature on institutional theory, Lawrence and
Suddaby (2006) offer a typology of forms of institutional work. This typology identifies three main categories of institutional work: creating institutions,
maintaining institutions and disrupting institutions. Each type of institutional
work includes several activities or sub-sets. These are summarized in Table 4.1.

The concept of institutional work has also been used in sustainability
accounting research. For example, Lawrence and Suddaby (2006, p. 221)
describe advocacy as 'the mobilization of political and regulatory support
through direct and deliberate techniques of social suasion'. This involves a
concerted effort to gain legitimacy (see Suchman 1995) for the new institution and is undertaken in several different ways, including: lobbying, advertising and litigation (Lawrence and Suddaby 2006). For example, Brown et al.
(2009) examine the institutionalization of the GRI standards which have
become the most established sustainability reporting standards in the world.
The researchers attribute the GRI's success to the ability of the GRI's found-
ers to mobilize a wide range of stakeholders to participate in the development of standards. However, the participation of companies and financial
institutions was greater than that of NGOs and activists as these stakeholders
had access to greater financial resources. Consequently, many argue that the
GRI project leaned more towards these more powerful stakeholders. In this
way, the study shows how social actors must mobilize key stakeholders and
resources (tangible and intangible)[1] to achieve their objectives (see also Fligstein 1997; Seo and Creed 2002).

Lawrence and Suddaby (2006) define mimicry as "leveraging existing sets of
taken-for-granted practices, technologies and rules, if they are able to associate
the new with the old in some way that eases adoption" (Lawrence and Suddaby
2006, p. 225). Such efforts are designed to take advantage of key social actors'
familiarity and comfort with existing institutionalized practices and in this way,
overcome their resistance to new practices. This may involve using discursive
strategies such as analogies, similes, metaphors and rhetoric (Etzion and Ferraro
2010; Mills 1940; Oaks et al. 1998; Suddaby and Greenwood 2005; Suddaby
et al. 2015). An example is provided in Etzion and Ferraro's (2010) study of
how the GRI used analogies to support the rapid global adoption of the GRI
standards. The similarities between financial and sustainability reporting was
emphasized (see also Brown et al. 2009). Once their global reach had been
established the GRI switched tactics and began to focus more on highlighting
the "dissimilarity and incongruence with financial reporting" (ibid, p. 1093).

Educating work involves 'educating of actors in skills and knowledge necessary to support the new institution or the new institutional form' (Lawrence
and Suddaby 2006, p. 227). A new institution will involve innovation, and key
social actors will need to be equipped with the skills necessary to support the
new structures. The sustainability reporting literature highlights how one of
the greatest challenges affecting the introduction of sustainability reporting is

Table 4.1 Forms of institutional work

Creating institutions	
Advocacy	Promoting a new institution using a range of direct and deliberate techniques which involve leveraging political and regulatory support for the new institution
Defining	Constructing a system of rules which grant status, establish boundaries of membership or create hierarchies within a field
Vesting	Creating rule structures that grant property rights
Constructing identities	Establishing a social actor's identity within the field in which the social actor operates
Changing normative associations	Remodelling the norms underlying a practice or certain practices
Constructing normative networks	Creating inter-organizational relationships which form groups with authority and responsibility over monitoring, evaluating and ensuring compliance with institutional practices and norms
Mimicry	Drawing similarities with existing institutionalized practices in order to make adoption of a new institution easier
Theorizing	Creating abstract categories and developing details around a chain of cause and effect
Educating	Providing key social actors with the skills and knowledge necessary to adopt the new institution
Maintaining institutions	
Enabling work	Introducing rules and regulations (including organizational roles and structures) which are designed to support the functioning on an institution
Policing	Monitoring and checking to ensure that the new institution is being complied with
Deterring	Creating barriers which will prevent institutional change
Valorizing and demonizing	Providing social actors with examples (including stories) of what normatively acceptable and unacceptable practice
Mythologizing	Maintaining the norms underlying an institution by creating myths around its history
Embedding and routinizing	Embedding the norms of the institution in the day-to-day routines of social actors and/or organizational operations
Disrupting institutions	
Disconnecting sanctions	Disconnecting the rewards and/or penalties related to an institution
Disassociating moral foundations	Destroying the moral foundation of an institution
Undermining assumptions and beliefs	Reducing the risk associated with adopting something new and different by undermining

Adapted from Lawrence and Suddaby (2006, pp. 221, 230, 235)

the lack of education and experience of managers at reporting entities (Adams and McNicholas 2007).

As a final example, efforts referred to as 'enabling work' involve the 'creation of rules that facilitate, supplement and support institutions' (Lawrence and Suddaby 2006, p. 230). New roles are created to carry out institutional routines, and agents are given expanded authority to support the continued functioning of the institution. Brown et al. (2009) highlight how the GRI secretariat played a key role in the success of the GRI standards. The secretariat was instrumental in keeping interest in the GRI project alive. The secretariat adopted an inclusive approach which helped in 'building a sense of shared ownership of the new rules and practices' (ibid p. 571). Furthermore, new versions of the standard were regularly introduced and each round of revision led to fresh rounds of stakeholder engagement which provided 'a mechanism for maintaining the discussion well into the future' (ibid., p. 571).

Conclusion

Institutional theory offers a useful framework for examining sustainability accounting. The theory comprises two main branches which examine the relationship between institutions and social actors. The first branch explores how institutions exert isomorphic pressure which force social actors to adopt similar patterns of behaviour. These isomorphic pressures include coercive (e.g., the introduction of legislation mandating sustainability reporting), mimetic (e.g., smaller companies copying the sustainability reporting practices of their larger counterparts) and normative pressures (e.g., the introduction of sustainability reporting standards). The second branch explores how social actors work to change or transform institutions. Forms of institutional work include creating new institutions, maintaining existing institutions and disrupting institutions.

Note

1 Tangible resources, such as funding, are essential for lobbying and advertising efforts, while intangible resources include the social actors' social capital (i.e., reputation and credibility) (Battilana et al. 2009; Coleman 1988).

References

Adams, C. A. and McNicholas, P., 2007. Making a difference: sustainability reporting, accountability and organisational change. *Accounting, Auditing & Accountability Journal*, 20 (3), 382–402.

Atkins, J.F., Atkins, B., Thomson, I. and Maroun, W., 2015a. 'Good' news from nowhere: imagining utopian sustainable accounting. *Accounting, Auditing & Accountability Journal*, 28 (5), 651–670.

Atkins, J., Barone, E., Maroun, W. and Atkins, B., 2016. Bee accounting and accountability in the UK. *In:* K. Atkins and B. Atkins, eds. *The business of bees: an integrated approach to bee decline and corporate responsibility.* Sheffield, UK: Greenleaf Publishers.

Atkins, J. F. and Maroun, W., 2014. *South African institutional investors' perceptions of integrated reporting.* London: The Association of Chartered Certified Accountants.

Atkins, J. F. and Maroun, W., 2015. Integrated reporting in South Africa in 2012: perspectives from South African institutional investors. *Meditari Accountancy Research,* 23 (2), 197–221.

Atkins, J. F., Solomon, A., Norton, S. and Joseph, N. L., 2015. The emergence of integrated private reporting. *Meditari Accountancy Research,* 23 (1), 28–61.

Battilana, J., Leca, B. and Boxenbaum, B., 2009. How actors change institutions: towards a theory of institutional entrepreneurship. *The Academy of Management Annals,* 3 (1), 65–107.

Bebbington, J., Larrinaga, C. and Moneva, J. M., 2008. Corporate social reporting and reputation risk management. *Accounting, Auditing & Accountability Journal,* 21 (3), 337–361.

Berger, T. L. and Luckmann, T., 1976. *The social construction of reality: a treatise on the sociology of knowledge.* Harmondsworth, UK: Penguin.

Brennan, N. and Merkl-Davies, D., 2014. Rhetoric and argument in social and environmental reporting: the Dirty Laundry case. *Accounting, Auditing & Accountability Journal,* 27 (4), 602–633.

Brown, H. S., de Jong, M., and Lessidrenska, T., 2009. The rise of the Global Reporting Initiative: a case of institutional entrepreneurship. *Environmental Politics,* 18 (2), 182–200.

Brown, J. and Dillard, J., 2014. Integrated reporting: on the need for broadening out and opening up. *Accounting, Auditing & Accountability Journal,* 27 (7), 1120–1156.

Burns, J., and Scapens, R. W., 2000. Conceptualizing management accounting change: an institutional framework. *Management Accounting Research,* 11 (1), 3–25.

Carruthers, B. G., 1995. Accounting, ambiguity, and the new institutionalism. *Accounting, Organizations and Society,* 20 (4), 313–328.

Cho, C. H., Roberts, R. W. and Patten, D. M., 2010. The language of US corporate environmental disclosure. *Accounting, Organizations and Society,* 35 (4), 431–443.

Coleman, J. S., 1988. Social capital in the creation of human capital. *American Journal of Sociology,* 94, 95–120.

De Klerk, M. and De Villiers, C., 2012. The value relevance of corporate responsibility reporting: South African evidence. *Meditari Accountancy Research,* 20 (1), 21–38.

De Villiers, C. J. and Alexander, D., 2014. The institutionalisation of corporate social responsibility reporting. *The British Accounting Review,* 46 (2), 198–212.

De Villiers, C. J. and Barnard, P., 2000. Environmental reporting in South Africa from 1994 to 1999: a research note. *Meditari Accountancy Research,* 8 (1), 15–23.

De Villiers, C. J., Low, M. and Samkin, G., 2014a. The institutionalisation of mining company sustainability disclosures. *Journal of Cleaner Production,* 84, 51–58.

De Villiers, C. J. and Marques, A., 2016. Corporate social responsibility, country-level predispositions, and the consequences of choosing a level of disclosure. *Accounting and Business Research,* 46 (2), 167–195.

De Villiers, C. J., Rinaldi, L. and Unerman, J., 2014b. Integrated reporting: insights, gaps and an agenda for future research. *Accounting, Auditing & Accountability Journal,* 27 (7), 1042–1067.

Dillard, J. and Reynolds, M., 2008. Green Owl and the Corn Maiden. *Accounting, Auditing & Accountability Journal,* 21 (4), 556–579.

DiMaggio, P. J., 1983. State expansion and organization fields. *In:* R. H. Hall and R. E. Quinn, eds. *Organization theory and public policy.* Beverly Hills, CA: Sage, 147–161.

DiMaggio, P. and Powell, W., 1983. The Iron Cage revisited: institutional isomorphism and collective rationality in organizational fields. *American Sociology Review,* 48 (2), 147–160.

Dowling, J. and Pfeffer, J., 1975. Organizational legitimacy: social values and organizational behavior. *The Pacific Sociological Review*, 18 (1), 122–136.

Etzion, D., and Ferraro, F., 2010. The role of analogy in the institutionalization of sustainability reporting. *Organization Science*, 21 (5), 1092–1107.

Fligstein, N., 1997. Social skill and institutional theory. *American Behavioural Scientist*, 40 (4), 397–405.

Flower, J., 2015. The international integrated reporting council: a story of failure. *Critical Perspectives on Accounting*, 27, 1–17.

Fogarty, T. J., 1992. Organizational socialization in accounting firms: a theoretical framework and agenda for future research. *Accounting, Organizations and Society*, 17 (2), 129–149.

Gray, R., 2006. Social, environmental and sustainability reporting and organisational value creation? Whose value? Whose creation? *Accounting, Auditing & Accountability Journal*, 19 (6), 793–819.

Gray, R., Walters, D., Bebbington, J. and Thompson, I., 1995. The greening of enterprise: an exploration of the (NON) role of environmental accounting and environmental accountants in organizational change. *Critical Perspectives on Accounting*, 6 (3), 211–239.

Greenwood, R., Oliver, C., Sahlin, K. and Suddaby, R., 2008. Introduction. *In:* R. Greenwood, C. Oliver, K. Sahlin, and R. Suddaby, eds. *The Sage handbook of organizational institutionalism*. Los Angle: Sage, 1–46.

Greenwood, R. and Suddaby, R., 2006. Institutional entrepreneurship in mature fields: the Big Five accounting firms. *Academy of Management Journal*, 49 (1), 27–48.

Higgins, C., Stubbs, W. and Love, T., 2014. Walking the talk(s): organisational narratives of integrated reporting. *Accounting, Auditing & Accountability Journal*, 27 (7), 1090–1119.

Higgins, C. and Walker, R., 2012. Ethos, logos, pathos: Strategies of persuasion in social/environmental reports. *Accounting Forum*, 36 (3), 194–208.

Hughen, L., Lulseged, A. and Upton, D., 2014. Improving stakeholder value through sustainability and integrated reporting. *CPA Journal*, March, 57–61.

IIRC, 2013. *The international framework: integrated reporting*. Available: www.theiirc.org/wp-content/uploads/2013/12/13-12-08-THE-INTERNATIONAL-IR-FRAMEWORK-2-1.pdf [Accessed 1 October 2013].

Intergovernmental Panel on Climate Change, 2013. *Climate change 2013: the physical science basis*. Available: www.ipcc.ch/report/ar5/wg1/ [Accessed 1 June 2015].

Jepperson, R. L., 1991. Institutions, institutional effects, and institutional practice. *In:* W. W. Powell and P. J. DiMaggio, eds. *The new institutionalism in organizational analysis*. Chicago: Chicago University Press, 143–163.

Jonäll, K. and Rimmel, G., 2016. Corporate bee accountability among Sweedish companies. *In:* K. Atkins and B. Atkins, eds. *The business of bees: an integrated approach to bee decline and corporate responsibility*. Sheffield, UK: Greenleaf Publishers.

Jones, M. J. and Solomon, J. F., 2013. Problematising accounting for biodiversity. *Accounting, Auditing & Accountability Journal*, 26 (5), 668–687.

KPMG, 2011. *Integrated reporting: performance insight through better business reporting*. Available: www.kpmg.com/Global/en/IssuesAndInsights/ArticlesPublications/Documents/road-to-integrated-reporting.pdf [Accessed 26 November 2011].

KPMG, 2015. *Currents of change: The KPMG survey of corporate responsibility reporting 2015.* Available: https://assets.kpmg.com/content/dam/kpmg/pdf/2016/02/kpmg-international-survey-of-corporate-responsibility-reporting-2015.pdf [Accessed 11 December 2016].

Laine, M., 2009a. Ensuring legitimacy through rhetorical changes? A longitudinal interpretation of the environmental disclosures of a leading Finnish chemical company. *Accounting, Auditing & Accountability Journal*, 22 (7), 1029–1054.

Laine, M., 2009b. Towards sustaining the status quo: business talk of sustainability in Finnish corporate disclosures 1987–2005. *European Accounting Review*, 19 (2), 247–274.

Lawrence, T. B. and Suddaby, R., 2006. Institutions and institutional work. *In:* S. R. Clegg, C. Hardy, T. B. Lawrence, and W. R. Nord, eds. *Handbook of organizational studies*. London: Sage, 215–254.

Lawrence, T., Suddaby, R. and Leca, B., 2011. Institutional work: refocusing institutional. *Studies of Organization*, 20 (1), 52–58.

Lounsbury, M., 2008. Institutional rationality and practice variation: new directions in institutional analysis of practice. *Accounting, Organizations and Society*, 33 (4/5), 349–361.

Malsch, B., 2013. Politicizing the expertise of the accounting industry in the realm of corporate social responsibility. *Accounting, Organizations and Society*, 38 (2), 149–168.

Mansoor, H. and Maroun, W., 2016. An initial review of biodiversity reporting by South African corporates – the case of the food and mining sectors. *South African Journal of Economic and Management Sciences*, 19 (4), 592–614.

Marcia, A., Maroun, W. and Callaghan, C., 2015. Value relevance and corporate responsibility reporting in the South African context: an alternate view post King-III. *South African Journal of Economic and Management Sciences*, 18 (4), 500–518.

Maroun, W., 2016. No bees in their bonnet: on the absence of bee reporting by South African listed companies. *In:* K. Atkins and B. Atkins, eds. *The business of bees: an integrated approach to bee decline and corporate responsibility*. Sheffield, UK: Greenleaf Publishers.

Maroun, W., Coldwell, D. and Segal, M., 2014. SOX and the transition from apartheid to democracy: South African auditing developments through the lens of modernity theory. *International Journal of Auditing*, 18 (3), 206–212.

Maroun, W. and van Zijl, W., 2016. Isomorphism and resistance in implementing IFRS 10 and IFRS 12. *The British Accounting Review*, 48 (2), 220–239.

Meyer, J. W. and Rowan, B., 1977. Institutionalized organizations: formal structure as myth and ceremony. *American Journal of Sociology*, 83 (2), 340–363.

Meyer, J. W., Scott, W. R. and Deal, T. E., 1981. Institutional and technical sources of organizational structure: explaining the structure of educational organizations. *In:* H. D. Stein, ed. *Organizations and the human services*. Philadelphia: Temple University Press.

Michelon, G., Pilonato, S. and Ricceri, F., 2015. CSR reporting practices and the quality of disclosure: an empirical analysis. *Critical Perspectives on Accounting*, 33, 59–78.

Mills, C. W., 1940. Situated actions and vocabularies of motive. *American Sociological Review*, 5 (6), 904–913.

Oaks, L. S., Townley, B. and Cooper, D. J., 1998. Business planning as pedagogy: language and control in a changing institutional field. *Administrative Science Quarterly*, 43 (2), 257–292.

O'Donovan, G., 2002. Environmental disclosures in the annual report. *Accounting, Auditing & Accountability Journal*, 15 (3), 344–371.

Patten, D. M., 2002. The relation between environmental performance and environmental disclosure: a research note. *Accounting, Organizations and Society*, 27 (8), 763–773.

Perego, P. and Kolk, A., 2012. Multinationals' accountability on sustainability: The evolution of third-party assurance of sustainability reports. *Journal of Business Ethics*, 110 (2), 173–190.

Powell, W. W., 1988. Institutional effects on organizational structure and performance. *In:* L. G. Zucker, ed. *Institutional patterns and organizations: culture and environment*. Cambridge, MA: Ballinger, 3–22.

PwC, 2015. *Integrated reporting where to next?* Available: www.pwc.co.za/en/assets/pdf/integrated-reporting-survey-2015.pdf [Accessed 16 February 2016].

Romi, A. and Longing, S., 2016. Accounting for bees: evidence from disclosures by US listed companies. *In:* K. Atkins and B. Atkins, eds. *The business of bees: an integrated approach to bee decline and corporate responsibility*. Sheffield, UK: Greenleaf Publishers.

Scott, W. R., 2008. *Institutions and organizations: ideas and interests.* Thousand Oaks, CA: Sage Publications.

Seo, M., and Creed, W. E., 2002. Institutional contradictions, praxis and institutional change: a dialectical perspective. *Academy of Management Review*, 27 (2), 222–247.

Sharma, U., Lawrence, S. and Lowe, A., 2014. Accountants as institutional entrepreneurs: changing routines in a telecommunications company. *Qualitative Research in Accounting & Management*, 11 (3), 190–214.

Solomon, J. and Maroun, W., 2012. *Integrated reporting: the new face of social, ethical and environmental reporting in South Africa?* London: The Association of Chartered Certified Accountants.

Solomon, J. F., Solomon, A., Joseph, N. L. and Norton, S. D., 2013. Impression management, myth creation and fabrication in private social and environmental reporting: insights from Erving Goffman. *Accounting, Organizations and Society*, 38 (3), 195–213.

Stent, W. and Dowler, T., 2015. Early assessments of the gap between integrated reporting and current corporate reporting. *Meditari Accountancy Research*, 23 (1), 92–117.

Stubbs, W. and Higgins, C., 2014. Integrated reporting and internal mechanisms of change. *Accounting, Auditing & Accountability Journal*, 27 (7), 1068–1089.

Suchman, M. C., 1995. Managing legitimacy: strategic and institutional approaches. *The Academy of Management Review*, 20 (3), 571–610.

Suddaby, R., 2010. Challenges for institutional theory. *Journal of Management Inquiry*, 19 (1), 14–20.

Suddaby, R. and Greenwood, R., 2005. Rhetorical strategies of legitimacy. *Administrative Science Quarterly*, 50 (1), 35–67.

Suddaby, R., Saxton, G. D. and Gunz, S., 2015. Twittering change: the institutional work of domain change in accounting expertise. *Accounting, Organizations and Society*, 45, 52–68.

Thomson, I., 2015. 'But does sustainability need capitalism or an integrated report' a commentary on 'The International Integrated Reporting Council: a story of failure' by Flower, J. *Critical Perspectives on Accounting*, 27, 18–22.

Tregidga, H., 2013. Biodiversity offsetting: problematisation of an emerging governance regime. *Accounting, Auditing & Accountability Journal*, 26 (5), 806–832.

Tregidga, H., Milne, M. and Kearins, K., 2014. (Re)presenting 'sustainable organizations'. *Accounting, Organizations and Society*, 39 (6), 477–494.

van Liempd, D. and Busch, J., 2013. Biodiversity reporting in Denmark. *Accounting, Auditing & Accountability Journal*, 26 (5), 833–872.

Venter, E. and De Villiers, C., 2013. The accounting profession's influence on academe: South African evidence. *Accounting, Auditing & Accountability Journal*, 26 (8), 1246–1278.

Zucker, L. G., 1977. The role of institutionalization in cultural persistence. *American Journal of Sociology*, 42 (5), 726–743.

5 Why organizations voluntarily report – agency theory

Charl DE VILLIERS
The University of Auckland, and University of Pretoria

Pei-Chi Kelly HSIAO
The University of Auckland

Abstract

Agency theory explains voluntary disclosures and the need for the assurance of the information through the concept of information asymmetry. Information asymmetry arises from the separation of ownership (principals or shareholders) and control (agents or managers). Agency theory assumes that both shareholders and managers are economically rational and self-interested. Shareholders monitor the behaviour of managers through disclosures. Managers voluntarily disclose additional information to reveal positive information and may do so in self-serving ways. Agency theory focuses on managers' motivations to disclose information rather than organizations' 'motivations'.

Introduction

Agency theory addresses problems that arise from conflicts of interest between principals and agents. In a corporate context, shareholders are the principals and corporate management are the agents. Shareholders are traditionally viewed as corporate owners who elect directors to manage operations and monitor performance on their behalf. Delegation of authority exemplifies a separation of ownership and control. This separation leads to agency problems and agency costs, which arise when the interests of managers and shareholders diverge. From an agency perspective, the existence of voluntary disclosures coincides with the problem of asymmetric information. Voluntary disclosures can act as a monitoring mechanism to mitigate agency problems. Alternatively, managers may exploit information asymmetry and use voluntary disclosures as a tool for self-serving purposes. The need to enhance the credibility of information because of the presence of asymmetric information contributes to the demand for disclosure assurance. Agency theory focuses on managers' motivations and how these influence decisions; this contrasts with social theories, such as legitimacy theory and stakeholder theory, which look at corporations as a whole rather than the individuals running the organization.

This chapter introduces agency theory and interprets voluntary disclosures through this theoretical lens. The next section provides an overview of agency theory and critiques of its assumptions and introduces political cost as an additional motivator for disclosures. Then issues relating to the relationship between voluntary disclosures and corporate governance, the potential for voluntary disclosures to be used as an impression management tool and the demand for disclosure assurance from an agency perspective are discussed. The final section concludes the chapter.

Agency theory

Overview of agency theory

Agency theory is a positive accounting theory as opposed to a normative theory, meaning it seeks to understand and explain what happens in practice rather than prescribing what ought to happen. Agency theory is founded on the existence of agency relationships, which arise when there is a contract delegating decision-making authority from principals to agents (Jensen and Meckling 1976). In a principal-agent relationship, it is expected that agents act on the instructions and in the interests of the principals, and there is a fiduciary relationship of confidence and trust between the parties. However, agency theory infers that there are conflicts inherent in principal-agent relationships, based on the assumptions that individuals are economically rational and self-interested. Merkl-Davies and Brennan (2011) explain economic rationality as the assumption that economic actors are highly rational and seeks to maximize expected utility. Rational actors make choices that take into account all possible consequences that may result from a decision, and all choices are made intentionally and strictly opportunistically. To maximize expected utility, actors compute the likely effect of all possible actions on their total wealth and select the option that maximizes material gains. The assumptions of economic rationality and self-interest indicate that in circumstances where the interests of agents conflict with those of the principals, opportunistic behaviour will arise and agents will seek to maximize their own utility regardless of the impact their actions have on the principals (Fama and Jensen 1983). For instance, in situations where contracts are not enforced or when contracts do not cover the specific circumstance, self-interested managers may invest in high-risk capital projects or pay excessive compensation. Thereby, from an agency perspective, the relationship between shareholders and managers is characterized by contractual obligations and utility maximization.

Information asymmetry is an agency problem that results from the separation of ownership and control. It reflects an information gap that arises from managers possessing superior knowledge, relative to the investment community, regarding the true operations and performance of the corporation. Managers can exploit this knowledge and take actions to maximize their own utility. There are a number of incentives that motivate managers to disclose, distort, or conceal information. In terms of concealing information, for example, career concerns can motivate managers to withhold negative performance outcomes in the hope that such information will not be revealed during their planned tenures, or to buy time to resolve problems before the problems become apparent to shareholders (Song and Thakor 2006; Kothari et al. 2009). The presence of asymmetric information causes investors to demand an information risk premium, and information-deprived investors become less willing to trade (Graham et al. 2005; Dhaliwal et al. 2011). Agency theory predicts that corporations that experience high agency problems will attempt to reduce them by adopting various control mechanisms.

Agency costs include costs incurred to control the agency problem and costs associated with the consequences of not eliminating the problem fully. While construction of optimal contracts is a potential solution to agency problems, it can be costly and/or impossible to cover every circumstance that may occur. As framed by Jensen and Meckling (1976), agency costs are a function of monitoring costs, bonding costs and residual loss. Monitoring costs are incurred by the principals. They include costs related to efforts at monitoring, measuring, and controlling. Disclosure and assurance of information are examples of monitoring costs, along with the employment of independent outside directors to monitor executive behaviour. Bonding costs are incurred by the agents. These occur when agents employ or agree to certain control mechanisms as a guarantee that they will not act against the principals' interests or to ensure principals are compensated in the event of adverse behaviour. Bonding costs include costs associated with performance-based executive compensation and internal audits. While monitoring mechanisms and performance-based compensation contracts are used to align managers' incentives with shareholders' interests, such measures are often insufficient to perfectly resolve agency conflicts. Residual loss occurs when the agency problem is not managed or fully controlled, resulting in misuse of corporate funds or negligence of duties.

Critiques of agency theory

The assumptions of economic rationality and self-interest have been criticized as an oversimplification of human behaviour. Psychological biases in human behaviour prevent full awareness of situations and the rational use of information in decision-making, providing an argument against the assumption of economic rationality. Individuals may be influenced by personal and psychological traits, such as experience and overconfidence; these behavioural biases are commonly the subject of research in behavioural finance literature (see, for instance: Malmendier and Tate 2005; Graham et al. 2013). Furthermore, parties involved in the principal-agent relationship may not fully understand the asymmetric information they face in order to make perfectly rational decisions. The relationships between strategies and outcomes are dynamic, and in practice there is uncertainty and imperfect knowledge.

Another criticism lies in the assumption of self-interest, which may not be applicable to all managers. If the assumptions made by agency theory lie at one end of a spectrum, the assumptions of stewardship theory lie at the opposite end. Davis et al. (1997) identify stewardship theory as an alternative perspective for explaining the motivations driving management behaviours. Stewardship theory assumes that managers are motivated by the collective goals of the organization rather than self-serving behaviour. The steward perceives the utility gained from interest alignment and collaborative behaviour with the principal as higher than the utility gained through self-serving behaviours. Managers are stewards whose interests align with that of the corporation and its owners, and there is no inherent problem of divergent interests. A steward is motivated by intrinsic rewards rather than extrinsic rewards, and their utility function is maximized when shareholders' wealth is maximized. From the perspective of stewardship theory, agency problems cease to exist as the assumption that managers are stewards eliminates the divergence of interests that causes agency problems.

Theories do not exist in isolation, and there is no single theoretical model that can underpin all management behaviour or the reasons behind voluntary disclosures. However, theories can provide a clearer interpretation of the phenomenon under study when considered collectively. Agency theory provides a way of interpreting principal-agent relationships when there is divergence of interests. Agency theory posits that there will be attempts to mitigate agency problems using mechanisms such as voluntary disclosures.

Political costs

The costs of interactions between principals and agents are not the only costs borne by parties involved in a principal-agent relationship. In addition to agency costs, political costs constitute another form of contracting costs that may explain managers' attitudes towards disclosing information. Watts and Zimmerman (1978) assert that external groups such as interest groups, politicians and the government have power to affect corporate wealth redistribution by imposing regulations or corporate taxes, or engaging in product boycotts. Politically visible corporations, often those large in terms of size and profits, can be scrutinized by external groups. Corporations that are politically visible and subject to high political costs may voluntarily disclose information to reduce risks and political costs. De Villiers and Van Staden (2011) indicate that in the event of an environmental crisis, corporations disclose more environmental information on their websites to mitigate adverse political attention. This increase in voluntary disclosures is to reduce political costs by demonstrating that the issues are being adequately managed and do not require consumer action or regulatory intervention.

Voluntary disclosure as a monitoring mechanism

Corporate governance and voluntary disclosures are two monitoring mechanisms used to mitigate agency problems and protect shareholders. Corporate governance mechanisms are introduced to provide oversight over managerial decisions and to ensure efficient corporate operations on behalf of corporate shareholders. Corporate disclosures are a means for investors to supervise managerial actions. Along with information produced by intermediaries such as financial analysts and media reporters, voluntary disclosures address the issue of information asymmetry.

In situations where internal controls are ineffective, such as the presence of large controlling shareholders that dominate the boards and influence decision-making, there will be calls for additional monitoring. Voluntary disclosure is one of the potential control devices that can be used. However, in situations where internal controls are effective, the relationship between internal governance controls and voluntary disclosures can be either complementary or substitutive. Agency theory predicts that if the mechanisms are complementary, the adoption of more governance mechanisms strengthens internal control and managers are less likely to withhold information under an intensive monitoring environment. For instance, independent directors have an incentive to monitor management and facilitate further monitoring methods because their value as an outside director depends primarily on the performance of the companies they are involved in (Donnelly and Mulcahy 2008). This results in improvements in disclosure comprehensiveness and quality. On the other hand, the relationship may be substitutive if one of the two mechanisms is adequate to address the agency problem. Voluntary disclosures are not costless, and if agency conflicts and information asymmetry can be mitigated using alternative mechanisms, such as effective internal governance structures, there will be fewer or no calls for voluntary disclosures.

While there are studies that support the complementary argument, there are also studies that provide evidence supporting the substitutive argument. Research has shown a positive association between levels of voluntary disclosure and board characteristics and presence of an audit committee. In an Italian setting, Allegrini and Greco (2013) found a higher level of voluntary disclosure in firms with larger boards, and a positive impact of board and audit committee meeting frequency on the level of disclosure. Donnelly and Mulcahy (2008) examined the association between board independence and information asymmetry. The study found that in Ireland, voluntary disclosure increased with the number of non-executive directors on the board. Greater board independence is associated with greater transparency, better monitoring, and increased voluntary disclosures. Similar results were found in an Australian context (Lim et al. 2007). In contrast, Eng and Mak's (2003) study in Singapore found an increase in independent directors on boards reduced corporate disclosures, suggesting external directors play a substitute monitoring role in disclosures rather than a complementary role.

Impression management and exploitation of voluntary disclosures

While the provision of incremental information through voluntary disclosures can be viewed in a positive light, the presence of information asymmetry can also be interpreted as an opportunity for impression management. Impression management is concerned with how individuals present themselves to others to be perceived favourably. Agency theory is the dominant perspective on impression management in a corporate reporting context (Merkl-Davies and Brennan 2011). As agency theory assumes managers exhibit opportunistic behaviour, managers are motivated to engage in biased representation of information out of self-interest. Managers have economic incentives to manipulate the content and presentation of disclosures and convey positive performance more clearly than poor performance as their remuneration is linked to corporate performance. Managers can distort perceptions of other parties by directly manipulating financial statements, or they may indirectly manipulate using other corporate communications to alter the perception of performance. It is assumed that managers distort other parties' perceptions of corporate performance by concealing failures and emphasizing successes.

Corporations with weak corporate governance controls and poor financial performance have a greater tendency to engage in impression management. Leung et al. (2015) found corporations in Hong Kong that experience poor current performance, as measured by accounting or market-based measures, are more likely to engage in the concealment of voluntary narrative information. Corporations with higher bankruptcy risk also tend to obfuscate investors' perceptions by making minimal disclosures. Melloni et al. (2016) analysed the tone of business model disclosures in integrated reports, finding a significant association between positive tone and weak corporate governance and poor financial performance. This is supported by Osma and Guillamón-Saorín (2011), who found strong governance limits impression management; this is consistent with the explanation that governance monitoring effectively reduces self-serving disclosures by managers. Monitoring corporate communication strategy can reduce biases in the preparation, presentation and dissemination of information, resulting in lower potential for erroneous decision-making by outsiders. The study also found that corporations with strong corporate governance are more likely to include negative information in their press releases.

Demand for voluntary disclosure assurance

The demand for assurance relates to the need to mitigate agency costs associated with information asymmetry. As management behaviour is generally unobservable by shareholders and creditors, assurance of information through an independent third party increases the credibility of the information provided by the agent. Assurance therefore contributes to reducing information asymmetry and agency costs. However, as independent assurance is a costly process, it is expected that corporations will assure disclosures only if the anticipated benefits outweigh the assurance costs.

Research suggests that corporations operating in settings with a greater need to enhance credibility have a higher tendency to engage in voluntary assurance. Simnett et al. (2009) found corporations operating in industries with greater environmental or social impacts, and those that are more exposed to environmental and social risks, have a greater tendency to purchase assurance for sustainability disclosures. Assurance is demanded to increase user confidence in the credibility of the information contained in their reports. Kolk and Perego (2010) provided a similar explanation in a country-level context. Auditing and governance mechanisms can act as substitutes for weak country-level institutional mechanisms. There is strong evidence that the voluntary demand for assurance services is significantly influenced by the quality of enforcement in the legal environment in which a firm operates. Nevertheless, the study found that the decision to purchase a sustainability assurance service depends on the level of awareness about sustainability that exists in a country. Ruhnke and Gabriel (2013) found that larger firm size and greater dispersion of share ownership positively influence assurance demand, suggesting agency costs play an important role in the decision to seek voluntary assurance. Moreover, voluntary assurance is driven by a self-selection mechanism; corporations that have a sustainability department and generate more comprehensive reports are more likely to seek external assurance.

Conclusion

Corporations use a number of control mechanisms to ensure their agents act in the interest of the principals. From an agency perspective, voluntary disclosures are a monitoring mechanism to address information asymmetry, and they may either complement or substitute for other control mechanisms. In an environment with high agency problems and poor control systems, opportunistic managers may exploit the information gap and produce biased disclosures to modify perceptions of corporate performance. Corporations will engage in voluntary assurance if there is a perceived need to enhance the credibility of information for external users. Agency theory provides a perspective from which to view the principal-agent relationship and offers useful explanations regarding the existence of voluntary disclosures and assurance.

References

Allegrini, M. and Greco, G., 2013. Corporate boards, audit committees and voluntary disclosure: evidence from Italian Listed Companies. *Journal of Management and Governance*, 17 (1), 187–216.

Davis, J. H., Schoorman, F. D. and Donaldson, L., 1997. Toward a stewardship theory of management. *Academy of Management Review*, 22 (1), 20–47.

De Villiers, C. and Van Staden, C. J., 2011. Where firms choose to disclose voluntary environmental information. *Journal of Accounting and Public Policy*, 30 (6), 504–525.

Dhaliwal, D. S., Li, O. Z., Tsang, A. and Yang, Y. G., 2011. Voluntary nonfinancial disclosure and the cost of equity capital: the initiation of corporate social responsibility reporting. *The Accounting Review*, 86 (1), 59–100.

Donnelly, R. and Mulcahy, M., 2008. Board structure, ownership, and voluntary disclosure in Ireland. *Corporate Governance: An International Review*, 16 (5), 416–429.

Eng, L. L. and Mak, Y. T., 2003. Corporate governance and voluntary disclosure. *Journal of Accounting and Public Policy*, 22 (4), 325–345.

Fama, E. F. and Jensen, M. C., 1983. Separation of ownership and control. *The Journal of Law & Economics*, 26 (2), 301–325.

Graham, J. R., Harvey, C. R. and Puri, M., 2013. Managerial attitudes and corporate actions. *Journal of Financial Economics*, 109 (1), 103–121.

Graham, J. R., Harvey, C. R. and Rajgopal, S., 2005. The economic implications of corporate financial reporting. *Journal of Accounting and Economics*, 40 (1–3), 3–73.

Jensen, M. C. and Meckling, W. H., 1976. Theory of the firm: managerial behavior, agency costs and ownership structure. *Journal of Financial Economics*, 3 (4), 305–360.

Kolk, A. and Perego, P., 2010. Determinants of the adoption of sustainability assurance statements: an international investigation. *Business Strategy and the Environment*, 19 (3), 182–198.

Kothari, S. P., Shu, S. and Wysocki, P. D., 2009. Do managers withhold bad news? *Journal of Accounting Research*, 47 (1), 241–276.

Leung, S., Parker, L. and Courtis, J., 2015. Impression management through minimal narrative disclosure in annual reports. *British Accounting Review*, 47 (3), 275–289.

Lim, S., Matolcsy, Z. and Chow, D., 2007. The association between board composition and different types of voluntary disclosure. *European Accounting Review*, 16 (3), 555–583.

Malmendier, U. and Tate, G., 2005. CEO overconfidence and corporate investment. *The Journal of Finance*, 60 (6), 2661–2700.

Melloni, G., Stacchezzini, R. and Lai, A., 2016. The tone of business model disclosure: an impression management analysis of the integrated reports. *Journal of Management & Governance*, 20 (2), 295–320.

Merkl-Davies, D. M. and Brennan, N. M., 2011. A conceptual framework of impression management: new insights from psychology, sociology and critical perspectives. *Accounting and Business Research*, 41 (5), 415–437.

Osma, B. G. and Guillamón-Saorín, E., 2011. Corporate governance and impression management in annual results press releases. *Accounting, Organizations and Society*, 36 (4–5), 187–208.

Ruhnke, K. and Gabriel, A., 2013. Determinants of voluntary assurance on sustainability reports: an empirical analysis. *Journal of Business Economics*, 83 (9), 1063–1091.

Simnett, R., Vanstraelen, A. and Chua, W. F., 2009. Assurance on sustainability reports: an international comparison. *The Accounting Review*, 84 (3), 937–967.

Song, F. and Thakor, A. V., 2006. Information control, career concerns, and corporate governance. *The Journal of Finance*, 61 (4), 1845–1896.

Watts, R. L. and Zimmerman, J. L., 1978. Towards a positive theory of the determination of accounting standards. *The Accounting Review*, 53 (1), 112–134.

6 Stakeholder requirements for sustainability reporting

Charl DE VILLIERS

The University of Auckland, and University of Pretoria

Abstract

Investors need sustainability information in order to fully understand companies' future prospects, including future cash flows and the associated risks. Apart from private and institutional investors, investment professionals, such as analysts and financial advisors, also use the information. These investment-related stakeholders often rely on corporate disclosures for sustainability information. Managers, employees, auditors, customers, pressure groups (for example, environmental groups) and the media have all been shown to demand sustainability information. Stakeholders tend to rely on corporate sustainability and integrated reports for periodic assessments, referring to organizational websites for current information as important matters, such as an environmental crisis, unfold.

Introduction

Chapter 1 explained how sustainability reporting developed as a result of stakeholder demands for more social and environmental information, resulting in companies and other organizations feeling the need to explain their activities. Therefore, stakeholder demands have always been central to sustainability reporting and more recently, integrated reporting. This chapter will discuss what is known about stakeholder demands for social and environmental information.

Evidence has long been gathering that several different stakeholders regard social and environmental disclosures as important; information is sought from corporate disclosures, and this non-financial information is used in investment decision making. The Global Reporting Initiative standards and the Integrated Reporting framework require that organizations establish who their stakeholders are and then engage with stakeholders to ascertain what material sustainability information should be disclosed.

Shareholders' social and environmental disclosure needs

Milne and Chan (1999) and Solomon and Solomon (2006) review shareholder surveys dating back to the 1970s and 1980s, showing that shareholders had little interest in environmental disclosure at that stage. However, market reaction studies already provided clear evidence that markets reacted to environmental events and disclosures (Blacconiere and Patten 1994; Patten and Nance 1998; Shane and Spicer 1983). During the 1990s, shareholders started to demand environmental disclosure. For example, Deegan and Rankin (1997) report that 72 percent of Australian shareholders regard environmental information as material and thus needed for investment decision-making. According to Epstein and Freedman (1994, p. 104), "the economic impact [of social and environmental disclosure items] is most important" to US shareholders. Between 62 percent and 75 percent of New Zealand shareholders rated seven types of corporate environmental disclosure as important (Goodwin et al. 1996). Experiments also show that analysts and individual shareholders take environmental information into account in investment decision-making (Chan and Milne 1999; Holm and Rikhardsson 2008; Liyanarachchi and Milne 2005; Milne and Chan 1999; Milne and Patten 2002; Rikhardsson and Holm 2008).

De Villiers and Van Staden (2010a, 2010b, 2011a, 2012) surveyed individual shareholders, who mostly make their own investment decisions, in the US, the UK, Australia, New Zealand and South Africa, regarding their corporate environmental disclosure requirements. It is important to realise that environmental disclosures are a subset of sustainability disclosures and that individual shareholders who make their own investment decisions are a subset of all investors, with institutional investors, individual investors who rely on advice from others in their investment decisions, lenders such as banks and analysts all playing important roles in the investment information environment.

Table 6.1 Summary of key findings regarding shareholders' environmental disclosure needs based on survey evidence

	US	UK	Australia	New Zealand	South Africa
	Percentage of shareholders who agreed				
The following environmental information should be disclosed by companies:					
1. Major environmental risks and impacts described	83	84	92	87	97
2. Environmental policy	86	81	93	86	94
3. Measurable targets based on environmental policy	66	65	77	67	78
4. Actual performance against targets	69	66	80	68	81
5. Environmental costs by category	75	61	76	62	80
6. Independent audit/assurance	53	55	70	53	75
Environmental disclosure by companies should be compulsory	68	67	69	72	90
Environmental disclosures by companies should be provided:					
1. In the annual report	87	80	91	88	90
2. On the corporate website	76	75	84	72	82

Source: Summarized from De Villiers and Van Staden (2010a, 2010b, 2011a, 2012)

Given that environmental disclosure could potentially be costly, in terms of focusing attention on failures and increasing the likelihood that companies will be held accountable and be forced to take remedial action, it is probably safe to assume that shareholders might be focused on maximizing returns and be the least likely of all stakeholders to be positive about their companies disclosing environmental information. However, De Villiers and Van Staden (2010a, 2010b, 2011a, 2012) find a surprisingly high level of support for corporate environmental disclosure among shareholders. Figure 6.1 shows a summary of some of the key findings of De Villiers and Van Staden (2010a, 2010b, 2011a, 2012). Note the support of between 67 percent and 90 percent of respondents for making environmental disclosures compulsory, as well as the high percentages of support for environmental disclosures in annual reports and on corporate websites.

Archival evidence also shows that the provision of additional social and environmental disclosures is associated with lower cost of capital (Dhaliwal et al. 2011), lower analyst forecast dispersion (Dhaliwal et al. 2012), higher firm values (Cahan et al. 2016) and higher share prices (De Villiers and Marques 2016; De Klerk and De Villiers 2012; De Klerk et al. 2015). In addition, institutional investors show an interest in environmental information and go so far as to acquire additional private environmental information (Solomon and Solomon 2006). Therefore, we can deduce that institutional investors are interested in environmental and other non-financial disclosures voluntarily provided by firms.

Indeed, evidence is mounting that environmental, social and governance (ESG) information is being used by investment professionals. According to a Radley Yeldar (2012) survey, investors and analysts use the voluntary non-financial disclosures provided by firms in their investment decision-making, reporting that "over 80% of [respondents] believe that extra-financial information is . . . relevant to their investment decision-making" (p. 3), that more than 80 percent believe integrated reporting will "deliver benefits to their analysis and company assessments" (p. 4), and that 70 percent use information based on the Global Reporting Initiative Sustainability Reporting Framework (p. 4). One of the most revealing pieces of information from the report is the statement that: "Every respondent in our sample states that they assess extra-financial information as part of their research, analysis or investment decision-making" (Radley Yeldar 2012, p. 16). The kinds of sustainability information that investors and analysts consider relevant to their decision-making processes include information relating to governance, natural resources and social, human and intellectual capital (Radley Yeldar 2012). Respondents favour corporate sustainability reports and integrated reports as the preferred source of extra-financial information, but in addition to corporate disclosures, independent sources of information such as indexes were also mentioned as a source of information; for example, the FTSE4Good index series and the Dow Jones Sustainability Index (Radley Yeldar 2012).

The provision of ESG information by Bloomberg and others, such as RepRisk and Asset4, is also indicative of the demand for sustainability information. The increased prevalence of the supply of this kind of information evidences the market for and the usefulness of such information for investment professionals, who are the leading consumers of these databases and indexes.

Additional evidence that investors, including lenders, use sustainability information, i provided by Dhaliwal et al. (2011), who report that companies are more likely to initiate a stand-alone Corporate Social Responsibility report for the first time when they are about to acquire additional capital from the market.

RobecoSAM (2017, p. 1) explains why investors are interested in sustainability information:

> Sustainability challenges are shaping companies' competitive landscape, and companies that take the lead in seizing opportunities and managing risks associated with these challenges are best-positioned to outperform their peers. . . . [T]he integration of . . . sustainability information into our investment decisions helps us to evaluate companies' quality of management and future performance potential.

RobecoSAM (2015) provides detailed examples of the precise methods whereby sustainability information is incorporated into valuation models. These methods involve valuing a company using traditional methods and data sources (mostly financial in nature), before adding the additional insights provided by sustainability, social and environmental or non-financial data sources. The first step is to graph the likelihood of an impact and the potential size of an impact from social and environmental sources on the company's industry. On this basis, the issues that are deemed to be most likely to have a major influence on the industry are identified. For example, RobecoSAM (2015) identifies product stewardship, environmental management and innovation as the three critical factors for the chemical industry. All sources of sustainability information, including the company's sustainability and integrated reports, are then analysed for information regarding these critical factors. The company's rating compared to its peers in the industry is then used to modify the initial valuation of the company. The modification can be based on additional risk factors or additional opportunities that are identified. Additional risks would generally lead to an increased required rate of return, and thereby to a lowering of the initial valuation, whereas additional opportunities would generally lead to an increased estimation of future revenues and/or increased cost efficiency, translating to increased cash flows, thereby leading to an increase in the initial valuation (RobecoSAM 2015). With this explanation in mind, the increased demand for sustainability information from investors and investment professionals can be understood.

Other stakeholders' requirements

The Global Reporting Initiative standards and the Integrated Reporting framework require extensive stakeholder engagement processes to determine organizations' impacts and which impacts are to be considered material (GRI 2016; IIRC 2013). Material impacts are then expected to be disclosed in sustainability and integrated reports. These requirements acknowledge the information needs of stakeholders and indeed their right to such disclosures. It is also instructive to note that stakeholders are defined broadly and include all groups that are affected by the organization, such as employees, customers, local communities and activists and NGOs interested in specific impacts, such as environmental or health impacts (GRI 2016; IIRC 2013).

De Villiers and Vorster (1995) surveyed auditors, managers and members of several professional accounting bodies. These stakeholders were quite positive about corporate environmental disclosures, for example agreeing with the need for companies to disclose more environmental information on a voluntary basis (65 percent of auditors, 63 percent of managers and 66 percent of accounting professionals) (De Villiers and Vorster 1995). De Villiers (1998) reports similar survey-based findings; for example, 95 percent of managers, 87 percent of auditors and 84 percent of users of corporate disclosures were reported to be in favour of companies disclosing their environmental policies. Using an interview approach, De Villiers (1999) provides evidence that managers involved in the decision to disclose environmental information regard the satisfaction of stakeholders' social and environmental information needs as a major reason for providing these disclosures. De Villiers (2003) provides further evidence that managers support corporate environmental disclosures; for example, 95 percent of managers supported environmental disclosure in annual reports and 66 percent supported disclosure on corporate websites.

Employee-related disclosures form part of the Global Reporting Initiative standards. The requirements include the disclosure of the company's employment policies, the employment code of conduct subscribed to, and health and safety information. Even though employee-related disclosures are increasing, these disclosures are not always provided, even in labour-intensive industries such as mining (Faure and De Villiers 2004).

De Villiers and Van Staden (2011b) theorize that environmental activists, the media and other interested parties seek information regarding a crisis event, such as a major oil spill, on the website of the company involved. De Villiers and Van Staden (2011b) provide evidence that companies respond to these stakeholder needs by regularly updating their websites during a crisis event and that these elevated levels of disclosure are maintained for some time after the event.

Bradford et al. (2017) theorize that customers, as a stakeholder group, also need sustainability information. Bradford et al. (2017) compare customers' needs with the Global Reporting Initiative standards' disclosure items and conclude that the Global Reporting Initiative standards do not adequately cater for customers' sustainability information needs. Nevertheless, customers need sustainability disclosures (Bradford et al. 2017).

Conclusion

This chapter discussed the evidence establishing that stakeholders demand sustainability information and that investment professionals and investors use social, environmental and governance information in their investment decision making. In fact, there is a growing industry around the gathering and provision of sustainability information for investment decision making. However, investors still use companies' own sustainability disclosures as a major source of this kind of information. In addition, the promotion and adoption of integrated reporting indicates renewed interest in non-financial disclosures.

In addition to the information demands from the investment community, various stakeholders demand sustainability disclosures, and both the Global Reporting Initiative standards and the Integrated Reporting framework require the identification of and engagement with the organization's stakeholders to identify which sustainability matters are material and should be dealt with in disclosures.

Of course, not everything is known about stakeholders' sustainability information needs, and stakeholder requirements is one of the relatively under-researched areas in sustainability accounting and integrated reporting research. For example, exactly which types of information would be most valuable and sought after by different stakeholders, and how this might change depending on the circumstances (following an environmental crisis, or following a financial crisis), is not fully understood. Future research could provide insight into these matters.

References

Blacconiere, W. G. and Patten, D. M., 1994. Environmental disclosures, regulatory costs, and changes in firm value. *Journal of Accounting and Economics*, 18 (3), 357–377.

Bradford, M., Earp, J. B., Showalter, D. S. and Williams, P. F., 2017. Corporate sustainability reporting and stakeholder concerns: is there a disconnect? *Accounting Horizons*, 31 (1), 83–102.

Cahan, S., De Villiers, C., Jeter, D., Naiker, V. and Van Staden, C., 2016. Are CSR disclosures value relevant? Cross-country evidence. *European Accounting Review*, 25 (3), 579–611.

Chan, C. C. and Milne, M., 1999. Investor reactions to corporate environmental saints and sinners: an experimental analysis. *Accounting and Business Research*, 29 (4), 250–272.

Deegan, C. and Rankin, M., 1997. The materiality of environmental information to users of annual reports. *Accounting, Auditing & Accountability Journal*, 10 (4), 562–583.

De Klerk, M. and De Villiers, C., 2012. The value relevance of corporate responsibility reporting by South African companies. *Meditari Accountancy Research*, 20 (1), 21–38.

De Klerk, M., De Villiers, C. and Van Staden, C., 2015. The influence of corporate social responsibility disclosure on share prices: evidence from the United Kingdom. *Pacific Accounting Review*, 27 (2), 208–228.

De Villiers, C. J., 1998. The willingness of South Africans to support more green reporting. *South African Journal of Economic and Management Sciences*, NS 1 (1), 145–167.

De Villiers, C. J., 1999. The decision by management to disclose environmental information: a research note based on interviews. *Meditari Accountancy Research*, 7, 33–48.

De Villiers, C. J., 2003. Why do South African companies not report more environmental information when managers are so positive about this kind of reporting? *Meditari Accountancy Research*, 11 (1), 11–23.

De Villiers, C. and Marques, A., 2016. Corporate social responsibility, country-level predispositions, and the consequences of choosing a level of disclosure. *Accounting and Business Research*, 46 (2), 167–195.

De Villiers, C. and Van Staden, C., 2010a. Shareholders' requirements for corporate environmental disclosures: a cross country comparison. *British Accounting Review*, 42 (4), 227–240.

De Villiers, C. and Van Staden, C., 2010b. Why do shareholders require corporate environmental disclosure? *South African Journal of Economic and Management Sciences*, 13 (4), 436–445.

De Villiers, C. and Van Staden, C., 2011a. Shareholder requirements for compulsory environmental information in annual reports and on websites. *Australian Accounting Review*, 21 (4), 317–326.

De Villiers, C. and Van Staden, C., 2011b. Where firms choose to disclose voluntary environmental information. *Journal of Accounting and Public Policy*, 30 (6), 504–525.

De Villiers, C. and Van Staden, C., 2012. New Zealand shareholder attitudes towards corporate environmental disclosure. *Pacific Accounting Review*, 24 (2), 186–210.

De Villiers, C. J. and Vorster, Q., 1995. More corporate environmental reporting in South Africa? *Meditari Accountancy Research*, 3 (1), 44–66.

Dhaliwal, D. S., Li, O. Z., Tsang, A. H. and Yang, Y. G., 2011. Voluntary non-financial disclosure and the cost of equity capital: the case of corporate social responsibility. *Accounting Review*, 86 (1), 59–100.

Dhaliwal, D. S., Radhakrishnan, S., Tsang, A. and Yang, Y. G., 2012. Nonfinancial disclosure and analyst forecast accuracy: international evidence on corporate social responsibility disclosure. *Accounting Review*, 87 (3), 723–759.

Epstein, M. J. and Freedman, M., 1994. Social disclosure and the individual investor. *Accounting, Auditing & Accountability Journal*, 7 (4), 94–109.

Faure, G. and De Villiers, C. J., 2004. Employee-related disclosures in corporate annual reports and the King II Report recommendations. *Meditari Accountancy Research*, 12 (1), 61–75.

Goodwin, D., Goodwin, J. and Konieczny, K., 1996. The voluntary disclosure of environmental information – a comparison of investor and company perceptions. *Accounting Research Journal*, 9 (1), 29–39.

GRI, 2016. *Consolidated set of GRI sustainability reporting standards (2016)*. Available: www.globalreporting.org/standards/gri-standards-download-center/?g=ae2e23b8-4958-455c-a9df-ac372d6ed9a8 [Accessed 9 June 2017].

Holm, C. and Rikhardsson, P., 2008. Experienced and novice investors: does environmental information influence investment allocation decisions? *European Accounting* Review, 17 (3), 537–557.

IIRC, 2013. *The international <IR> framework*. International Integrated Reporting Council. Available: www.theiirc.org/international-ir-framework/ [Accessed 23 February 2014].

Liyanarachchi, G. and Milne, M., 2005. Comparing the investment decisions of accounting practitioners and students: an empirical study on the adequacy of student surrogates. *Accounting Forum*, 29 (2), 121–135.

Milne, M. J. and Chan, C., 1999. Narrative social disclosures: how much of a difference do they make to investor decision-making. *British Accounting Review*, 31 (4), 439–457.

Milne, M. J. and Patten, D. M., 2002. Securing organizational legitimacy: an experimental decision case examining the impact of environmental disclosures. *Accounting, Auditing & Accountability Journal*, 15 (3), 372–405.

Patten, D. M. and Nance, J. R., 1998. Regulatory cost effects in a good news environment: the intra-industry reaction to the Alaska oil spill. *Journal of Accounting and Public Policy*, 17 (4), 409–429.

Radley Yeldar, 2012. *The value of extra-financial disclosure: what investors and analysts said*. Report commissioned by Accounting for Sustainability and the Global Reporting Initiative. Available: www.globalreporting.org/resourcelibrary/The-value-of-extra-financial-disclosure. pdf [Accessed 9 June 2017].

Rikhardsson, P. and Holm, C., 2008. The effect of environmental information on investment allocation decisions – an experimental study. *Business Strategy and the Environment*, 17 (6), 382–397.

RobecoSAM, 2015. *The sustainability yearbook 2015*. Zurich, Switzerland: RobecoSAM.

RobecoSAM, 2017. *The corporate sustainability assessment at a glance*. Available: www.robecosam.com/en/sustainability-insights/about-sustainability/corporate-sustainability-assessment/index.jsp [Accessed 9 June 2017].

Shane, P. and Spicer, B., 1983. Market response to environmental information produced outside the firm. *Accounting Review*, 58 (3), 521–538.

Solomon, J. F. and Solomon, A., 2006. Private social, ethical and environmental disclosure. *Accounting, Auditing & Accountability Journal*, 19 (4), 564–591.

7 Sustainability reporting after a crisis

Warren MAROUN
University of the Witwatersrand

Abstract

An environmental or a social crisis can have a significant effect on a company's sustainability and/or integrated reporting. In general, companies increase in the extent of reporting in order to reassure stakeholders and ensure their continued support. In some cases, however, a decrease in the extent of reporting is important for downplaying adverse events, avoiding additional criticism and denying responsibility. Maintaining and repairing legitimacy is complex and subjective. As a result, there is no generally accepted approach for how companies should change their reporting to manage the effects of an event which undermines organizational legitimacy.

Introduction

When an unexpected event or circumstance occurs, stakeholders demand explanations and expect the organization to take steps to deal with adverse outcomes. At the same time, a negative event can highlight weaknesses, raise awareness of broader issues and result in demands for additional reforms. From a strategic perspective, the organization reacts to the adverse event using one or more of the legitimization strategies outlined in Chapter 3 (adapted from: Suchman 1995; O'Donovan 2002). The aim is to reduce the extent of incongruence between the organization's activities and the expectations of important stakeholders (Dowling and Pfeffer 1975; Suchman 1995). This chapter deals with this process in more detail. It examines how companies change their sustainability or integrated reporting in response to specific events or crises. The aim of this is not to provide a comprehensive summary of all of the applicable research. Instead, select examples are provided and used to illustrate different legitimatization strategies, many of which have been outlined in Chapter 3.

Case studies on sustainability reporting

The Exxon Valdez disaster

In March 1989, the super tanker *Exxon Valdez* ran aground in the Gulf of Alaska, resulting in a spill of approximately 11 million litres of crude oil. At the time, it was the worst environmental disaster caused directly by human activity. Environmental rehabilitation cost Exxon billions of dollars and resulted in significant public criticism (The Economist 1990). Patten (1992, p. 472) examines the company's reporting on the environmental crisis:

> It is not surprising, given the magnitude of the disaster, that Exxon allocated substantial coverage to the spill and the subsequent clean-up efforts in its 1989 annual report. Indeed, approximately 3.5 pages of the report were devoted to the Exxon Valdez accident. Interestingly, Exxon included another 2.5 pages of non-Valdez related environmental disclosures in the 1989 annual report. In contrast, only about 0.6 pages of environmental information had been included in the company's 1988 report.

The change in the company's disclosure trends is strong evidence of the relevance of legitimacy theory in action (see, for example, Deegan et al. 2002; De Villiers and Van Staden 2006; Cho et al. 2010). As discussed in Chapter 3, a company reacts to the destabilizing effect of a negative event by increasing the extent of reporting on the incident in order to allay stakeholders concerns and ensure continued investment.

Patten (1992) shows that an environmental disaster also has implications for other companies not directly involved in the oil spill. A review of the annual reports of 21 (of the 23) companies included in the petroleum segment of the Fortune 500 at the time shows a statistically significant increase in the number of social responsibility–related disclosures in the aftermath of the environmental disaster. The effect is more pronounced for larger firms and those with an ownership interest in the companies directly involved in the oil spill.

These findings provide further evidence of the relevance of legitimacy theory for understanding changes in non-financial reporting The oil spill results in additional public scrutiny of environmental practices and raises societal awareness of the importance of protecting the environment (see The Economist 1990). The effect is stronger for larger, more established organizations which attract more attention from stakeholders. In order to signal an awareness of environmental concerns, distance themselves from oil spill and inform stakeholders of their environmental performance, all of the firms in the petroleum sector provide additional environmental disclosures in their annual reports (Patten 1992).

Deepwater Horizon

In April 2010, an explosion on the Deepwater Horizon oilrig resulted in the discharge of 4.9 million barrels of oil from a well into the Gulf of Mexico. The disaster resulted in a loss of 11 lives, permanent ecological damage and adverse consequences for the local fishing and tourism industry (The Economist 2010). The Deepwater Horizon disaster replaced the Exxon Valdez spill as America's worst environmental disaster.

Summerhays and De Villiers (2012) deal with the corporate reporting implications. They examine the annual reports of the five largest oil companies by market capitalization at the time of the crisis. Similar to Patten's (1992) findings, the company directly involved in the oil spill increases the disclosure dealing specifically with the environmental disaster and with its environmental policies and actions in general. The researchers attribute this to a strategy designed to repair damaged legitimacy. The company acknowledges the crisis, commits to environmental rehabilitation and provides specific disclosures on its action plans. It also uses its sustainability reporting to reassure stakeholders of its overall commitment to the environment, deflect attention and shift some of the focus from the oil spill (see Suchman 1995; O'Donovan 2002). (Subsequently, Matejek and Gossling (2014) argue that the disconnect between environmental reporting and clear action went on to damage further the organization's legitimacy as stakeholders identified the reporting strategy as a symbolic rather than a substantive one.)

Similar to the effects of the *Exxon Valdez* disaster, Deepwater Horizon leads to negative media attention and additional scrutiny that other oil producers respond to by including environmental disclosures designed to portray the organizations' in a favourable light (Summerhays and De Villiers 2012). Sustainability reporting is used to demonstrate that these companies are aware of important environmental risks, have learned from their competitors' mistakes and are operating in a responsible manner (see Suchman 1995; O'Donovan 2002).

The Erika and AZF Toulouse

In 1999, one of Total's oil tankers, the *Erika*, sank off the coast of France, discharging crude oil into the ocean. There was material damage to ocean biology, and the spill's economic impact was estimated at between EUR 840 and EUR 960 million. In 2001, Total suffered a second disaster. There was an explosion at is *AZF Toulouse* chemical plant resulting in loss of life and significant damage to property (Cho 2009).

Consistent with Exxon and BP's reaction to *Exxon Valdez* and *Deepwater Horizon* respectively, Total responded to both incidents by increasing the extent of its environmental disclosures as part of a strategy aimed at repairing legitimacy. In addition, the close timing of the disasters has had an effect on reporting with the increase in disclosures after *AZF Toulouse* being more pronounced than after the *Erika* oil spill (Cho 2009). These results were complemented by findings from a qualitative review of the company's corporate reports to discern the specific legitimization tactics being employed.

In response to the *Erika* oil spill, the company relied primarily on image management. Total concentrated on demonstrating its commitment to the environment and provided specific details on how it planned to respond to the disaster. At the same time, Total attempted to manage blame and deflect some of the criticism for the oil spill but stopped short of denying responsibility. When dealing with *AZF Toulouse*, disclosures were also focused on managing the Total's image as a responsible corporate citizen, but there was more emphasis on distancing the organization from the disaster. The company did not deny responsibility for *AZF Toulouse* but two years after the oil spill, used this strategy for managing the remaining threat to legitimacy posed by the first environmental disaster (Cho 2009).

Airline disasters

Vourvachis et al. (2016) provide an account of how airline companies altered their corporate reporting in response to aviation disasters. The research deals with the following airplane crashes:

* July 2000: Air France Flight 4590
* October 2000: Singapore Airlines Flight 006
* October 2001: Scandinavian Airlines Flight SK686
* June 2009: Air France Flight 447

Contrary to prior findings which show an increase in reporting after an environmental disaster, Air France decreases total disclosures (including items of a positive nature) when dealing with the 2009 crash. This may reflect the effect of the 2008/2009 financial crisis (Vourvachis et al. 2016) and imply that managing legitimacy was not the dominant consideration (Guthrie and Parker 1989). According to Vourvachis et al. (2016), it is also possible that the results reflect the use of denial strategy in terms of which the company refuses to acknowledge accountability for the disaster (see Suchman 1995; O'Donovan 2002).

In the other cases, the affected companies deal specifically with the crashes in their annual reports. These reports show significant increases in the extent of corporate social responsibility (CSR) reporting, especially disclosures on health and safety (Vourvachis et al. 2016). Reporting also tends to emphasize positive CSR aspects (see Suchman 1995; Deegan 2002; O'Donovan 2002). The findings are consistent with the operation of legitimacy theory.

The end of Apartheid

The coming to power of the African National Congress (ANC) in South Africa's 1994 elections brought about the formal end of Apartheid but also ushered in a period of political and economic uncertainty. The ANC's political manifesto at the time questioned the philosophy of the Capitalist system and referred to the need to nationalize the banking and mining sectors in order to redistribute the country's wealth from an elite minority to the impoverished majority (Meznar et al. 1994; Hamilton et al. 2009). The implications for the country's business leaders are summarized by De Villiers and Van Staden (2006, p. 769):

> Managers were facing a situation where everything, including core values, was questioned. Not only did society, represented by the new government,

question the methods and motives of individual companies, but the system of allowing companies to operate, the for-profit motive and the free-market ethos, were questioned.

In response to a significant threat to the legitimacy, companies turned to increased social and environmental reporting. This was designed to signal that organizations were aligning with the social and environmental policies of the new government and providing value for *stakeholders* in addition to the providers of financial capital (De Villiers and Barnard 2000; De Villiers and Van Staden 2006). In the early 1990s, however, South African business had little experience with sustainability reporting. Consequently, managers resorted to replicating best international practice (De Villiers and Van Staden 2006; Maroun et al. 2014). In addition, in order to align the country with international expectations, South Africa adopted International Financial Reporting Standards and released the world's second code on corporate governance which stressed the importance of transparent business leadership and sustainability (Rossouw et al. 2002; Maroun et al. 2014). (These institutional perspectives on sustainability reporting are discussed in more detail in Chapter 4.)

By the early 2000s, many of the initial concerns about radical policy change by the ANC had dissipated. In particular, it had become clear that sustainable business management was not high on the ruling party's list of priorities. As a result, an initial increase in the extent of sustainability reporting by local mining and industrial companies from 1994 to 1999 was followed by a decline in disclosures (De Villiers and Van Staden 2006). As discussed in Chapter 3, companies continue to provide generic disclosures in their annual or sustainability reports to satisfy expectations for, at least, some non-financial reporting. At the same time, they decrease disclosures dealing with specific results, actions and plans in order to avoid drawing attention to otherwise unchallenged sustainability performance (see also Suchman 1995; Cho et al. 2015).

Reactions to violent strike actions

In August 2012, a year of unprecedented strike action in South Africa's platinum industry culminated in a confrontation between police and mineworkers in Marikana which left over 30 people dead and close to 100 injured (Farlam et al. 2015). The strike action was covered extensively by local and international media and resulted in significant criticism of the South African Police and the mining company directly involved in the unrest (for details see: Frankel 2012; Hill and Maroun 2015).

Dube and Maroun (2017) examine how local mining companies dealt with the unrest in their sustainability and integrated reports and provide one of the few examples of the link between non-financial reporting and legitimacy theory in the aftermath of a specific social crisis. Their results are partially consistent with the research examining changes in disclosures in response to environmental disasters (see Patten 1992; Summerhays and De Villiers 2012). The company directly involved in the strike action provides additional disclosure on the events unfolding at Marikana and management's response. This forms part of a legitimization strategy in terms of which management acknowledges problems, attempts to provide a normalizing account and reassures stakeholders that it is responding appropriately (see also Suchman 1995). Contrary to the findings of Patten (1992) and Summerhays and De Villiers (2012), however, the company *decreases* the extent of other sustainability disclosures. According to Dube and Maroun (2017, p. 17):

> This is not necessarily to withhold information from stakeholders but to ensure focus on the most significant event and suggest subtly that the event is extraordinary and not indicative of underlying problems at other operations or with the business model in general.

The finding is consistent with research carried out by De Villiers and Van Staden (2006), which suggested that legitimacy can be repaired or maintained by decreasing the extent of reporting. Most companies increase their corporate social responsibility disclosures and the extent of reporting on the strike action in their integrated, annual or sustainability reports. Almost a third decrease their disclosures, possibly in an effort to avoid additional scrutiny. It is also possible that reduced disclosures are used to signal that the existing governance structures are sound and are unaffected by Marikana (Dube and Maroun 2017).

The introduction of new legislation

There are a number of examples of how the promulgation of new laws or regulations prescribing minimum levels of sustainability performance has implications for organizational legitimacy and reporting strategies (O'Donovan 2002; Watson 2011; Alrazi et al. 2015; Atkins and Maroun 2015; du Toit et al. 2017; McNally et al. 2017). The aim of this chapter is not to summarize this body of work. As a result, one of the most recent examples is used as an illustration.

Cho et al. (2015) examine how two large oil and gas companies balance corporate reporting and sustainability performance while public debate on the extraction of natural resources in the Alaskan National Wildlife Refuge (ANWR) and a proposed environmental bill is taking place.

The two companies under review use their annual and sustainability reports and information on their websites to construct a rational façade 'which posits that oil and gas companies are sustainable from a core economic stakeholder perspective' (Cho et al. 2015, p. 86). The rational façade relies on the taken-for-granted centrality of the capital market and generally accepted position that, while an organization ought to play a responsible role in society, its primary objective is profit maximization (see Bebbington et al. 1999; Tregidga et al. 2014; Atkins et al. 2015).

Nevertheless, as concerns about the state of the planet mount, influential stakeholders expect organizations to take steps to improve environmental performance and align themselves with the latest views on and technological developments concerning the environment (for example, see Okereke 2007; Brown and Dillard 2014; Atkins et al. 2016). As a result, companies combine a market-oriented focus in their corporate reports with rhetoric pointing to the need for improvement and reform:

> In an oil and gas industry setting, challenges related to the core business are acknowledged, but are rep resented as manageable using proactive tactics. Similarly, future initiatives are presented as potential avenues through which encountered challenges will be solved and possible environmental and social consequences will be mitigated.
>
> (Cho et al. 2015, p. 88)

This progressive façade is important for demonstrating that a company is aware of important environmental challenges and is taking steps to develop a more sustainable business model. Cho et al. (2015), however, also find that sustainability disclosures are framed as broad commitments and seldom deal with specific plans of action. In addition, the disclosures are designed to achieve a 'temporal distance'. This involves acknowledging the need to change business processes in the interest of long-term sustainability but deferring significant reforms, which might impact short-term financial considerations, to the distant future (see also Malsch 2013; Tregidga et al. 2014).

A reputation façade complements the rational façade. Similar to the legitimization tactics discussed in Chapter 3, a reputational façade is used to construct an image of a responsible organization which cares about the planet. Disclosures in annual reports or on websites are used to suggest that important social and environmental issues are an integral part of the companies' values and that the provisions of the respective environmental laws are adhered to and respected (Malsch 2013; Cho et al. 2015).

The construction of rational, progressive and reputation façades is important for allowing organizations to respond to the competing expectations of different stakeholders. As explained by Cho et al. (2015, p. 91):

> These practices allow corporations to frame their commitment to sustainability as economically beneficial (rational façade), embracing of new technologies (progressive façade) and sensitive to society and the environment.
>
> (reputation façade)

In other words, the three façades address the importance of economic considerations at the heart of the capital market while recognizing that social and environmental issues have to be dealt with to satisfy the expectations of the relevant influential stakeholders. Unfortunately, the reporting practice involves deferring substantial reform to the long-term and may be an example of how sustainability reporting is contributing to a less-sustainable world (see also Gray 2006).

Unfavourable media attention

This sub-section discusses some of the prior research dealing with the effect of increased media attention or lobbying by non-governmental organizations (NGOs) on companies' sustainability reporting.

Using media agenda setting theory, Brown and Deegan (1998) argue that media are effective in creating an awareness of social or environmental issues and driving concern about organizations' sustainability performance. As predicted by legitimacy theory, companies respond by increasing the extent of related disclosures in order to allay stakeholders' concerns and reassure them that their continued support remains justified. The study is based on Australian data from 1981 to 1994 and is an early example of research dealing with the relevance of legitimacy theory for understanding changes in sustainability reporting.

A more recent study examines how organizations in the fashion industry respond to a conflict with Greenpeace over the release of dangerous chemicals reported in the popular press. The firms in question concede to the NGO's demands but also persuade stakeholders about the reasonableness of their planned response. In particular, environmental reporting is used to present the cause of the pollution and remedial process as complex. This is important for rationalizing the negative environmental event and providing the time needed to develop a more comprehensive plan of action (Brennan and Merkl-Davies 2014).

As a final illustration, Deegan and Blomquist (2006) deal with the interactions between the WWF-Australia and the Minerals Council of Australia (MCA). During 1999, the NGO completed an evaluation of the environmental reports of 11 large Australian mining companies which had signed the *Australian Minerals Industry Code for Environmental Management* issued by the MCA. The researchers' findings suggest that the evaluation of environmental reports by the WWF challenged the companies' social license to operate (see Chapter 3) and resulted in a constructive engagement between the NGO, MCA and mining companies. The mining houses made some effort to alter their behaviour and to conform to the WWF's expectations. In addition, the WWF's concerns appear to have been taken into account in revisions to the industry's environmental code.

On the one hand, this may reflect a legitimization strategy based on changing perceptions and managing expectations, rather than on adopting a policy of significant business reform (consider Dowling and Pfeffer 1975; Tregidga et al. 2014). The adoption of and conformance to the environmental code can be seen as a type of symbolic display which creates the appearance of an industry attempting to improve its sustainability performance (Deegan and Blomquist 2006). The need for substantial change is acknowledged but successfully deferred as increased environmental reporting placates stakeholders and business models, core policies and actual operating activities are left largely unaltered (see also Tregidga et al. 2014; Atkins et al. 2015; Cho et al. 2015). On the other hand, changes to industry standards and reporting practices can be interpreted more favourably. They show how companies may genuinely react

Table 7.1 Summary of crises

Crisis	Paper	Theoretical framework(s)	Companies involved directly in the crisis		Other industry players	
			Disaster-specific disclosure	Related and/or total disclosures	Disaster-specific disclosure	Related and/or total disclosures
Exxon Valdez oil spill	Patten (1992)	Legitimacy theory	Increase	Increase	Not specified	Increase
Deepwater Horizon oil spill	Summerhays and De Villiers (2012)	Legitimacy theory	Increase	Increase	Increase	Increases
The Erika and AZF Toulouse	Cho (2009)	Legitimacy theory	Increase of select disclosures	Increase	Not specified	
Airline disasters	Vourvachis et al. (2016)	Legitimacy theory	Increase	Generally increase	Not specified	
The end of Apartheid and change in South Africa's socio-economic policies	De Villiers and Van Staden (2006)	Legitimacy theory	N/A	N/A	An initial increase in disclosure followed by an emphasis on generic disclosure and a reduction in specific disclosures	
Labour unrest	Dube and Maroun (2017)	Legitimacy theory	Increase	Decrease	Mixed	Mixed
Introduction of new environmental laws	Cho et al. (2015)	Organized hypocrisy	Increase of select disclosures		Increase of generic disclosures	
Media coverage of environmental issues	Brown and Deegan (1998)	Media agenda setting theory & legitimacy theory	N/A	N/A	Increase of select disclosures	
Lobbying by NGO's	Brennan and Merkl-Davies (2014) Deegan and Blomquist (2006)	Legitimacy theory & the use of metaphor in corporate reporting	Increase	Not specified	Increase	

to a threat to legitimacy by engaging with stakeholders and taking some steps to address their concerns (Deegan and Blomquist 2006; Atkins et al. 2016). As summarized by Deegan and Blomquist (2006), if organizations are prepared to at least acknowledge stakeholders' concerns, improved environmental and social performance may be possible.

Summary and conclusion

- Early examples of papers dealing with sustainability reporting as a means of legitimizing organization are based on the assumption that companies react to a negative event by increasing the amount of information provided to stakeholders (Patten 1992).
- More recent studies have shown that the legitimization process is complex and that companies can adopt different strategies for reacting to an event which threatens their credibility. Most notably, De Villiers and Van Staden (2006) provide one of the first accounts of how companies decrease the extent of reporting to avoid public scrutiny and maintain legitimacy. The results are confirmed by Dube and Maroun (2017). This paper also shows variations in reporting strategies, with some companies increasing the information included in their integrated/sustainability reports in the aftermath of a social crisis while others decrease the extent of reporting.
- Predominantly quantitative studies on sustainability reporting are being complemented by more interpretive research. Brennan and Merkl-Davies (2014) and Cho et al. (2015) are examples. These studies do not focus on changes in the volume of reporting. They engage with the legitimization process more closely to deal with exactly how companies use non-financial reporting to maintain or repair legitimacy. As part of this process, a more refined theoretical framework is adopted. The essence of the research is concerned with the legitimization process, but organized hypocrisy and the use of metaphor in language is employed to provide a more detailed understanding of the functioning of sustainability reporting as a tool for securing organizational legitimacy.

References

Alrazi, B., De Villiers, C. and Van Staden, C. J., 2015. A comprehensive literature review on, and the construction of a framework for, environmental legitimacy, accountability and proactivity. *Journal of Cleaner Production*, 102, 44–57.

Atkins, J., Atkins, B., Thomson, I. and Maroun, W., 2015. 'Good' news from nowhere: imagining utopian sustainable accounting. *Accounting, Auditing & Accountability Journal*, 28 (5), 651–670.

Atkins, J., Barone, E., Maroun, W. and Atkins, B., 2016. Bee accounting and accountability in the UK. *In:* K. Atkins and B. Atkins, eds. *The business of bees: an integrated approach to bee decline and corporate responsibility.* Sheffield, UK: Greenleaf Publishers.

Atkins, J. and Maroun, W., 2015. Integrated reporting in South Africa in 2012: perspectives from South African institutional investors. *Meditari Accountancy Research*, 23 (2), 197–221.

Bebbington, J., Gray, R. and Owen, D., 1999. Seeing the wood for the trees: taking the pulse of social and environmental accounting. *Accounting, Auditing & Accountability Journal*, 12 (1), 47–52.

Brennan, N. and Merkl-Davies, D., 2014. Rhetoric and argument in social and environmental reporting: the Dirty Laundry case. *Accounting, Auditing & Accountability Journal*, 27 (4), 602–633.

Brown, J. and Dillard, J., 2014. Integrated reporting: on the need for broadening out and opening up. *Accounting, Auditing & Accountability Journal*, 27 (7), 1120–1156.

Brown, N. and Deegan, C., 1998. The public disclosure of environmental performance information – a dual test of media agenda setting theory and legitimacy theory. *Accounting and Business Research*, 29 (1), 21–41.

Cho, C. H., 2009. Legitimation strategies used in response to environmental disaster: a French case study of total SA's Erika and AZF incidents. *European Accounting Review*, 18 (1), 33–62.

Cho, C. H., Laine, M., Roberts, R. W. and Rodrigue, M., 2015. Organized hypocrisy, organizational façades, and sustainability reporting. *Accounting, Organizations and Society*, 40 (0), 78–94.

Cho, C. H., Roberts, R. W. and Patten, D. M., 2010. The language of US corporate environmental disclosure. *Accounting, Organizations and Society*, 35 (4), 431–443.

Deegan, C., 2002. Introduction: the legitimising effect of social and environmental disclosures – a theoretical foundation. *Accounting, Auditing & Accountability Journal*, 15 (3), 282–311.

Deegan, C. and Blomquist, C., 2006. Stakeholder influence on corporate reporting: an exploration of the interaction between WWF-Australia and the Australian minerals industry. *Accounting, Organizations and Society*, 31 (4–5), 343–372.

Deegan, C., Rankin, M. and Tobin, J., 2002. An examination of the corporate social and environmental disclosures of BHP from 1983–1997. *Accounting, Auditing & Accountability Journal*, 15 (3), 312–343.

De Villiers, C. J. and Barnard, P., 2000. Environmental reporting in South Africa from 1994 to 1999: a research note. *Meditari Accountancy Research*, 8 (1), 15–23.

De Villiers, C. and Van Staden, C. J., 2006. Can less environmental disclosure have a legitimising effect? Evidence from Africa. *Accounting, Organizations and Society*, 31 (8), 763–781.

Dowling, J. and Pfeffer, J., 1975. Organizational legitimacy: social values and organizational behavior. *The Pacific Sociological Review*, 18 (1), 122–136.

Dube, S. and Maroun, W., 2017. Corporate social responsibility reporting by South African mining companies: evidence of legitimacy theory. *South African Journal of Business Management*, 48 (1), 23–34.

du Toit, E., van Zyl, R. and Schutte, G., 2017. Integrated reporting by South African companies: a case study. *Meditari Accountancy Research*, 25 (4).

The Economist, 1990. *In the wake of the Exxon Valdez: the devastating impact of the Alaska Oil Spill*. *The Economist* [Online]. Available: www.highbeam.com/doc/1G1-9037399.html [Accessed 10 February 2017].

The Economist, 2010. The oil well and the damage done. *The Economist* [Online]. Available: www.economist.com/node/16381032 [Accessed 10 February 2017].

Farlam, I., Hemraj, P. and Tokota, B., 2015. *Marikana commission of inquiry: report on matters of public, national and international concern arising out of the tragic incidents at the Lonmin Mine in Marikana, in the North West Province*. Pretoria: Government Printers.

Frankel, P., 2012. Marikana: 20 years in the making. *Business report* [Online]. Available: www.iol.co.za/business/opinion/marikana-20-years-in-the-making-1.1407448 [Accessed 30 March 2013].

Gray, R., 2006. Social, environmental and sustainability reporting and organisational value creation? Whose value? Whose creation? *Accounting, Auditing & Accountability Journal*, 19 (6), 793–819.

Guthrie, J. and Parker, L. D., 1989. Corporate social reporting: a rebuttal of legitimacy theory. *Accounting and Business Research*, 19 (76), 343–352.

Hamilton, C., Mbenga, B. and Ross, R., 2009. *The Cambridge history of South Africa*. Cambridge, UK: Cambridge University Press.

Hill, N. and Maroun, W., 2015. Assessing the potential impact of the Marikana incident on South African mining companies: an event method study. *South African Journal of Economic and Management Sciences*, 18 (4), 586–607.

Malsch, B., 2013. Politicizing the expertise of the accounting industry in the realm of corporate social responsibility. *Accounting, Organizations and Society*, 38 (2), 149–168.

Maroun, W., Coldwell, D. and Segal, M., 2014. SOX and the transition from apartheid to democracy: South African auditing developments through the lens of modernity theory. *International Journal of Auditing*, 18 (3), 206–212.

Matejek, S. and Gossling, T., 2014. Beyond legitimacy: a case study in BP's "Green Lashing". *Journal of Business Ethics*, 20 (4), 571–584.

McNally, M.-A., Cerbone, D. and Maroun, W., 2017. Exploring the challenges of preparing an integrated report. *Meditari Accountancy Research*, 25 (4).

Meznar, M. B., Nigh, D. and Kwok, C. C.Y., 1994. Effect of announcements of withdrawal from South Africa on s. *Academy of Management Journal*, 37 (6), 1633.

O'Donovan, G., 2002. Environmental disclosures in the annual report. *Accounting, Auditing & Accountability Journal*, 15 (3), 344–371.

Okereke, C., 2007. An exploration of motivations, drivers and barriers to carbon management: The UK FTSE 100. *European Management Journal*, 25 (6), 475–486.

Patten, D. M., 1992. Intra-industry environmental disclosures in response to the Alaskan oil spill: a note on legitimacy theory. *Accounting, Organizations and Society*, 17 (5), 471–475.

Rossouw, G. J., van der Watt, A. and Malan, D. P., 2002. Corporate governance in South Africa. *Journal of Business Ethics*, 37 (3), 289–302.

Suchman, M. C., 1995. Managing legitimacy: strategic and institutional approaches. *The Academy of Management Review*, 20 (3), 571–610.

Summerhays, K. and De Villiers, C., 2012. Oil company annual report disclosure responses to the 2010 Gulf of Mexico Oil Spill. *Journal of the Asia-Pacific Centre for Environmental Accountability*, 18 (2), 103–130.

Tregidga, H., Milne, M. and Kearins, K., 2014. (Re)presenting 'sustainable organizations'. *Accounting, Organizations and Society*, 39 (6), 477–494.

Vourvachis, P., Woodward, T., Woodward, D. G. and Patten, D. M., 2016. CSR disclosure in response to major airline accidents: a legitimacy-based exploration. *Sustainability Accounting, Management and Policy Journal*, 7 (1), 26–43.

Watson, S., 2011. Conflict diamonds, legitimacy and media agenda: an examination of annual report disclosures. *Meditari Accountancy Research*, 19 (1/2), 94–111.

8 Determinants of reporting

Warren MAROUN
University of the Witwatersrand

Abstract

A large body of research examines determinants of sustainability reporting. Examples include company-specific features such as size, strategic attitude, organizational culture and financial performance. External forces (including industry characteristics and country level governance and culture) and stakeholder pressures are also relevant. Collectively, these factors have a direct impact on sustainability proactivity, specifically the sophistication of companies' management protocols, accounting systems and stakeholder engagement processes. If these proactivity elements are well established, the organization is more likely to achieve higher levels of accountability leading to improved sustainability and integrated reporting and ultimately, organizational legitimacy.

Introduction

A large body of research adopts a deterministic perspective on sustainability reporting. This involves identifying different variables or factors which are correlated or show a causal connection with sustainability disclosures (Cho et al. 2012; Guidry and Patten 2012). The model proposed by Alrazi et al. (2015) is an example which focused on environmental reporting, but their environmental legitimacy, accountability and proactivity model can be modified to provide a broad understanding of the determinants of sustainability and integrated reporting. The modified version, first introduced in Chapter 1, is shown in Figure 8.1. It highlights several company features, stakeholder pressures and external factors which influence the nature and extent of sustainability and integrated reporting.

Starting from the right-hand side, the model assumes that organizational legitimacy is a primary objective (see Chapter 6). This is achieved when there is congruence between the organization's strategy, processes and related outcomes and the expectations of stakeholders (O'Donovan 2002), giving rise to stakeholder satisfaction.

To satisfy its stakeholders, the organization must accept accountability for sustainability-related issues. This requires responsible performance and high-quality sustainability and integrated reporting which is supported by appropriate

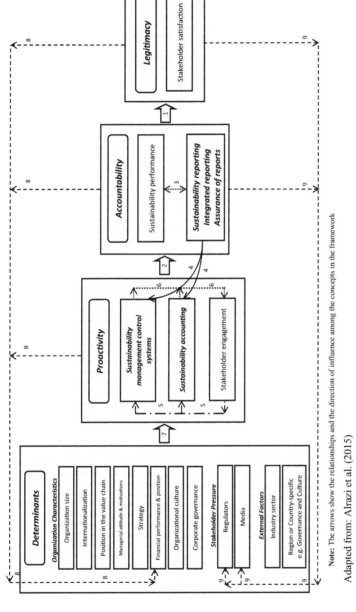

Note: The arrows show the relationships and the direction of influence among the concepts in the framework

Adapted from: Alrazi et al. (2015)

Figure 8.1 Framework of sustainability accounting and integrated reporting influences

assurance of the reports. A company can secure some legitimacy by using its sustainability or integrated report to construct an image of a responsible corporate citizen (for example, see Higgins and Walker 2012; Cho et al. 2015). In the long run, however, corporate rhetoric has to be supported by substantive plans, programs and actions which result in sustainable performance (see Higgins et al. 2014; Matejek and Gossling 2014; Atkins and Maroun 2015). This can only be achieved if the organization has a proactive approach to sustainability management and engagement.

Figure 8.1 shows three elements of proactivity: management and control systems, sustainability accounting and stakeholder engagement. Collectively these elements provide a framework for identifying social and environmental issues, managing them accordingly and collecting the relevant data for measuring performance and reporting to stakeholders (Jones 2010; Alrazi et al. 2015). These are influenced by multiple variables or determinants which can be classified as company factors, stakeholder pressures and external factors. Each of the elements in Figure 8.1 is discussed in more detail below

Determinants – company factors

Various determinants will affect an organization's sustainability management and reporting systems and in turn, its sustainability or integrated report. Company factors are an example. The prior research finds that

> a higher degree of involvement in environmental initiatives is more prevalent among companies that are larger in size, multinational, closer to end consumers, receiving top management support, and more proactive to market stimuli.
>
> (Alrazi et al. 2015, p. 51)

This is probably the result of increased stakeholder pressure/engagement and the resources to develop and maintain comprehensive internal management and reporting systems to support high-quality integrated and sustainability reporting. In particular, environmental or social initiatives can be costly, implying that only firms with adequate financial capital can support sustainability management projects and a comprehensive reporting infrastructure (Alrazi et al. 2015). The research on the relevance of financial performance as a determinant of sustainability reporting has, however, produced mixed results. An alternate view is that firms with lower profitability can take advantage of sustainability projects to lower costs, enhance reputation and improve efficiency, implying that they have a greater incentive to engage in proactive sustainability management (see Porter and van der Linda 1995).

The importance of firm culture and related closely to this, corporate governance should not be overlooked. Senior management are responsible for providing strategic direction, monitoring performance and ensuring long-term sustainability (Solomon 2010; IOD 2016). A firm culture which promotes a dynamic and innovative approach to business is more likely to appreciate the importance of sustainability performance and take a proactive approach to sustainability management and reporting (see Stubbs and Higgins 2014; Massa et al. 2015; De Villiers et al. 2016; du Toit et al. 2017; Dumay and Dai 2017). At the same time, most codes of corporate governance maintain that management has a duty of responsibility for the environment and society (Solomon 2010; IOD 2016). A good example is South Africa's recently released *King-IV Report on Corporate Governance*. This requires those charged with an organization's governance to ensure compliance with laws and regulations which prescribe minimum levels of environmental performance and reporting; to take social and environmental issues into consideration when developing corporate strategies and monitoring performance; and to report transparently on economic, environmental and social dimensions (IOD 2016).

Finally, there is evidence of some companies understanding that social and environmental concerns are not just 'soft issues' which need to be reported to placate stakeholders. So-called non-financial metrics are relevant for an organization's strategy and ability to generate returns (Atkins and Maroun 2015; King 2016; McNally et al. 2017). For example, Porter and van der Linda (1995) argue that companies interpreting environmental issues at the strategic level can incorporate associated risks and opportunities in their business models, leading to innovative approaches to business, reduced costs and increased competitiveness. The researchers maintain that environmental responsibility can be reframed as a drive for productive and efficient utilization of resources and an important opportunity for a company to differentiate itself from its less-sustainable competitors (see also Eccles and Krzus 2010; Mansoor and Maroun 2016). Similarly, Haller and Van Staden (2014) suggest that companies can articulate an integrated business model using a value-added approach. This entails managing and accounting for different capital transformations and the distributions of value to stakeholders to report clearly how the business model generates benefits for stakeholders. As a result, a strategic and innovative approach to business is associated with a proactive approach to sustainability, a sense of environmental and social accountability and improved integrated or sustainability reporting (consider Eccles et al. 2012; Alrazi et al. 2015; Atkins and Maroun 2015).

Stakeholder pressures

Stakeholder activism is likely to drive firms to be proactive about managing their sustainability performance and communicating this information in their integrated or sustainability reports. From a legitimacy theory perspective, Chapter 6 explained that firms operate under a social license which requires them to be mindful of influential stakeholders' needs and to operate according to prevailing social norms (see Dowling and Pfeffer 1975; Suchman 1995; O'Donovan 2002). Higher levels of public scrutiny (Brown and Deegan 1998), active monitoring of and engagement on firms' performance (Atkins and Maroun 2015) and monitoring by regulatory agencies and NGOs (Brennan and Merkl-Davies 2014) can result in changes in the volume and type of information reported to the public (De Villiers and Van Staden 2010).

In essence, all stakeholders have some interest in a firm's environmental or social impact. Even providers of financial capital, including institutional investors, are starting to realize that sustainability and financial performance are closely related (for examples see: Porter and van der Linda 1995; De Villiers and Van Staden 2010; IOD 2011; Atkins and Maroun 2015). As such, investors in Australia, New Zealand, South Africa, the UK and the USA expect companies to provide high-quality non-financial information to complement their financial statements (De Villiers and Barnard 2000; De Villiers and Van Staden 2010; Atkins and Maroun 2015). There are also calls for sustainability or integrated reporting to be mandated and regulated more closely (De Villiers and Van Staden 2011).

The relevance of stakeholder engagement for management proactivity, accountability and sustainability/integrated reporting is discussed in more detail below.

External factors

Companies which are subject to greater regulation/political scrutiny (Solomon and Lewis 2002; Williamson et al. 2006)[1] and have a greater environmental or social impact usually manage sustainability performance more actively (Alrazi et al. 2015; Alrazi et al. 2016) and provide more extensive disclosures in their integrated or sustainability reports (De Villiers and Barnard 2000; Cho et al. 2010).[2] For example, Patten (1992) and Summerhays and De Villiers (2012) document increases in the extent of environmental reporting in the aftermath of the *Exxon Valdez* (1989) and Gulf of Mexico (2010) oil spills respectively. Patten (2002) and Loate et al. (2015) find that companies or industries with poor environmental track records included more environmental information in their corporate reports. Similarly, when faced with a social crisis, the extent of reporting on human capital management increases in an effort to reassure stakeholders and ensure continued support for the affected organizations (Maroun 2016; Dube and Maroun 2017). (Refer to Chapter 7 for more information on how companies change their sustainability reporting in times of crisis.)

The nature of the industry sector is an additional factor to consider. For example, Alrazi et al. (2015, p. 51) explain that:

> Companies in more concentrated industries are able to pass on price increases (due to environmental in- vestments) to their customers. However, companies operating in less concentrated industries may see environmental proactivity as a differentiation strategy and thus an opportunity to gain a competitive advantage.
>
> (see also Porter and van der Linda 1995)

There is also evidence on the relevance of geographical location for the extent and type of information included in sustainability or integrated reports. For

Table 8.1 Summary of cultural elements as determinants of sustainability reporting

Cultural element	Explanation	Relationship with sustainability reporting	
		Low	*High*
Individualism	The degree of integration among members of society and extent to which self-interest is advanced	'Companies realizing good financial performance in low individualist countries share their profits with all stakeholders by undertaking social and environmental actions and disclose information about them to increase their legitimacy' (p. 309).	Reduced levels of social and environmental reporting, possibly as a result of a sense of reduced integration as part of the social context
Masculinity	Firms in a masculine society are more results-orientated, competitive and aggressive.	In a more feminine context, there is a greater sense of solidarity and equality which goes hand-in-hand with non-financial reporting	Management places the emphasis on their own success and returns for investors. ESG metrics are perceived as less relevant and disclosures are reduced.
Tolerance levels	The extent to which firms are able to tolerate or react to changing circumstances	Firms operating in low-tolerance environments rely on rules and regulations to drive their integrated and sustainability reporting.	Firms operate in more flexible/principles-based environment which is willing to adapt to dynamic contexts. This should provide higher-quality integrated or sustainability reports, although the prior research provides mixed results.
Power distance	A description of society's hierarchies. A large power distance shows significant variations in the power status of different parts of society.	The prior research has produced mixed results, but it is expected that firms operating in social settings where power is less stratified enjoy more flexibility and would focus on higher-quality sustainability reporting.	Theoretically, high power distance is associated with more rigid environment which would not be conducive to high-quality sustainability or integrated reporting. The prior research is not, however, conclusive.
Long-term orientation	The extent to which long-term considerations are taken into account by society	Environmental and social issues are often seen as beyond the control or time frame of the organization. As a result, there is less investment in ESG initiatives and reduced reporting.	Profitable companies with a long-term focus try to build stakeholder relationships. They undertake social and environmental initiatives and report on these in their annual or sustainability reports.

(Adapted from Khlif et al. 2015)

example, companies located far from major urban centres or rich biodiversity areas may have a low environmental impact and devote less attention to environmental metrics in their corporate reporting (Alrazi et al. 2015; Mansoor and Maroun 2016). Similarly, variations in the regulatory environment may impact the extent to which companies feel accountable for environmental performance and in turn, the extent of disclosures designed to discharge organizations' accountability to the users of sustainability reports (Solomon and Lewis 2002; Holland and Boon Foo 2003). This becomes more complex for multinationals which need to take into consideration the reporting requirements and expectations of their home countries and those of the numerous jurisdictions in which they operate (Newson and Deegan 2002).

Differences in corporate governance systems, reporting frameworks and national institutions may also be relevant for the explaining variations in the nature and extent of sustainability reporting in different countries (De Klerk et al. 2015; Cahan et al. 2016; De Villiers and Marques 2016). For example, companies operating in countries which champion investor protection, democracy, investor activism and quality corporate governance regulation usually have superior sustainability reporting practices and outperform their peers in terms of return on capital (Cahan et al. 2016; De Villiers and Marques 2016). Similarly, companies conducting business in jurisdictions with mature environmental laws, regulations and reporting guidelines are more likely to provide comprehensive reporting on their environmental performance and management (Cahan et al. 2016).

Finally, there is a growing body of research which deals with the relevance of national cultures for explaining variations in sustainability reporting (Fifka 2013; Kamal and Deegan 2013; Khlif et al. 2015; Maroun 2015). A recent meta-analysis by Khlif et al. (2015) and García-Sánchez et al. (2013) summarizes the relevance of three important cultural elements for predicting the extent of sustainability reporting.

Proactivity

An organization's management systems, accounting function and extent of stakeholder engagement are essential for proactive sustainability management. The prior research usually deals with these elements in the context of environmental reporting, but the principles discussed below will be equally relevant in a broader sustainability context.

Sustainability management control systems

Sustainability management control systems comprise planning and operating practices. They include:

the formal systems and database which [integrate] procedures and processes for the training of personnel, monitoring, summarising, and reporting of specialized environmental performance information to internal and external stakeholders of the firm.

(Melnyk et al. 2003, p. 332)

Effective management systems are important for defining sustainability-related challenges and risks, developing appropriate policies and procedures for managing corporate sustainability and monitoring performance against targets or plans (Alrazi et al. 2015). The benefits of sustainability management and control systems are enhanced when the organization understands sustainability as a strategic issue and monitors sustainability performance at the highest levels (Jones and Solomon 2013; IOD 2016). Where this is the case, sustainability forms part of the organization's core. Disclosures provided in the integrated or sustainability report provide a clear explanation of how the organization is managing material ESG issues and allow stakeholders to assess the organization's ability to generate sustainable returns (IIRC 2013; Atkins and Maroun 2015; King 2016).

Sustainability accounting

Sustainability accounting refers to the system for measuring and reporting on an organization's social and environmental impact. In a financial accounting context, this could include measures of environmental contingencies and provisions and associated financial liabilities (see IASB 1998; IASB 2004). From a management accounting perspective, the environmental and social implications of product costing, project evaluation and performance measurement would be tracked and used for internal decision-making purposes (Botten 2009; Eccles et al. 2012). This is complemented by the use of formal assurance services designed to attest to specific environmental or social measures, such as quantity of CO_2 emissions, water consumption, safety statistics and compliance with non-financial reporting guidelines (Jones and Solomon 2010; Maroun and Atkins 2015; Green et al. 2017). Environmental accounting can also take the form of qualitative or narrative information designed to present the company in a particular light, explain the management of non-financial capital or outline environmental and social objectives (Jones 2010; Jones and Solomon 2013; Atkins et al. 2015).

The financial and management accounting research has shown that the 'calculable infrastructure' of conventional accounting systems can be used to define minimum levels of performance, enhance monitoring and control and allow for corrective action where actual and expected performance differ (see, for example, Cowton and Dopson 2002; Mennicken and Miller 2012; van Zijl and Maroun 2016). The same may apply in a sustainability accounting and reporting context. For example, Alrazi et al. (2015) assert that detailed environmental management systems are usually supported by an accounting infrastructure which allows for the collection and analysis of data to monitor sustainability performance, correct unsatisfactory performance and report results to senior management and external stakeholders. It also possible that the accounting process leads to changes in the management systems. As explained by Frost and Seamer (2002) and Alrazi et al. (2015, p. 51), 'organizations reporting on environmental performance may find it necessary to manage their operations in order to meet the expectations established by the reporting process'.

In some cases, management systems and reporting protocols are underdeveloped. Many companies are producing sustainability (or integrated) reports, but the quality of disclosures has been criticized. For example, the ESG information is often generic, repetitive and not linked sufficiently closely to the organizations' strategy and actual operations (see Solomon and Maroun 2012; KPMG 2015; PwC 2015; Raemaekers et al. 2016). Weak management systems and reporting protocols are part of the reason for this. They make the collection, analysis and distribution of data challenging (Solomon and Lewis 2002; Alrazi et al. 2015). Consequently, a number of reporting guidelines have been released to assist companies to decide what information to include in their sustainability/integrated reports. Examples include the Global Reporting Initiative, the UN Global Compact, the Carbon Disclosure Project and the *International Framework: Integrated Reporting*. In addition, companies are making use of external assurance services to improve compliance with reporting guidelines and the quality of their integrated or sustainability reports (Jones and Solomon 2010; Simnett and Huggins 2015; Farooq and De Villiers 2017).

Stakeholder engagement

Stakeholder engagement involves an organization interacting with its stakeholders to determine their views, information needs and reasonable expectations. Stakeholder engagement has become a key part of codes of corporate governance and a primary consideration in effective sustainability or integrated reporting (see Atkins and Maroun 2015; IOD 2016).

Stakeholders can be defined differently. For both financial and integrated reporting purposes, providers of financial capital are seen as the primary group of stakeholders (see IASB 2010; IIRC 2013). It is assumed that the information needs of other stakeholders are satisfied by addressing the expectations of the primary stakeholders (ibid.). This has been criticized for over-emphasizing the role of financial capital to the detriment of the sustainability agenda which ought to champion environmental and social considerations (Adams 2015; Flower 2015). A review of the definition of 'stakeholders' in a corporate reporting context is, however, beyond the scope of this chapter. In practical terms, an organization would identify its most influential/powerful stakeholders and ensure that their most urgent or material information needs are appropriately addressed (Botten 2009; Alrazi et al. 2015).

Engagement with these stakeholders is essential for understanding their concerns, expectations and requirements. In turn, the focus of information included in integrated and sustainability reports can be adjusted to meet specific information needs, address criticism of the reports and ultimately, ensure higher quality integrated/sustainability reporting (Adams 2002; Alrazi et al. 2015). This can feed back to the underlying management and accounting systems as the organization improves its internal processes and controls to refine information reported to stakeholders (Alrazi et al. 2015). Opportunities for stakeholders to interact with management can also be useful for addressing emerging concerns, bolstering confidence in the organization and providing a complete and transparent account of the business. As a result, effective stakeholder engagement is seen as a key part of sustainability performance and accountability.

Outcomes

If sustainability is integrated in business processes, systems and management philosophies, sustainability and integrated reporting may drive improved sustainability performance and *vice versa*. Where this is the case, the reporting entity demonstrates that its commitment to sustainability is more than just symbolic and legitimacy results. The outcomes of accountability and legitimacy are discussed in more detail in Chapter 9.

Summary and conclusion

- Determinants of sustainability reporting can be categorized as company-specific, external forces and the result of stakeholder pressures. Company size, strategic attitude, organizational culture and financial performance are examples of company features. External forces include, *inter alia*, industry characteristics and the level of public scrutiny. Pressures to provide sustainability-related disclosures can result from the actions of governments, regulators, NGOs, shareholders or other stakeholders.
- Collectively, internal/company-specific features, external factors and stakeholder pressures have a direct impact on sustainability proactivity and are usually associated with more detailed sustainability and integrated reporting.
- In order for a firm to produce a high-quality sustainability or integrated report, a carefully designed management control system is essential. This defines the relationship between internal operations, activities and performance and in turn, influences the scope of the accounting system. If this system is well-designed and supported by stakeholder engagement, the organization is more likely to achieve higher levels of accountability. Ultimately, high levels of accountability yield organizational legitimacy and other positive outcomes, as discussed in more detail in Chapter 9.

Notes

1 Williamson et al. (2006) argue that some companies may ignore sustainability disclosures. They may only report on sustainability performance if this is mandatory.
2 Additional reporting may not always be driven by accountability. Companies may include more information in their integrated or sustainability reports to obfuscate negative performance, manage impressions and deflect criticism. This is discussed in more detail in Chapter 6.

References

Adams, C. A., 2002. Internal organisational factors influencing corporate social and ethical reporting. *Accounting, Auditing & Accountability Journal*, 15 (2), 223–250.

Adams, C. A., 2015. The international integrated reporting council: a call to action. *Critical Perspectives on Accounting*, 27, 23–28.

Alrazi, B., De Villiers, C. and Van Staden, C. J., 2015. A comprehensive literature review on, and the construction of a framework for, environmental legitimacy, accountability and proactivity. *Journal of Cleaner Production*, 102, 44–57.

Alrazi, B., De Villiers, C. and Van Staden, C. J., 2016. The environmental disclosures of the electricity generation industry: a global perspective. *Accounting and Business Research*, 46 (6), 665–701.

Atkins, J., Atkins, B., Thomson, I. and Maroun, W., 2015. 'Good' news from nowhere: imagining utopian sustainable accounting. *Accounting, Auditing & Accountability Journal*, 28 (5), 651–670.

Atkins, J. and Maroun, W., 2015. Integrated reporting in South Africa in 2012: perspectives from South African institutional investors. *Meditari Accountancy Research*, 23 (2), 197–221.

Botten, N., 2009. *Management accounting business strategy*, 2009 ed. Oxford, UK: CIMA Publishing.

Brennan, N. and Merkl-Davies, D., 2014. Rhetoric and argument in social and environmental reporting: the Dirty Laundry case. *Accounting, Auditing & Accountability Journal*, 27 (4), 602–633.

Brown, N. and Deegan, C., 1998. The public disclosure of environmental performance information – a dual test of media agenda setting theory and legitimacy theory. *Accounting and Business Research*, 29 (1), 21–41.

Cahan, S. F., De Villiers, C., Jeter, D. C., Naiker, V. and Van Staden, C. J., 2016. Are CSR disclosures value relevant? Cross-country evidence. *European Accounting Review*, 25 (3), 579–611.

Cho, C. H., Guidry, R. P., Hageman, A. M. and Patten, D. M., 2012. Do actions speak louder than words? An empirical investigation of corporate environmental reputation. *Accounting, Organizations and Society*, 37 (1), 14–25.

Cho, C. H., Laine, M., Roberts, R. W. and Rodrigue, M., 2015. Organized hypocrisy, organizational façades, and sustainability reporting. *Accounting, Organizations and Society*, 40, 78–94.

Cho, C. H., Roberts, R. W. and Patten, D. M., 2010. The language of US corporate environmental disclosure. *Accounting, Organizations and Society*, 35 (4), 431–443.

Cowton, C. J. and Dopson, S., 2002. Foucault's prison? Management control in an automotive distributor. *Management Accounting Research*, 13 (2), 191–213.

De Klerk, M., De Villiers, C. and Van Staden, C., 2015. The influence of corporate social responsibility disclosure on share prices: evidence from the United Kingdom. *Pacific Accounting Review*, 27 (2), 208–228.

De Villiers, C. J. and Barnard, P., 2000. Environmental reporting in South Africa from 1994 to 1999: a research note. *Meditari Accountancy Research*, 8 (1), 15–23.

De Villiers, C. and Marques, A., 2016. Corporate social responsibility, country-level predispositions, and the consequences of choosing a level of disclosure. *Accounting and Business Research*, 46 (2), 167–195.

De Villiers, C., Rouse, P. and Kerr, J., 2016. A new conceptual model of influences driving sustainability based on case evidence of the integration of corporate sustainability management control and reporting. *Journal of Cleaner Production*.

De Villiers, C. and Van Staden, C. J., 2010. Shareholders' requirements for corporate environmental disclosures: a cross country comparison. *The British Accounting Review*, 42 (4), 227–240.

De Villiers, C. and Van Staden, C. J., 2011. Where firms choose to disclose voluntary environmental information. *Journal of Accounting and Public Policy*, 30 (6), 504–525.

Dowling, J. and Pfeffer, J., 1975. Organizational legitimacy: social values and organizational behavior. *The Pacific Sociological Review*, 18 (1), 122–136.

du Toit, E., van Zyl, R. and Schutte, G., 2017. Integrated reporting by South African companies: a case study. *Meditari Accountancy Research*, 25 (4).

Dube, S. and Maroun, W., 2017. Corporate social responsibility reporting by South African mining companies: evidence of legitimacy theory. *South African Journal of Business Management*, 48 (1), 23–34.

Dumay, J. and Dai, T., 2017. Integrated thinking as a cultural control? *Meditari Accountancy Research*, 25 (4).

Eccles, R. G., Ioannou, I. and Serafeim, G., 2012. The impact of corporate sustainability on organisational processes and performance. *NBER WORKING PAPER SERIES* [Online]. Available: www.nber.org/papers/w17950.pdf

Eccles, R. G. and Krzus, M. P., 2010. *Integrated reporting for a sustainable strategy*. Available: www.financialexecutives.org/KenticoCMS/Financial-Executive-Magazine/2010_03/Financial-Reporting-Feature – March-2010.aspx#axzz48iuAkAHV [Accessed 26 November 2012].

Farooq, M. B. and De Villiers, C., 2017. The market for sustainability assurance services: a comprehensive literature review and future avenues for research. *Pacific Accounting Review*, 29 (1), 79–106.

Fifka, M. S., 2013. Corporate responsibility reporting and its determinants in comparative perspective – a review of the empirical literature and a meta-analysis. *Business Strategy and the Environment*, 22 (1), 1–35.

Flower, J., 2015. The international integrated reporting council: a story of failure. *Critical Perspectives on Accounting*, 27, 1–17.

Frost, G. R. and Seamer, M., 2002. Adoption of environmental reporting and management practices: an analysis of New South Wales public sector entities. *Financial Accountability & Management*, 18 (2), 103–127.

García-Sánchez, I.-M., Rodríguez-Ariza, L. and Frías-Aceituno, J.-V., 2013. The cultural system and integrated reporting. *International Business Review*, 22 (5), 828–838.

Green, W., Taylor, S. and Wu, J., 2017. Determinants of greenhouse gas assurance provider choice. *Meditari Accountancy Research*, 25 (1).

Guidry, R. P. and Patten, D. M., 2012. Voluntary disclosure theory and financial control variables: an assessment of recent environmental disclosure research. *Accounting Forum*, 36 (2), 81–90.

Haller, A. and Van Staden, C., 2014. The value added statement – an appropriate instrument for Integrated Reporting. *Accounting, Auditing & Accountability Journal*, 27 (7), 1190–1216.

Higgins, C., Stubbs, W. and Love, T., 2014. Walking the talk(s): organisational narratives of integrated reporting. *Accounting, Auditing & Accountability Journal*, 27 (7), 1090–1119.

Higgins, C. and Walker, R., 2012. Ethos, logos, pathos: strategies of persuasion in social/environmental reports. *Accounting Forum*, 36 (3), 194–208.

Holland, L. and Boon Foo, Y., 2003. Differences in environmental reporting practices in the UK and the US: the legal and regulatory context. *The British Accounting Review*, 35 (1), 1–18.

IASB, 1998. *International accounting standard 37: provisions, contingent liabilities and contingent assets*. Available: http://eifrs.ifrs.org/eifrs/files/238/bv2012_ias08_part%20a_149.pdf [Accessed 29 January 2013].

IASB, 2004. *IFRIC interpretation 1: changes in existing decommissioning, restoration and similar liabilities*. Available: http://eifrs.ifrs.org/eifrs/files/238/bv2012_ifrs13_part%20a_135.pdf [Accessed 29 January 2013].

IASB, 2010. *The conceptual framework for financial reporting.* Available: http://eifrs.ifrs.org/eifrs/files/238/bv2012_conceptual_framework_part%20a_161.pdf [Accessed 29 January 2013].

IIRC, 2013. *The international framework: integrated reporting.* Available: www.theiirc.org/wp-content/uploads/2013/12/13-12-08-THE-INTERNATIONAL-IR-FRAMEWORK-2-1.pdf [Accessed 1 October 2013].

IOD, 2011. *Code for responsible investing in South Africa.* Johannesburg, South Africa: Lexis Nexus South Africa.

IOD, 2016. *King IV report on corporate governance in South Africa.* Johannesburg, South Africa: Lexis Nexus South Africa.

Jones, M. J., 2010. Accounting for the environment: towards a theoretical perspective for environmental accounting and reporting. *Accounting Forum,* 34 (2), 123–138.

Jones, M. J. and Solomon, J. F., 2010. Social and environmental report assurance: some interview evidence. *Accounting Forum,* 34 (1), 20–31.

Jones, M. J. and Solomon, J. F., 2013. Problematising accounting for biodiversity. *Accounting, Auditing & Accountability Journal,* 26 (5), 668–687.

Kamal, Y. and Deegan, C., 2013. Corporate social and environment-related governance disclosure practices in the textile and garment industry: evidence from a developing country. *Australian Accounting Review,* 23 (2), 117–134.

Khlif, H., Hussainey, K. and Achek, I., 2015. The effect of national culture on the association between profitability and corporate social and environmental disclosure: a meta-analysis. *Meditari Accountancy Research,* 23 (3), 296–321.

King, M., 2016. Comments on: *integrated reporting, GARI Conference,* Henley on Thames, UK, 23 October.

KPMG, 2015. *Currents of change: The KPMG survey of corporate responsibility reporting 2015.* Available: https://assets.kpmg.com/content/dam/kpmg/pdf/2016/02/kpmg-international-survey-of-corporate-responsibility-reporting-2015.pdf [Accessed 11 December 2016].

Loate, B., Padia, N. and Maroun, W., 2015. Acid mine drainage in South Africa: a test of legitimacy theory. *Journal of Governance and Regulation,* 4 (2), 26–40.

Mansoor, H. and Maroun, W., 2016. An initial review of biodiversity reporting by South African corporates – the case of the food and mining sectors. *South African Journal of Economic and Management Sciences,* 19 (4), 592–614.

Maroun, W., 2015. Culture, profitability, non-financial reporting and a meta-analysis: comments and observations. *Meditari Accountancy Research,* 23 (3), 322–330.

Maroun, W., 2016. A preliminary study on corporate social responsibility reporting by South African mining companies and the relevance of legitimacy theory. *Meditari Accountancy Research Conference.* University of South Africa, Pillansberg, South Africa.

Maroun, W. and Atkins, J., 2015. *The challenges of assuring integrated reports: views from the South African auditing community.* London: The Association of Chartered Certified Accountants.

Massa, L., Farneti, F. and Scappini, B., 2015. Developing a sustainability report in a small to medium enterprise: process and consequences. *Meditari Accountancy Research,* 23 (1), 62–91.

Matejek, S. and Gossling, T., 2014. Beyond legitimacy: a case study in BP's "Green Lashing". *Journal of Business Ethics,* 20 (4), 571–584.

McNally, M.-A., Cerbone, D. and Maroun, W., 2017. Exploring the challenges of preparing an integrated report. *Meditari Accountancy Research,* 25 (4).

Melnyk, S. A., Sroufe, R. P. and Calantone, R., 2003. Assessing the impact of environmental management systems on corporate and environmental performance. *Journal of Operations Management,* 21 (3), 329–351.

Mennicken, A. and Miller, P., 2012. Accounting, territorialization and power. *Foucault Studies,* 13, 4–24.

Newson, M. and Deegan, C., 2002. Global expectations and their association with corporate social disclosure practices in Australia, Singapore, and South Korea. *The International Journal of Accounting*, 37 (2), 183–213.

O'Donovan, G., 2002. Environmental disclosures in the annual report. *Accounting, Auditing & Accountability Journal*, 15 (3), 344–371.

Patten, D. M., 1992. Intra-industry environmental disclosures in response to the Alaskan oil spill: a note on legitimacy theory. *Accounting, Organizations and Society*, 17 (5), 471–475.

Patten, D. M., 2002. The relation between environmental performance and environmental disclosure: a research note. *Accounting, Organizations and Society*, 27 (8), 763–773.

Porter, E. and van der Linda, C., 1995. Green and competitive: ending the stalemate. *Harvard Business Review* [Online], September–October. Available: https://hbr.org/1995/09/green-and-competitive-ending-the-stalemate [Accessed 1 February 2017].

PwC, 2015. *Integrated reporting where to next?* Available: www.pwc.co.za/en/assets/pdf/integrated-reporting-survey-2015.pdf [Accessed 16 February 2016].

Raemaekers, K., Maroun, W. and Padia, N., 2016. Risk disclosures by South African listed companies post-King III. *South African Journal of Accounting Research*, 30 (1), 41–60.

Simnett, R. and Huggins, A. L., 2015. Integrated reporting and assurance: where can research add value? *Sustainability Accounting, Management and Policy Journal*, 6 (1), 29–53.

Solomon, A. and Lewis, L., 2002. Incentives and disincentives for corporate environmental disclosure. *Business Strategy and the Environment*, 11 (3), 154–169.

Solomon, J., 2010. *Corporate governance and accountability*, 3rd ed. West Susex, UK: John Wiley and Sons Ltd.

Solomon, J. and Maroun, W., 2012. *Integrated reporting: the new face of social, ethical and environmental reporting in South Africa?* London: The Association of Chartered Certified Accountants.

Stubbs, W. and Higgins, C., 2014. Integrated Reporting and internal mechanisms of change. *Accounting, Auditing & Accountability Journal*, 27 (7), 1068–1089.

Suchman, M. C., 1995. Managing legitimacy: strategic and institutional approaches. *The Academy of Management Review*, 20 (3), 571–610.

Summerhays, K. and De Villiers, C., 2012. Oil company annual report disclosure responses to the 2010 Gulf of Mexico Oil Spill. *Journal of the Asia-Pacific Centre for Environmental Accountability*, 18 (2), 103–130.

van Zijl, W. and Maroun, W., 2016. Discipline and punish: exploring the application of IFRS 10 and IFRS 12. *Critical Perspectives on Accounting*.

Williamson, D., Lynch-Wood, G. and Ramsay, J., 2006. Drivers of environmental behaviour in manufacturing SMEs and the implications for CSR. *Journal of Business Ethics*, 67 (3), 317–330.

9   Consequences of reporting

Warren MAROUN

University of the Witwatersrand

Abstract

Chapter 8 presented a model showing a relationship between determinants of sustainability reporting, a company's management and accounting systems and stakeholder engagement. When these factors interact and reinforce each other, the result is more detailed sustainability or integrated reporting. As reporting quality improves, higher levels of accountability are achieved and organizational legitimacy is enhanced. Other positive outcomes of effective sustainability/integrated reporting include: improved profitability/performance, reduced information asymmetry and effective discharge of fiduciary responsibility by those charged with an organization's governance.

Introduction

Chapter 8 dealt with the determinants of sustainability reporting and, by analogy, integrated reporting. These included:

- Different company-specific features (Alrazi et al. 2015; Massa et al. 2015);
- the characteristics of the relevant industry or jurisdiction in which the organization operates (Khlif et al. 2015; Maroun 2015);
- stakeholder pressures (De Villiers and Van Staden 2010);
- the robustness of the underlying accounting infrastructure (Melnyk et al. 2003; McNally et al. 2017); and
- the maturity of sustainability management system (De Villiers et al. 2016; Dumay and Dai 2017).

Turning to the consequences of sustainability accounting and integrated reporting, where there are significant pressures to take cognizance of sustainability-related issues and high levels of environmental proactivity, accountability for sustainability performance and reporting results. This, in turn, leads to stakeholder satisfaction and to organizational legitimacy (see Chapter 3). The outcomes are discussed in detail below.

Accountability

There is no generally accepted definition of 'accountability' in a sustainability reporting context. According to Burritt and Welch (1997, p. 534) environmental accountability relates to 'the actions made on behalf of organizations and the impacts of resulting activities on ecological systems'. Accountability is only possible with high-quality reporting which allows performance to be monitored. Similarly, Dowling and Pfeffer (1975) and Suchman (1995) maintain that organizations are obligated to operate according to prevailing societal norms and demonstrate compliance with societal expectations (see Chapters 3 and 4 for details). In periods of late modernity, this takes into account the growing demand for social and environmental responsibility and transparent corporate reporting on these so-called non-financial issues (see Jones and Solomon 2013; Bebbington and Larrinaga 2014; Atkins and Maroun 2015). Consequently, 'accountability' is a function of an organization's actions or performance and the communication of results to stakeholders (Roberts 1991; Jones and Solomon 2010; Alrazi et al. 2015).

In some cases, corporate reporting may be used to obscure negative sustainability performance or manage impressions (Merkl-Davies et al. 2011; Solomon et al. 2013; Atkins et al. 2015b; Cho et al. 2015). For example, Patten (2002), Cho et al. (2010) and Leung et al. (2015) show that firms with poor environmental track records increase the amount of environmental disclosures but reduce details on specific plans and actions (see Chapter 7 for details). In these cases, sustainability reporting becomes an exercise in managing legitimacy, rather than ensuring accountability (Alrazi et al. 2015). In other instances, however, non-financial reporting can be used to highlight important social and environmental issues, draw an organization's attention to the need for action and give rise to positive changes in systems and processes (see Dillard and Reynolds 2008; Brown and Dillard 2014; Atkins et al. 2015a). For example, Atkins et al. (2016) and Jonäll and Rimmel (2016) show how a decline in pollinator populations has been identified as an emerging environmental risk for the food industry. Disclosures found in integrated and sustainability reports are being used to create public awareness and to explore possible solutions for a complex scientific problem. Similarly, Annandale et al. (2004) argue that environmental reporting provides an account of an organization's environmental impact, which highlights key strategic issues for management's attention and provides a benchmark for tracking performance and implementing internal controls. In other words, non-financial reporting formalizes an account of social and environmental indicators and highlights new domains for management control and review which might otherwise go unnoticed (see Burchell et al. 1980; Hopwood 1987).

The relationship between accountability and reporting is further illustrated by the case of integrated reporting. The IIRC's framework on integrated reporting suggests that management are accountable for more than just the generation of short-term financial returns (King 2016). Organizations need to manage and accept responsibility for multiple types of capital. These include financial, human, intellectual, manufactured, natural and social/relationship capital. Each of these capitals needs to be seen as an integral part of the business model and relevant for the strategic direction of the firm and its approach to reducing and capitalizing on risks and opportunities respectively (IIRC 2013; IOD 2016). This integrated approach to business management is expected to result in improved processes and returns (Eccles et al. 2012); enhanced stakeholder awareness (Atkins and Maroun 2015) and long-term sustainability (King 2016). Management is, therefore, accountable for ensuring that these material benefits for both the organization and its stakeholders are realized.

For stakeholders to be aware of management's plans for ensuring sustainability and to evaluate actual performance against those plans, high-quality corporate reporting is required. As explained by King (in IRCSA 2011) an effective integrated report:

> incorporates, in clear language, material information . . . to enable stakeholders to evaluate the organisation's performance and to make an informed assessment about its ability to create and sustain value. An integrated report should provide stakeholders with a concise overview of an organisation, integrating and connecting important information about strategy, risks and opportunities and relating them to social, environmental, economic and financial issues. By its very nature an integrated report cannot simply be a reporting by-product. It needs to flow from the heart of the organisation.
>
> (Mervyn King's foreword, Integrated Reporting Committee of South Africa [IRCSA] 2011, p. 1)

In other words, high-quality reporting should explain comprehensively the organization's value creation process, reduce information asymmetry and allow stakeholders to hold management accountable for sustainability performance (Eccles et al. 2012; Atkins and Maroun 2015). In addition:

> by its very nature an integrated report cannot simply be a reporting by-product. It needs to flow from the heart of the organisation.
>
> (Mervyn King's foreword, Integrated Reporting Committee of South Africa [IRCSA] 2011, p. 1)

In line with a predicted relationship between proactivity and accountability outlined in Chapter 8 (Alrazi et al. 2015), the reporting process is not only a compliance exercise. Internal policies, plans and controls are required to identify material financial and non-financial capital, monitor their transformations and ensure long-term sustainability. This integrated approach to business management, founded on a broad duty of accountability for multidimensional capital management, informs the preparation of the integrated report (Eccles and Krzus 2010; Atkins and Maroun 2015; Massa et al. 2015). In this way, the prior research has produced mixed results, but it is possible that a sense of accountability for society and environment can drive a more responsible approach to business management. In turn, this can lead to more balanced reporting on how an organization generates value (see Gray et al. 1995; Brown and Dillard 2014; Stubbs and Higgins 2014; Atkins et al. 2015a).

Legitimacy

Chapter 3 explained that companies operate under a social contract which requires them to function according to social values, norms and beliefs. A failure to maintain legitimacy can have serious implications. As explained by Alrazi et al. (2015, p. 53):

> Un-satisfied stakeholders could have a direct impact on the business financial performance and position through shifting to other suppliers (customers), withdrawals of investment (shareholders), and imposing higher interest rates (creditors). Other stakeholders cannot act in this way and for these other stakeholders, their concerns are more likely to be heard through other mechanisms, such as lobbying the regulators for punitive action and engaging the media to create public awareness.

For these reasons, organizations are expected to devote considerable attention to managing and reporting on their sustainability performance. This is designed to meet the information needs of important stakeholders; to demonstrate that the organization is aligned with prevailing social norms/values and ultimately, to secure organizational legitimacy (see Brown and Deegan 1998; O'Donovan 2002; Bansal and Clelland 2004; De Villiers and Van Staden 2006; Atkins and Maroun 2015). The different strategies on which integrated reports rely to gain, maintain or repair legitimacy are discussed in Chapter 3 and Chapter 7.

Other consequences of sustainability reporting

Alrazi et al. (2015) points out that the model discussed in Chapter 8 is not intended to suggest that legitimacy is the only consideration which drives sustainability or integrated reporting. Organizations engage in sustainability management and different types of non-financial reporting for a number of reasons including economic pressures, strategic motives or profitability (see, for example, Porter and van der Linda 1995; Solomon and Lewis 2002; Okereke 2007; Solomon and Maroun 2012). These can be thought of as part of a broader legitimization process (Alrazi et al. 2015) or can be seen as consequences of non-financial reporting in their own right.

Profitability and value-relevance

As touched on in Chapter 8, effective social and environmental management can be used to provide an organization with a competitive advantage, lead to improved efficiency and increase financial performance (Porter and van der Linda 1995). These effects are depicted by arrow 8 in Figure 9.1 of Chapter 8. For example, Eccles et al. (2012) find that companies adopting sustainability policies are more likely to focus on long-term performance, engage actively with stakeholders, manage internal processes and in turn, outperform their counterparts in terms of both return on capital and accounting profit measures. Similarly, Okereke (2007) argues that companies are beginning to make a clear link between climate change and business risk in an effort to develop more comprehensive strategies and ensure long-term profitability (see also Brønn and Vidaver-Cohen 2009). There is also evidence of an initial change in market perception on ESG factors. These are no longer seen as 'soft issues' but important capitals which need to be managed effectively and relevant indicators of a company's ability to generate superior and responsible returns (see Solomon and Lewis 2002; IOD 2011; Atkins and Maroun 2015; du Toit et al. 2017; McNally et al. 2017).

Consequently, there is a significant body of research pointing to the value relevance of ESG reporting. For example, De Klerk and De Villiers (2012), Eccles et al. (2012), De Klerk et al. (2015) and De Villiers and Marques (2016) find statistically significant relationships between different measures of sustainability reporting and performance and the financial or economic performance of multiple organizations in different jurisdictions. The research also reports that factors such as the quality of disclosures, sophistication of the local capital market and the strength of national institutions[1] have a positive impact on the value relevance of ESG disclosures (Jones et al. 2007; Atkins et al. 2015a; Alrazi et al. 2016; Cahan et al. 2016). There are some examples disputing the argument that non-financial reporting is value relevant (for examples, see Hassel et al. 2005; Stubbs and Higgins 2014; Marcia et al. 2015). Nevertheless, the conceptual link between sustainability and economic performance (Porter and van der Linda 1995); significant growth in sustainability and integrated reporting (Hughen et al. 2014) and increasing demands for high-quality disclosures on ESG factors (De Villiers and Van Staden 2010) provides a strong business case for sustainability reporting.

Reducing information asymmetry

Linked closely to the argument that sustainability reporting is value relevant is the possibility that ESG disclosures contribute to the reduction of information asymmetry. The general position is that high-quality financial reporting can be used to manage agency risks, improve accountability and lower the cost of capital (Watts and Zimmerman 1976). 'If the centrality of the shareholder [at the heart of] agency theory is relaxed, and provision is made for a broader group of stakeholders, a similar conclusion is reached regarding the development of non-financial disclosures' (Marcia et al. 2015, p. 502; Zhou et al. 2017). The GRI, IIRC and most codes on corporate governance champion sustainability/ integrated reporting as a way of complementing financial statements by providing a more balanced account of how an organization generates value (Solomon 2010; IIRC 2013; Atkins and Maroun 2014; GRI 2016). Effective integrated (or sustainability) reporting can provide important information about business ethics, environmental awareness and social considerations which are essential for assessing risk, evaluating returns and concluding on an organization's sustainability (IOD 2016). The result is a reduction in cost of capital and increase in firm value (Zhou et al. 2017).

Fiduciary responsibility

There are a number of examples of sustainability considerations being identified as a fiduciary concern for those charged with an organization's governance. Okereke (2007) explains how global warming has been highlighted as a key business consideration by leading petroleum companies. The directors of these organizations are acknowledging some responsibility for managing carbon emissions on ethical grounds and to ensure that their companies are not disadvantaged by possible future action on climate change. Similarly, Atkins et al. (2016) report that companies in the food industry are acknowledging the importance of developing more sustainable agricultural practices and are identifying issues such habitat destruction and extinction of species as requiring urgent attention.

These findings are in line with an emerging view of directors' responsibilities. This holds that those charged with an organization's governance owe a fiduciary duty to their companies to ensure that they generate sustainable returns in the short and long term and take the legitimate interests of stakeholders into account when acting for their firms (Esser and Du Plessis 2007; IOD 2016). This means that a stakeholder-inclusive approach to business can result in situations where a decision by a board of directors is in the best interest of an organization as a whole but is to the immediate disadvantage of shareholders (IOD 2016). It is also possible that ineffective sustainability performance and reporting will lead to legal consequences for boards of directors and their organizations as society places ever more emphasis on the importance of ESG issues (ibid.).

Internal change

The prior literature examining the change potential of sustainability and integrated reporting has produced conflicting results on whether non-financial reporting practices yield positive change at the operational level. For example, Stubbs and Higgins (2014) find that integrated reporting has resulted in only superficial change. While companies provide more ESG information in their integrated reports, underlying processes and operations remain largely unaltered. The results are consistent with those reported by Gray et al. (1995), O' Dwyer (2002), Adams and McNicholas (2007), Adams and Frost (2008) and Raemaekers et al. (2016). These papers suggest that managers interpret non-financial reporting as part of a compliance process and are not consistently incorporating sustainability metrics in their organization's strategy, risk assessment and business processes.

In other cases, the research points to a more optimistic outcome. De Villiers et al. (2016) find that some firms are seeing the advantages of incorporating aspects of sustainability reporting with management control systems and the possibility of this providing a mechanism for external stakeholders to influence the determination of performance measures. Similarly, while Gray et al. (1995) and Adams and Frost (2008) have reservations about the change potential of sustainability reporting, they acknowledge that sustainability reporting can promote an awareness of important social and environmental issues. In turn, at least some companies are developing indicators for measuring sustainability performance and incorporating results in their decision-making, planning and performance evaluation.

Summary and conclusion

- Chapter 8 presented a model showing the relationship between determinants of sustainability reporting and a company's accounting and management systems (referred to collectively as proactivity). This chapter explains how these determinants interact with the accounting and management control infrastructure resulting in accountability and legitimacy.
- In the first instance, being accountable entails more than just descriptive reporting on material sustainability indicators. Where an organization has internalized the importance of sustainability-related issues for understanding business risks, developing strategy and managing business processes, high-quality integrated reporting results. This presents underlying social and environmental issues as more than just non-financial indicators but as an integral part of the business model which needs to be effectively managed to generate long-term returns.
- Where companies proactively monitor sustainability indicators, it is possible for sustainability reporting to inform changes to business processes and practices. While the prior research has challenged this change potential, there is a growing body of evidence which suggests that, as sustainability and integrated reporting systems mature, they may have a positive effect on how companies do business.
- Accountability for sustainability performance and reporting translates into organizational legitimacy. This is, arguably, longer-lasting than legitimacy built on ceremonial displays (see Chapters 3 and 4) because an organization

is able to support an image of a socially responsible citizen with clearly defined policies, plans and actions which supports long-term sustainability.

• In addition to legitimacy, there is a direct business case for high-quality integrated and sustainability reporting. Reporting on different environmental, social and governance aspects can reduce information asymmetry, demonstrate how boards of directors are discharging their fiduciary duties to stakeholders and ultimately, contribute to improved financial returns.

Note

1 These include those committed to enhancing/defending principles such as democracy, freedom of speech, corporate transparency and environmental accountability (Cahan et al. 2016).

References

Adams, C. A. and Frost, G. R., 2008. Integrating sustainability reporting into management practices. *Accounting Forum*, 32 (4), 288–302.

Adams, C. A. and McNicholas, P., 2007. Making a difference: sustainability reporting, accountability and organisational change. *Accounting, Auditing & Accountability Journal*, 20 (3), 382–402.

Alrazi, B., De Villiers, C. and Van Staden, C. J., 2015. A comprehensive literature review on, and the construction of a framework for, environmental legitimacy, accountability and proactivity. *Journal of Cleaner Production*, 102, 44–57.

Alrazi, B., De Villiers, C. and Van Staden, C. J., 2016. The environmental disclosures of the electricity generation industry: a global perspective. *Accounting and Business Research*, 46 (6), 665–701.

Annandale, D., Morrison-Saunders, A. and Bouma, G., 2004. The impact of voluntary environmental protection instruments on company environmental performance. *Business Strategy and the Environment*, 13 (1), 1–12.

Atkins, J. F., Atkins, B., Thomson, I. and Maroun, W., 2015a. 'Good' news from nowhere: imagining utopian sustainable accounting. *Accounting, Auditing & Accountability Journal*, 28 (5), 651–670.

Atkins, J. F., Barone, E., Maroun, W. and Atkins, B., 2016. Bee accounting and accountability in the UK. *In:* K. Atkins and B. Atkins, eds. *The business of bees: an integrated approach to bee decline and corporate responsibility*. Sheffield, UK: Greenleaf Publishers.

Atkins, J. F. and Maroun, W., 2014. *South African institutional investors' perceptions of integrated reporting*. London: The Association of Chartered Certified Accountants.

Atkins, J. F. and Maroun, W., 2015. Integrated reporting in South Africa in 2012: perspectives from South African institutional investors. *Meditari Accountancy Research*, 23 (2), 197–221.

Atkins, J. F., Solomon, A., Norton, S. and Joseph, N. L., 2015b. The emergence of integrated private reporting. *Meditari Accountancy Research*, 23 (1), 28–61.

Bansal, P. and Clelland, I., 2004. Talking trash: legitimacy, impression management, and unsystematic risk in the context of the natural environment. *Academy of Management Journal*, 47 (1), 93–103.

Bebbington, J. and Larrinaga, C., 2014. Accounting and sustainable development: an exploration. *Accounting, Organizations and Society*, 39 (6), 395–413.

Brønn, P. S. and Vidaver-Cohen, D., 2009. Corporate motives for social initiative: legitimacy, sustainability, or the bottom line? *Journal of Business Ethics*, 87 (1), 91–109.

Brown, J. and Dillard, J., 2014. Integrated reporting: on the need for broadening out and opening up. *Accounting, Auditing & Accountability Journal*, 27 (7), 1120–1156.

Brown, N. and Deegan, C., 1998. The public disclosure of environmental performance information – a dual test of media agenda setting theory and legitimacy theory. *Accounting and Business Research*, 29 (1), 21–41.

Burchell, S., Clubb, C., Hopwood, A., Hughes, J. and Nahapiet, J., 1980. The roles of accounting in organizations and society. *Accounting, Organizations and Society*, 5 (1), 5–27.

Burritt, R. L. and Welch, S., 1997. Accountability for environmental performance of the Australian Commonwealth public sector. *Accounting, Auditing & Accountability Journal*, 10 (4), 532–561.

Cahan, S. F., De Villiers, C., Jeter, D. C., Naiker, V. and Van Staden, C. J., 2016. Are CSR disclosures value relevant? Cross-country evidence. *European Accounting Review*, 25 (3), 579–611.

Cho, C. H., Laine, M., Roberts, R. W. and Rodrigue, M., 2015. Organized hypocrisy, organizational façades, and sustainability reporting. *Accounting, Organizations and Society*, 40 (0), 78–94.

Cho, C. H., Roberts, R. W. and Patten, D. M., 2010. The language of US corporate environmental disclosure. *Accounting, Organizations and Society*, 35 (4), 431–443.

De Klerk, M. and De Villiers, C., 2012. The value relevance of corporate responsibility reporting: South African evidence. *Meditari Accountancy Research*, 20 (1), 21–38.

De Klerk, M., De Villiers, C. and Van Staden, C., 2015. The influence of corporate social responsibility disclosure on share prices: evidence from the United Kingdom. *Pacific Accounting Review*, 27 (2), 208–228.

De Villiers, C. and Marques, A., 2016. Corporate social responsibility, country-level predispositions, and the consequences of choosing a level of disclosure. *Accounting and Business Research*, 46 (2), 167–195.

De Villiers, C., Rouse, P. and Kerr, J., 2016. A new conceptual model of influences driving sustainability based on case evidence of the integration of corporate sustainability management control and reporting. *Journal of Cleaner Production*.

De Villiers, C. and Van Staden, C. J., 2006. Can less environmental disclosure have a legitimising effect? Evidence from Africa. *Accounting, Organizations and Society*, 31 (8), 763–781.

De Villiers, C. and Van Staden, C. J., 2010. Shareholders' requirements for corporate environmental disclosures: a cross country comparison. *The British Accounting Review*, 42 (4), 227–240.

Dillard, J. and Reynolds, M., 2008. Green Owl and the Corn Maiden. *Accounting, Auditing & Accountability Journal*, 21 (4), 556–579.

Dowling, J. and Pfeffer, J., 1975. Organizational legitimacy: social values and organizational behavior. *The Pacific Sociological Review*, 18 (1), 122–136.

du Toit, E., van Zyl, R. and Schutte, G., 2017. Integrated reporting by South African companies: a case study. *Meditari Accountancy Research*, 25 (4).

Dumay, J. and Dai, T., 2017. Integrated thinking as a cultural control? *Meditari Accountancy Research*, 25 (4).

Eccles, R., Ioannou, I. and Serafeim, G., 2012. The impact of corporate sustainability on organisational processes and performance. *NBER WORKING PAPER SERIES* [Online]. Available: www.nber.org/papers/w17950.pdf

Eccles, R. G. and Krzus, M. P., 2010. *Integrated reporting for a sustainable strategy*. Available: www.financialexecutives.org/KenticoCMS/Financial-Executive-Magazine/2010_03/Finan cial-Reporting-Feature – March-2010.aspx#axzz48iuAkAHV [Accessed 26 November 2012].

Esser, I. and Du Plessis, J., 2007. The stakeholder debate and directors' fiduciary duties. *SA Mercantile Law Journal*, 19 (3), 346–363.

Gray, R., Walters, D., Bebbington, J. and Thompson, I., 1995. The greening of enterprise: an exploration of the (NON) role of environmental accounting and environmental accountants in organizational change. *Critical Perspectives on Accounting*, 6 (3), 211–239.

GRI, 2016. *Consolidated set of GRI sustainability reporting standards (2016)*. Available: www.globalreporting.org/standards/gri-standards-download-center/?g=ae2e23b8-4958-455c-a9df-ac372d6ed9a8 www.globalreporting.org/reporting/g4/Pages/default.aspx [Accessed 10 February 2017].

Hassel, L., Nilsson, H. and Nyquist, S., 2005. The value relevance of environmental performance. *European Accounting Review*, 14 (1), 41–61.

Hopwood, A. G., 1987. The archaeology of accounting systems. *Accounting, Organizations and Society*, 12 (3), 207–234.

Hughen, L., Lulseged, A. and Upton, D., 2014. Improving stakeholder value through sustainability and integrated reporting. *CPA Journal*, March, 57–61.

IIRC, 2013. *The international framework: integrated reporting*. Available: www.theiirc.org/wp-content/uploads/2013/12/13-12-08-THE-INTERNATIONAL-IR-FRAME WORK-2-1.pdf [Accessed 1 October 2013].

IOD, 2011. *Code for responsible investing in South Africa*. Johannesburg, South Africa: Lexis Nexus South Africa.

IOD, 2016. *King IV report on corporate governance in South Africa*. Johannesburg, South Africa: Lexis Nexus South Africa.

IRCSA, 2011. *Framework for integrated reporting and the integrated report*. Available: www.sustainabilitysa.org [Accessed 5 June 2012].

Jonäll, K. and Rimmel, G., 2016. Corporate bee accountability among Swedish companies. *In:* K. Atkins and B. Atkins, eds. *The business of bees: an integrated approach to bee decline and corporate responsibility*. Sheffield, UK: Greenleaf Publishers.

Jones, M. J. and Solomon, J. F., 2010. Social and environmental report assurance: some interview evidence. *Accounting Forum*, 34 (1), 20–31.

Jones, M. J. and Solomon, J. F., 2013. Problematising accounting for biodiversity. *Accounting, Auditing & Accountability Journal*, 26 (5), 668–687.

Jones, S., Frost, G., Loftus, J. and Van Der Laan, S., 2007. An empirical examination of the market returns and financial performance of entities engaged in sustainability reporting. *Australian Accounting Review*, 17 (41), 78–87.

Khlif, H., Hussainey, K. and Achek, I., 2015. The effect of national culture on the association between profitability and corporate social and environmental disclosure: a meta-analysis. *Meditari Accountancy Research*, 23 (3), 296–321.

King, M., 2016. Comments on: *integrated reporting*, *GARI Conference*, Henley on Thames, UK, 23 October.

Leung, S., Parker, L. and Courtis, J., 2015. Impression management through minimal narrative disclosure in annual reports. *The British Accounting Review*, 47 (3), 275–289.

Marcia, A., Maroun, W. and Callaghan, C., 2015. Value relevance and corporate responsibility in the South African context: an alternate view post King-III. *South African Journal of Economic and Management Sciences*, 18 (4), 500–519.

Maroun, W., 2015. Culture, profitability, non-financial reporting and a meta-analysis: comments and observations. *Meditari Accountancy Research*, 23 (3), 322–330.

Massa, L., Farneti, F. and Scappini, B., 2015. Developing a sustainability report in a small to medium enterprise: process and consequences. *Meditari Accountancy Research*, 23 (1), 62–91.

McNally, M.-A., Cerbone, D. and Maroun, W., 2017. Exploring the challenges of preparing an integrated report. *Meditari Accountancy Research*, 25 (4).

Melnyk, S. A., Sroufe, R. P. and Calantone, R., 2003. Assessing the impact of environmental management systems on corporate and environmental performance. *Journal of Operations Management*, 21 (3), 329–351.

Merkl-Davies, D. M., Brennan, N. M. and McLeay, S. J., 2011. Impression management and retrospective sense-making in corporate narratives: a social psychology perspective. *Accounting, Auditing & Accountability Journal*, 24 (3), 315–344.

O'Donovan, G., 2002. Environmental disclosures in the annual report. *Accounting, Auditing & Accountability Journal*, 15 (3), 344–371.

O'Dwyer, B., 2002. Managerial perceptions of corporate social disclosure: an Irish story. *Accounting, Auditing & Accountability Journal*, 15 (3), 406–436.

Okereke, C., 2007. An exploration of motivations, drivers and barriers to carbon management: the UK FTSE 100. *European Management Journal*, 25 (6), 475–486.

Patten, D. M., 2002. The relation between environmental performance and environmental disclosure: a research note. *Accounting, Organizations and Society*, 27 (8), 763–773.

Porter, E. and van der Linda, C., 1995. Green and competitive: ending the stalemate. *Harvard Business Review* [Online], September–October. Available: https://hbr.org/1995/09/green-and-competitive-ending-the-stalemate [Accessed 1 February 2017].

Raemaekers, K., Maroun, W. and Padia, N., 2016. Risk disclosures by South African listed companies post-King III. *South African Journal of Accounting Research*, 30 (1), 41–60.

Roberts, J., 1991. The possibilities of accountability. *Accounting, Organizations and Society*, 16 (4), 355–368.

Solomon, A. and Lewis, L., 2002. Incentives and disincentives for corporate environmental disclosure. *Business Strategy and the Environment*, 11 (3), 154–169.

Solomon, J., 2010. *Corporate governance and accountability*, 3rd ed., West Susex, UK: John Wiley and Sons Ltd.

Solomon, J. F. and Maroun, W., 2012. *Integrated reporting: the new face of social, ethical and environmental reporting in South Africa?* London: The Association of Chartered Certified Accountants.

Solomon, J. F., Solomon, A., Joseph, N. L. and Norton, S. D., 2013. Impression management, myth creation and fabrication in private social and environmental reporting: insights from Erving Goffman. *Accounting, Organizations and Society*, 38 (3), 195–213.

Stubbs, W. and Higgins, C., 2014. Integrated reporting and internal mechanisms of change. *Accounting, Auditing & Accountability Journal*, 27 (7), 1068–1089.

Suchman, M. C., 1995. Managing legitimacy: strategic and institutional approaches. *The Academy of Management Review*, 20 (3), 571–610.

Watts, R. L. and Zimmerman, J. L., 1976. *Positive accounting theory*. Upper Saddle River, NJ: Prentice-Hall.

Zhou, S., Simnett, R. and Green, W., 2017. Does integrated reporting matter to the capital market? *Abacus*, 53 (1), 94–132.

10 Sustainability and integrated reporting by the public sector and not-for-profit organizations

Warren MAROUN

University of the Witwatersrand, South Africa

Sumit LODHIA

Centre for Sustainability Governance, University of South Australia, Australia

Abstract

Drivers and outcomes of effective reporting (Chapter 8 and 9) in the private sector are usually applicable for the public/not-for-profit sector. There are, however, some important differences. Accountability and transparency are especially relevant for the latter given their position as providers of essential goods and services to the public. The use of integrated and sustainability reporting frameworks by entities which are not required to generate financial returns for stakeholders also needs to be carefully considered. Overall, there is a lack of integrated and sustainability reporting research by the public and not-for-profit sectors despite their important position in the global economy.

Introduction

The public sector, which is traditionally government-owned or controlled (Broadbent and Guthrie 1992), is characterized by the Global Reporting Initiative (GRI) (2016, p. 7–8) as 'significant employers, providers of services, and consumers of resources' which 'also [have] a major impact on national and global progress towards sustainable development' (GRI 2005, pp. 7 and 8). This sector often constitutes a national or federal government which governs the entire nation, governments in particular jurisdictions such as states, cities, provinces or counties, as well as local governments, such as councils. The public sector is often larger than the private sector in terms of size, influence and economic activity, resulting in a significant impact on the environment, society and the economy (Ball and Grubnic 2007). As explained by Guthrie et al. (2010, p. 451):

> government agencies and public sector institutions often exist to mitigate negative externalities and other market failures, or in some instances to influence directly the course of sustainable development through the regulation of business.

Public sector organizations (PSOs) have a civic responsibility to manage public goods, promote access to essential services and ensure application of basic levels of justice (Farneti and Guthrie 2009; Dumay et al. 2010; Guthrie et al. 2010). As a result, they occupy a unique position in contemporary society which is characterized by a high level of public interest and associated closely with this, an expectation for high levels of accountability (Broadbent and Guthrie 1992; Lodhia et al. 2012).

The public sector is not guided by the profitability motive driving corporations. This has resulted in a need to operate in an environmentally and socially sustainable manner, heightening their public accountability. The interaction between the public interest, accountability and sustainability has spurred a growing interest in sustainability reporting by PSOs (Lodhia and Burritt 2004; Guthrie and Farneti 2008; Guthrie et al. 2010). This is especially true because sustainability reporting by these organizations is still in its early stages when compared to the developments in sustainability and integrated reporting in the private sectors (Farneti and Guthrie 2009). However, some authors argue that sustainability reporting by corporations has failed to address sustainability of the planet with limited progress made in reducing sustainability impacts (Hopwood 2009, Milne and Gray 2013). This has led to increasing attention on the public sector as a custodian of the sustainability of resources. Consequently, an emerging body of research examines what PSOs are including in their sustainability reports (or equivalents), the challenges being encountered and the factors which influence the type and extent of reporting by the public sector.

Reporting by the public sector

Generally, public organizations such as schools, hospitals and youth centres are concerned with the provision of goods and services to members of the public and not only with the generation of financial returns for investors (GRI 2013, Institute of Directors in Southern Africa [IOD] 2016). As a result, reporting is typically focused on service delivery, accountability and physical resource management rather than on financial capital maintenance (Lodhia et al. 2012).

PSOs rely on a variety of reporting frameworks (such as those issued by AccountAbility and the United Nations), generally accepted practices which have developed over time, and internal considerations when preparing their reports (Burritt and Welch 1997b; Farneti and Guthrie 2009). Like the private sector, specific disclosures are also informed extensively by the Global Reporting Initiative (GRI) even though only a limited number of PSOs formally register their sustainability reports (or equivalents) with the GRI (Guthrie and Farneti 2008; Dumay et al. 2010; Lodhia et al. 2012). While there are criticisms that the use of the GRI overemphasizes managerial elements to the detriment of social justice (Dumay et al. 2010), codified reporting guidelines have the potential to improve transparency and accountability by ensuring that important sustainability performance information is being publically disclosed (GRI 2012). In addition, a generally accepted sustainability reporting framework can be used to improve comparability among public institutions, reduce the burden of reporting and ensure more efficient regulation at a global level (GRI 2012; King 2016).

Disclosures are provided according to the GRI's 'universals standards' (GRI101, GRI102 and GRI103) complemented by applicable economic (GRI200), environmental (GRI300) and social (GRI400) issues (see Guthrie and Farneti 2008; Lodhia et al. 2012; GRI 2016). Examples include: anti-corruption, energy, emissions, biodiversity impact, training and education and human rights assessments (Burritt and Welch 1997b; Guthrie and Farneti 2008; Lodhia et al. 2012). These are complemented by sector supplements such as those with tailored disclosures for energy providers, airports and non-governmental organizations (NGOs). In addition, in 2005, the GRI issued a pilot sector supplement to assist public agencies with their application of the relevant reporting standards.[1] Three broad reporting areas were identified: (1) organizational performance, (2) public policies and implementation measures and (3) the environmental context/state (GRI 2010).

Table 10.1 outlines common disclosures identified by the GRI in public sector organizations' sustainability reports.

Table 10.1 Examples of commonly found disclosure strategies/themes

Disclosure category	Description
Organizational profile	• An explanation of the relationship with other governments or public authorities including, where applicable, the position of the agency in the larger government structure
Public policies and implementation measures	• A definition of *sustainable development*, a sustainable development policy and an indication of the principles or frameworks used to develop that policy. • Outline of the organization's sustainability-related strategies, targets and/or objectives, including the process followed for setting these. • A detailed progress/implementation assessment for each goal, including, for example, key indicators used to measure progress, progress descriptions and steps taken to ensure continuous improvement. • Describe the role of and methods for ensuring effective stakeholder engagement.
Expenditures	• Gross expenditures analysed by type of payment and financial classification (including capital expenditure by financial classification). • Describe procurement policy of the public agency and how this is used to support organizational sustainability. • Describe economic, environmental and social variables used to evaluate procurements.
Procurement	• Explain how procurement is used to further organizational objectives/government policy. • An explanation of the proportion of goods or services sourced from sustainable suppliers.
Administrative efficiency	• Explain whether or not goods and services were provided efficiently and effectively and any plans for improving delivery

(GRI 2010, pp. 10–11)

Several reporting challenges have been identified:

- While there are a number of common disclosure requirements between the GRI and applicable regulatory provisions, this is not always the case (GRI 2012). In particular, legal requirements vary according to the type of public entity and country, making the development of universal public-sector reporting guidance particularly difficult.
- In addition to regulatory challenges, the GRI's guidelines may not always provide a useful reference for public sector entities wishing to prepare a sustainability report. This is evidenced by significant non-GRI disclosures included in PSOs' sustainability reports (Lodhia et al. 2012). It is possible that the reporting frameworks (including sector supplements issued by the GRI) are not sufficiently specific on how to report issues applicable to PSOs (Farneti and Guthrie 2009). Reporting frameworks have also been criticized for adopting a managerial approach to sustainability reporting by framing ESG metrics as operational considerations (see GRI 2016). Given the important role played by the public sector in providing essential services, a more ecological- and justice-oriented approach to reporting is required, one capable of stressing the centrality of social and environmental rather than financial and manufactured capital (Dumay et al. 2010).
- In this context, the pilot supplement issued by the GRI to guide public sector reporting was not widely adopted. At the time of carrying out their research (2010), the GRI found that only a minority of public organizations adopted the guidelines, and the majority of these were from Europe and Oceania. North America reported low levels of use while no PSOs in Africa made use of the pilot supplement (GRI 2010). This raises questions about the relevance of existing reporting guidelines for different types of public sector entities operating in different jurisdictions (see also Goswami and Lodhia 2014).
- Similar to the challenges being encountered with integrated and sustainability reporting by the private sector (De Villiers et al. 2014; Atkins and Maroun 2015), there is considerable variation in how the GRI's guidelines are interpreted and applied. In particular, rather than see the GRI's guidelines as a comprehensive reporting framework, entities are selective about the disclosure categories which they report on and the detail provided (Guthrie and Farneti 2008; GRI 2012). In addition, reporting can be generic and descriptive. The public sector appears reluctant to provide detailed policy descriptions, implementation measures and quantified assessments of performance against defined objectives (Burritt and Welch 1997b; Guthrie and Farneti 2008; GRI 2010).
- Like their private sector counterparts (see Brown and Dillard 2014; Stubbs and Higgins 2014), public organizations are struggling to apply disclosure guidelines as part of an integrated approach to sustainability management (King 2016). Although the public sector is not subject to the same financial pressures as commercial organizations, identifying and reporting on the interconnections between different types of capitals/resources under their control, associated risks and how GRI indicators are linked to the service

delivery model is proving challenging (Mahomed 2015; IOD 2016; King 2016).

- Limited stakeholder engagement provides a possible explanation for the reporting difficulties encountered by PSOs. Effective stakeholder engagement has been identified as an essential aspect of the reporting model (Botten 2009; Atkins and Maroun 2015) but detailed information on how stakeholders and their legitimate information needs are identified and managed is often not provided (GRI 2010; Kaur and Lodhia 2014). Kaur and Lodhia (2016) suggest that a lack of managerial commitment and professional bodies' support limit stakeholder engagement in sustainability reporting.
- Finally, there is no guarantee that sustainability reporting (even if aligned with the GRI or other reporting frameworks) necessarily results in improved sustainability performance (Dumay et al. 2010). The criticism that the sustainability report is frequently employed as an impression management tool (Moneva et al. 2006; Solomon et al. 2013) is also relevant in the public sector space. Compliance with reporting guidelines may be more about appeasing social expectations for a certain type of reporting than driving actual changes in public sector management (see Gray 2006; Milne et al. 2009; Dumay et al. 2010).

Drivers of sustainability reporting in the public sector

Many of the principles discussed in Chapter 3 and Chapter 8 are equally relevant when it comes to understanding why the public sector engages in different types of sustainability/integrated reporting. Report drivers are discussed below.

Regulation: coercive and normative pressures

Regulatory pressures often play a key role in driving the extent and type of reporting by PSOs. For example, in Australia, Italy and South Africa, public sector entities are required to report certain environmental policies and practices under statute (Burritt and Welch 1997a; Dumay et al. 2010; Lodhia et al. 2012; Mahomed 2015). Operating licenses, community service obligations and explicit mandates can also influence what information PSOs report to stakeholders (Farneti and Guthrie 2009; Lodhia and Jacobs 2013). These legal requirements act as a source of coercive isomorphic pressure (DiMaggio and Powell 1983) which, as explained in Chapter 6, means that at least some sustainability reporting is compliance-driven (Kaur and Lodhia 2016).

There is also evidence of the public sector being sensitive to normative isomorphic pressures. Compliance with already established institutional frameworks is an important means for organizations seeking to demonstrate that they are aligned with prevailing societal expectations (see DiMaggio and Powell 1983; Suchman 1995). The pressures at work in the private sector may not be the same for the public sector but PSOs subject to high levels of public scrutiny or specifically charged with a social or environmental mandate are more likely to adopt generally accepted reporting frameworks such as those issued by the GRI (Lodhia et al. 2012).

Efficiency considerations

Not all environmental and social disclosures provided by PSOs are required by laws and regulations and, in many cases, sustainability reporting is carried out voluntarily (Farneti and Guthrie 2009). In these instances, Australian-based research suggests that the public sector engages in sustainability reporting to satisfy stakeholder information needs, including those of government ministers, local communities and environmental groups (ibid.). In doing so, sustainability reporting plays a role in addressing the risk of the personal interests of politicians and bureaucrats conflicting with the public interest by promoting a transparent system of accounting and accountability (Burritt and Welch 1997a). This is consistent with the prior literature which suggests that accounting developments in the public sector space have focused on establishing or improving formal management control and reporting systems and facilitating performance-based audits as part of a broad accountability agenda (Broadbent and Guthrie 1992; Power 1994).

Sustainability reporting may also be used to improve monitoring and performance and to contribute to more efficient service delivery (Farneti and Guthrie 2009; Dumay et al. 2010), but research on how sustainability/integrated reporting is used to drive internal change at PSOs is limited (see also Broadbent and Guthrie 1992; Stubbs and Higgins 2014; Alrazi et al. 2015; De Villiers et al. 2016).

Stakeholder engagement

Effective stakeholder engagement is identified as a key requirement for high-quality sustainability (GRI 2016) and integrated reporting (International Integrated Reporting Council [IIRC] 2013). According to Kaur and Lodhia (2014, p. 55), this is true in the case of the public sector because of the 'close relationship with the community and other stakeholders' and essential services provided to citizens (Farneti and Guthrie 2009; Lynch 2010; IOD 2016).

Prior research identifies major stakeholder groups for PSOs as:

- Regulators – including parliaments and their advisory bodies;
- Agencies of parliaments – groups/agencies/institutions which implement, monitor and enforce policies and regulations;
- Those undertaking activities with environmental or social consequences (for example, industry groups, managers and natural resource planners);
- Those affected by PSOs' activities (including local and international communities);
- Professional bodies (such as, for example, local government associations, reporting awards bodies)
- Non-governmental organizations (NGOs)
- Internal stakeholders (executives, managers, employees)

(Burritt and Welch 1997a)

Results from a study on sustainability reporting by Australian local councils show that only a small proportion provide detailed disclosure on stakeholder engagement processes in their official reports (Lodhia et al. 2012), but this does not necessarily mean stakeholders' input is not being taken into consideration (see Association of Chartered Certified Accountants [ACCA] 2007). On the contrary, local councils identify their communities as a primary stakeholder suggesting direct accountability to residents/taxpayers. They rely on a number of methods to engage with these stakeholders, including newspapers, face-to-face discussions and public forums. This indicates that stakeholder engagement is more than a superficial process designed to manage expectations. Instead, the local councils interact with stakeholders to identify their legitimate concerns, understand the applicable social and environmental issues more clearly and inform the nature and extent of information being included in official reports (Kaur and Lodhia 2014). While the practice of stakeholder engagement for sustainability reporting by public sector entities is limited (Kaur and Lodhia 2014), recent research illustrates how certain local councils in Australia are leading this practice (Kaur and Lodhia forthcoming).

Sustainability champions

There is some evidence to suggest that sustainability reporting may be driven by key individuals at PSOs who understand its value and, therefore, take responsibility for championing high-quality sustainability reporting. These may be employees in charge of a particular project with specific social or environmental impacts, elected officials who have campaigned for a healthier environment or other internal stakeholders (Farneti and Guthrie 2009). A critical constraint on the public sector is the turnover of such staff who are often attracted to higher-paid and career-advancing positions in the commercial sector (Lodhia and Jacobs 2013).

The relevance of legitimacy

As discussed in Chapter 3 and Chapter 7, a large body of research has demonstrated how companies react to specific environmental or social issues which threaten their legitimacy by altering the amount and type of information included in their annual, integrated or sustainability reports (see, for example, Patten 2002; De Villiers and Van Staden 2006; Dube and Maroun 2017). Burritt and Welch (1997a) and Lodhia et al. (2012) argue that legitimacy continues to be a relevant consideration for PSOs. Like their private sector counterparts, these react to underlying accountability pressures and associated public scrutiny by providing additional information on the applicable environmental or social issues which they are expected to manage. In particular PSOs which have an explicit social or environmental mandate are subject to significant public pressures and associated legitimacy concerns. These may influence the type and extent of sustainability disclosures and propensity to adopt and comply with well-established reporting frameworks such as those issued by the GRI (Farneti and Guthrie 2009; Lodhia and Martin 2011; Lodhia et al. 2012; Lodhia and Jacobs 2013).

The public sector as a role model

According to Guthrie et al. (2010) and Lodhia et al. (2012), the public sector may identify itself as a type of role model for environmental management, with the result that their environmental reporting is designed to encourage environmental responsibility by private organizations. In this context, the aim of sustainability reporting is not only to secure legitimacy as part of an accountability-management initiative: the public sector relies on high-quality reporting to establish its sustainability credentials (see also Lodhia and Jacobs 2013). In doing so, it is able to position its sustainability reporting as the dominant practice. This serves as a significant source of normative iso-morphic pressure which encourages the private sector to adopt a particular sustainability agenda or reporting discourse (see DiMaggio and Powell 1983; Suchman 1995).

Impression management

Impression management in a sustainability reporting context has been exam-ined in detail (Merkl-Davies et al. 2011; Solomon et al. 2013). In contrast, how PSOs may be using sustainability or integrated reporting to similar ends has not been addressed. There are, however, some indications that sustainability reporting can be used as part of an image management process designed to win confidence in or support for a PSO. For example, Farneti and Guthrie (2009) suggest that compliance with the GRI – as an internationally recog-nized reporting standard – can be used to accord legitimacy to PSOs, even if actual sustainability operations are left unaltered (see Chapter 3 and "decou-pling" in Chapter 4). Similarly, sustainability reporting can be motivated by the desire to win public recognition, which contributes significantly to the 'sym-bolic capital' of the PSO (Lodhia and Jacobs 2013; p. 610). This allows PSOs to generate or to be allocated additional funds and adds to the reputation of individual public servants and politicians (see also: Suchman 1995; Bebbington et al. 2009).

Internal drivers of reporting practices

Not all of the prior research confirms the relevance of legitimacy theory for explaining variations in the extent and type of reporting by the public sector. Internal drivers may be more relevant for explaining public sector reporting practices (Lodhia et al. 2012). Many of these are similar to the determinations

Table 10.2 Organizational features affecting sustainability reporting

Feature	Discussion
Size of the organization	As predicted by legitimacy theory, large public institutions and those responsible for providing essential services are more likely to be subject to public scrutiny and provide additional disclosure as a method of managing expectations for enhanced transparency and accountability (consider Deegan 2002; Alrazi et al. 2015). Large government departments are also more complex. They may have multiple mandates; integrated service delivery models or multiple resources under their control. This necessitates more detailed reporting on the applicable environmental and social concerns (Lodhia et al. 2012; IOD 2016).
Managerial systems, practices/attitudes	In the private sector, organizations which identify sustainability considerations as a strategic issue and have proactive managers tend to produce higher-quality sustainability reports (Alrazi et al. 2015; De Villiers et al. 2016). The same may apply in the public sector. The research on the relevance of managerial practices and attitudes at PSOs for sustainability performance and reporting is less developed, but there is some evidence that PSOs which are, for example, aware of environmental issues and have positive managerial attitudes towards the environment have higher levels of environmental management and reporting (Toh and Frost 1998). Similarly, PSOs with more developed environmental accounting and performance systems may be more likely to provide more detailed environmental reporting (Frost and Seamer 2002). In contrast, where commitment to the sustainability agenda is weak, managerial attitudes can constrain sustainability engagement and lower the extent and quality of reporting (O'Dwyer 2005).
Proactivity associated with environmental or social mandates	Chapter 11 explains that organizations with a developed reporting system, sound stakeholder engagement practices and a clear understanding of sustainability performance drivers (referred to collectively as 'proactivity') are normally able to produce higher-quality sustainability or integrated reports than their counterparts (Alrazi et al. 2015; De Villiers et al. 2016). In a PSO context, sustainability proactivity may also be influenced by the organization's mandate. In addition to acting as a source of coercive isomorphic pressure (as discussed earlier), PSOs with a specific environmental or social mandate are more likely to identify respective sustainability considerations as a core part of their service delivery models, develop performance systems and report applicable indicators than other PSOs (Lodhia and Jacobs 2013).
Governance	An inclusive approach to governance which recognizes the importance of balanced authority for managing PSOs' operations and the relevance of high-quality reporting reinforces sustainability proactivity (IOD 2016). Conversely, where governance mechanisms are weak, it is possible for those charged with the management of the PSO to abuse their authority. This undermines sustainability performance and reporting (O'Dwyer 2005).

(*Continued*)

Table 10.2 (Continued)

Feature	Discussion
Source of funding	Based on findings from Australia, PSOs which are funded from budget appropriations (rather than market sources) are more inclined to provide environmental disclosures and place their reporting emphasis on internal channels. This is probably due to greater dependency on the relevant government department for future allocations of funds requiring these PSOs to use more detailed disclosures to demonstrate compliance with applicable government policies (Burritt and Welch 1997b).
	Similarly, non-budget PSOs provide less information about their internal operations than budget-funded PSOs. This suggests that, although environmental issues are growing in importance, commercial pressures on PSOs funded from market sources may be discouraging more detailed reporting (ibid.).
Availability of resources	PSOs which have more resources to maintain appropriate accounting systems, including experienced and competent staff, may provide more detailed sustainability reporting (Lynch 2010; Lodhia and Jacobs 2013; King 2016).
Extent of stakeholder engagement	Alrazi et al. (2015) explains that stakeholder engagement is an important determinant of sustainability reporting and proactivity in the private sector. The same applies in the public sector (Kaur and Lodhia 2014) where external stakeholder engagement is complemented by the actions of internal stakeholders (such as employees, project managers or sustainability champions) who encourage or promote sustainability reporting (Farneti and Guthrie 2009). Conversely, where external and internal stakeholders have limited interaction with PSOs on the relevance of sustainability issues, the detail and extent of reporting may decrease (Lynch 2010).

of sustainability proactivity and reporting by the private sector (see Chapter 11) and are summarized in Table 10.2.

Reporting by not-for-profit organizations

There is little research on the type and extent of reporting by the not-for-profit sector, despite the important role they play in society (Goddard and Juma Assad 2006; Glennie and Lodhia 2013). For the purpose of this chapter, the prior research is grouped into two broad areas. The first examines the role of the not-for-profit (NFPs) or non-governmental organization (NGOs) as a mechanism of accountability and for championing the sustainability agenda.[2] The second collection of research evaluates reporting by NGOs to a limited extent and identifies considerations for an effective reporting framework for these organizations.

NGOs as a mechanism of accountability and an agent of positive change

A large body of research deals with the role played by the not-for-profit sector in promoting higher levels of sustainability and accountability (O'Dwyer et al. 2005; Gondor and Morimoto 2011). For example, Brennan and Merkl-Davies (2014) examine reporting in the popular press by companies in the sportswear/fashion industry. The study focuses on reporting strategies used by Greenpeace to pressure these organizations to improve environmental standards. Similarly, Apostol (2015) evaluates how civil society groups generate counter-accounts in opposition to a gold-mining initiative driven by a Canadian company in Romania. These accounts are designed to highlight weaknesses in the mining company's plans for managing the adverse social and environmental impact of the operation and the propensity for state institutions to prioritize financial considerations over social imperatives and the environment.

A related body of work deals with the role of NGOs in the policy development space. For example, a case study dealing with the construction of a large commercial port in India examines the formulation of a sustainable development policy. The researchers find that policy formulation is an evolutionary process. It is driven by identification of existing challenges and advancement of recommendations by stakeholders, including members of civil society (Afreen and Kumar 2016). Deegan and Blomquist (2006) provide a comparable account of the role played by the WWF in reporting on environmental practices by Australian mining companies and driving changes to industry codes and these companies' reporting practices. From a slightly different perspective, Atkins et al. (2015) explain how NGOs play a key role in interpreting scientific evidence on looming environmental disasters to inform action plans and reporting strategies of regulators and commercial organizations.

The ability of NGOs to act as a mechanism of accountability and an agent of positive change is not without limitations. Availability of resources, unequal power distributions, differing world views and the direct relevance of environmental and social issues for commercial organizations and sustainability activists can limit an NGO's influence (Arts 2002; Lauwo et al. 2016). Nevertheless, the important role they play in raising awareness of important sustainability issues and campaigning change highlights the need for detailed reporting on their activities, their achievements and major challenges.

Reporting by NGOs

There is a large body of development economics research which deals with NGOs, including issues relevant to accounting practitioners and academics such as cost management, efficiency and accountability (see Unerman and O'Dwyer 2006).[3] The research does not, however, deal specifically with sustainability reporting (or equivalents) by NGOs (see Goddard and Juma Assad 2006; Jones and Roberts 2006; Glennie and Lodhia 2013).

Accountability of NGOs themselves (NGOs being accountable rather than holding others accountable) is far more complex than that existing in other sectors. This is due to accountability being comprised of upwards, downwards and internal dimensions (Boomsma and O'Dwyer 2014). Upwards accountability refers to accountability to those entities who provide funding to NGOs and have some power over them. This can include donors as well as governments. Downwards accountability infers accountability to those impacted by NGO operations and these can include communities and other beneficiaries. Internal accountability implies accountability within an NGO, such as to staff and partnering NGOs. There is, however, a lack of research into how such accountability is reported, especially in relation to sustainability issues.

The more limited research on the type and extent of reporting by NGOs has been conducted mainly in the USA and Australia and focuses on the importance of disclosing information on expenditures (Ryan and Irvine 2012a). Common metrics used to evaluate the NGOs include:

- A programme expense ratio – the ratio of program costs to total costs to demonstrate resources applied to specific projects/initiatives (Yetman and Yetman 2012).
- A fundraising expense ratio – the ratio of fundraising expenses to total expenses which gives a sense of the extent of resources expended on fundraising initiatives relative to core activities (Greenlee and Tuckman 2007).
- An administration expense ratio – the ratio of administrative to total costs designed to show how much of the total expenses is being used on administration as opposed to carrying out the core operations of the NGO (Greenlee and Tuckman 2007).
- A cost of fundraising measure – the ratio of fundraising to total funds raised which shows the extent to which donor funding is used to raise additional donations (Sargeant et al. 2009).

These can be complemented by measures designed to show donor concentrations, liquidity and gearing in order to highlight an NGO's ability to continue providing services. Measures of total surpluses and excess assets over claims can also provide a financial measure of organizational sustainability (Ryan and Irvine 2012b).

Details on how an NGO uses donor funds for managing its administrative infrastructure, collects additional funds and carries out its primary operations are seen as essential for evaluating its efficiency and effectiveness (Jones and Roberts 2006; Ryan and Irvine 2012a). At a minimum, this type of reporting can also be used to demonstrate a measure of accountability to donors and – as was the case with PSOs – secure legitimacy (Goddard and Juma Assad 2006; Ryan and Irvine 2012a).

Predominantly quantitative and cost-focused performance measures are not, however, without limitations. In particular, they provide a very narrow perspective on an NGO's activity (Ryan and Irvine 2012a) and are unsuitable for examining exactly how an NGO is managing different types of resources in

Table 10.3 An NGO reporting framework

Feature	Details
Detailed expense analysis	The reporting system needs to take into consideration the unique environment where incomes are from donations and costs management is paramount. As explained by Ryan and Irvine (2012a, p. 354), 'transparent disclosures of financial and narrative information about costs can inform stakeholders of the reasons behind expenditure, and assist organizations to discharge a more meaningful accountability, rather than a watered-down formulaic accountability'.
Balanced reporting based on qualitative and quantitative measures	As is the case with integrated reporting in general (IIRC 2013), disclosure of financial measures (including commonly used expense ratios) needs to be complemented with qualitative or narrative information which contextualizes the financial data and explains the relevance of that data for the NGO's operating model (Jones and Roberts 2006; Ryan and Irvine 2012a). The reporting needs to provide an account of positive and negative issues to avoid being perceived only as a publicity or marketing tool (Connolly and Hyndman 2003).
Integrated perspective	While the IIRC's (2013) does not refer specifically to NGOs, integrated reporting principles can be relevant for these types of organizations. For example, similar to the strategic analysis provided in a commercial entity's integrated report, an effective NGO report can include details on its philosophy, culture and values to provide a conceptual basis for understanding its mission and operations (see Goddard and Juma Assad 2006). Similarly, in explaining the relationship between donor funds and expenses, an integrated assessment could include details on the outcomes of the NGOs projects, operational challenges encountered, partnerships formed and risks preventing the NGO from achieving its objectives (consider: Eccles et al. 2012; Atkins and Maroun 2015).
Aligning reporting and practice	The reporting system needs to be aligned with the NGOs strategic objectives, risks and operating activities to ensure that it supports positive internal change and is not seen as only an administrative function (see Stubbs and Higgins 2014). For example, when it comes to detailed expense analysis and reporting, this should be done in a manner which highlights underlying operational factors and can be used to inform decisions on resource allocation and operational improvements (Arya and Mittendorf 2015).
Consistent reporting	As explained in Section 12.1, research on the PSO reporting trends finds inconsistent application of reporting guidelines and internally generated practices (Farneti and Guthrie 2009; GRI 2010). Similarly, in the absence of a prescriptive reporting framework, NGOs should ensure consistent reporting on material information to avoid obscuring important details and provide a comparable account of performance from period to period (see Ryan and Irvine 2012a).

(*Continued*)

Table 10.3 (Continued)

Feature	Details
Stakeholder-awareness and the importance of legitimacy	Any reporting system needs to take into account the type and extent of information required by donors in order to demonstrate accountability, maintain legitimacy and ensure continued financial support (Goddard and Juma Assad 2006; Ryan and Irvine 2012a). This can include demonstrating that the information being provided to stakeholders is credible and the underlying operations are sound by virtue of compliance with applicable laws and regulations, the use of an effective governance system, and reliance on different assurance services as required (see Goddard and Juma Assad 2006; IOD 2016; Maroun 2017). At the same time, accountability also needs to be demonstrated to users and beneficiaries. This can be achieved by complementing sustainability reports with expenditure accounts, progress reports, easy-to-understand explanations of services provided and presentation of details to communities serviced by the NGO (Awio et al. 2011).
Standardized reporting frameworks	Codification and standardization of sustainability disclosures by NGOs can improve the quality of reporting by driving comparability and prescribing minimum disclosure requirements. Care must, however, be taken to ensure that reporting guidelines are not too generic or over-emphasize financial and managerial perspectives. This can result in limited or ineffective application as was the case with PSOs (see Dumay et al. 2010; GRI 2010, 2013; Skouloudis et al. 2015). This is especially relevant given significant differences in NGOs' mandates, internal management, philosophies and stakeholder partnerships (Goddard and Juma Assad 2006; Kolk and Lenfant 2013).
Succinct reporting	The recommendation that an integrated or sustainability report should provide a clear explanation of an entity's business model in a succinct and easy-to-understand manner (Solomon and Maroun 2012; IIRC 2013) is equally applicable in the public sector and NGO context.
Upward, downwards and internal accountability	Reporting by NGOs should explicitly highlight accountability to donors and government (upward accountability), to communities and other beneficiaries (downwards accountability) and to staff and partners (internal accountability) (Boomsma and O'Dwyer 2014).
Cost versus benefit	A reporting system needs to be cognizant of the limited resources available to the NGO. While detailed and transparent reporting is essential for ensuring legitimacy, the management of the reporting system should not result in unnecessary diversion of donor funds from core operations to report systems management (Goddard and Juma Assad 2006; Ryan and Irvine 2012a). At the same time, the NGO needs to strike a balance between ensuring that the reporting system remains capable of servicing the organization and allowing it to become a primary focus which detracts from the organization's real purpose (ibid.).

order to achieve its objectives (consider Atkins and Maroun 2015; IOD 2016). In particular, to reassure donors that funds are being used as intended and that an NGO is making efficient use of resources, high quality reporting is imperative (GRI 2013). Features of an effective NGO reporting framework are summarized in Table 10.3

Integrated reporting by PSOs and NGOs

There is a lack of evidence of integrated reporting by PSOs and NGOs. When the reporting by these organizations is considered, this is normally part of a broader study focusing primarily on the private sector (see, for example, Hopwood et al. 2010; ICAA 2011). The unique context of the public and not-for-profit sector and the resulting impact for integrated reporting has not been addressed sufficiently.

There have been reports by public accounting bodies on integrated reporting in the public sector. The Chartered Institute of Management Accountants (CIMA 2016) provides insights into how integrated reporting could be beneficial for the public sector. The report suggests that:

> Although initially developed with corporate users in mind, the emphasis of <IR> on value beyond profit has many benefits for public sector organizations. Unlike traditional corporate reporting, this more flexible approach enables organizations to focus clearly on how they and their stakeholders define value in the short, medium and long term.
>
> (CIMA 2016, p. 6)

Similarly, the Chartered Institute of Public Finance and Accountancy (CIPFA 2016) suggests that integrated reporting provides opportunities for value creation in the public sector. Their report provides extensive guidance on adopting integrated reporting for PSOs. Brief case studies of integrated reporting in specific public sector entities in Russia, United Kingdom, New Zealand, Singapore and South Africa are provided in both CIMA (2016) and CIPFA (2016).

Adams and Simnett (2011) suggest that integrated reporting provides opportunities for the not-for-profit sector to engage in comprehensive and effective reporting, largely due to a lack of market-based pressures on its performance. This sector has greater scope for addressing its social and environmental responsibilities (when compared to corporations) through a focus on the six capitals advocated by the IIRC.

Summary and conclusion

- PSOs and NGOs play an important role in society by providing essential services, mitigating negative outcomes from the activities of profit-focused organizations and by acting as a type of role model for these entities. By virtue of their unique position, they contribute significantly to the sustainability agenda.

- Ironically, despite the significance of PSOs and NGOs, we know little about the type and extent of reporting by these organizations, including the factors which drive sustainability reporting. Most of the prior research is focused on sustainability and more recently, integrated reporting by the private sector.
- There is, however, some research which points to determinants of sustainability reporting by PSOs and NGOs. These are comparable to the factors discussed in Chapter 6 and Chapter 11 and include broad legitimacy and internal/operational considerations. Of particular importance for the public and not-for-profit sectors is the need to demonstrate accountability for the resources entrusted to them and to provide an account to stakeholders who are often significantly dependent on the goods and services provided by PSOs and NGOs.
- Formal guidance on how PSOs and NGOs should discharge their accountability by preparing sustainability reports (or equivalents) is limited. The GRI is the dominant international body responsible for issuing reporting guidelines but a number of challenges have been identified when attempting to apply these. Examples include the over-emphasis on managerial perspectives, significant variations in legal, contractual and other reporting requirements and differences in the philosophy and purpose of PSOs and NGOs which is not adequately addressed by the GRI.
- It should be noted that most of the research on sustainability reporting by PSOs and NGOs is based in the USA and Australia. To understand the type, extent and drivers of reporting by these organizations, additional information is needed about the not-for-profit and public sectors in other jurisdictions.
- Integrated reporting provides opportunities for the public and not-for-profit sectors to report more extensively on their accountability for sustainability impacts.

Notes

1 This supplement was not finalized. Work on a GRI sector supplement for the public sector is ongoing, even though more than a decade has elapsed since the initial development of this supplement.
2 In this chapter, no distinction is made between NFPs and NGOs.
3 A review of this literature is beyond the scope of this chapter.

References

Adams, S., and Simnett, R., 2011. Integrated reporting: an opportunity for Australia's not-for-profit sector. *Australian Accounting Review*, 21 (3), 292–301.
Afreen, S. and Kumar, S., 2016. Between a rock and a hard place: the dynamics of stakeholder interactions influencing corporate sustainability practices. *Sustainability Accounting, Management and Policy Journal*, 7 (3), 350–375.
Alrazi, B., De Villiers, C. and Van Staden, C. J., 2015. A comprehensive literature review on, and the construction of a framework for, environmental legitimacy, accountability and proactivity. *Journal of Cleaner Production*, 102, 44–57.

Apostol, O. M., 2015. A project for Romania? The role of the civil society's counter-accounts in facilitating democratic change in society. *Accounting, Auditing & Accountability Journal*, 28 (2), 210–241.

Arts, B., 2002. 'Green alliances' of business and NGOs. New styles of self-regulation or 'dead-end roads'? *Corporate Social Responsibility and Environmental Management*, 9 (1), 26–36.

Arya, A. and Mittendorf, B., 2015. Career concerns and accounting performance measures in nonprofit organizations. *Accounting, Organizations and Society*, 40, 1–12.

Association of Chartered Certified Accountants (ACCA)., 2007. *Disclosures on stakeholder engagement*. Sydney: Association of Chartered Certified Accountants. Out of circulation.

Atkins, J., Atkins, B., Thomson, I. and Maroun, W., 2015. 'Good' news from nowhere: imagining utopian sustainable accounting. *Accounting, Auditing & Accountability Journal*, 28 (5), 651–670.

Atkins, J., Barone, E., Gozman, D., Maroun, W. and Atkins, B., 2015. Exploring rhinoceros conservation and protection: corporate disclosures and extinction accounting by leading South African companies. *Meditari Accountancy Research Conference*. University of Bolognat, Folrli, Italy.

Atkins, J. and Maroun, W., 2015. Integrated reporting in South Africa in 2012: perspectives from South African institutional investors. *Meditari Accountancy Research*, 23 (2), 197–221.

Awio, G., Northcott, D. and Lawrence, S., 2011. Social capital and accountability in grass-roots NGOs: the case of the Ugandan community-led HIV/AIDS initiative. *Accounting, Auditing & Accountability Journal*, 24 (1), 63–92.

Ball, A. and Grubnic, S., 2007. Sustainability accounting and accountability in the public sector. *In:* J. Unerman, J. Bebbington, and B. O'Dwyer, eds. *Sustainability accounting and accountability*, 1st ed. London: Routledge.

Bebbington, J., Higgins, C. and Frame, B., 2009. Initiating sustainable development reporting: evidence from New Zealand. *Accounting, Auditing & Accountability Journal*, 22 (4), 588–625.

Boomsma, R. and O'Dwyer, B., 2014. The nature of NGO accountability: conceptions, motives, forms and mechanisms. *In:* J. Bebbington, J. Unerman, and B. O'Dwyer, eds. *Sustainability accounting and accountability*, 2nd ed. Oxon, UK: Routledge, 157–176.

Botten, N., 2009. *Management accounting business strategy*, 2009 ed. Oxford, UK: CIMA Publishing.

Brennan, N. and Merkl-Davies, D., 2014. Rhetoric and argument in social and environmental reporting: the Dirty Laundry case. *Accounting, Auditing & Accountability Journal*, 27 (4), 602–633.

Broadbent, J. and Guthrie, J., 1992. Changes in the public sector: a review of recent "Alternative" accounting research. *Accounting, Auditing & Accountability Journal*, 5 (2), null.

Brown, J. and Dillard, J., 2014. Integrated reporting: on the need for broadening out and opening up. *Accounting, Auditing & Accountability Journal*, 27 (7), 1120–1156.

Burritt, R. L. and Welch, S., 1997a. Accountability for environmental performance of the Australian Commonwealth public sector. *Accounting, Auditing & Accountability Journal*, 10 (4), 532–561.

Burritt, R. L. and Welch, S., 1997b. Australian commonwealth entities: an analysis of their environmental disclosures. *Abacus*, 33 (1), 69–87.

Chartered Institute of Management Accountants (CIMA), 2016. *Integrated reporting in the public sector*. United Kingdom: CIMA.

Chartered Institute of Public Finance and Accountancy (CIPFA), 2016. *Focusing on value creation in the public sector*. CIPFA, World Bank Group.

Connolly, C. and Hyndman, N., 2003. *Performance reporting by UK charities: approaches, difficulties and current practice*. Edinburgh: The Institute of Chartered Accountants of Scotland.

Deegan, C., 2002. Introduction: the legitimising effect of social and environmental disclosures – a theoretical foundation. *Accounting, Auditing & Accountability Journal*, 15 (3), 282–311.

Deegan, C. and Blomquist, C., 2006. Stakeholder influence on corporate reporting: an exploration of the interaction between WWF-Australia and the Australian minerals industry. *Accounting, Organizations and Society*, 31 (4–5), 343–372.

De Villiers, C., Rinaldi, L. and Unerman, J., 2014. Integrated reporting: insights, gaps and an agenda for future research. *Accounting, Auditing & Accountability Journal*, 27 (7), 1042–1067.

De Villiers, C., Rouse, P. and Kerr, J., 2016. A new conceptual model of influences driving sustainability based on case evidence of the integration of corporate sustainability management control and reporting. *Journal of Cleaner Production*.

De Villiers, C. and Van Staden, C. J., 2006. Can less environmental disclosure have a legitimising effect? Evidence from Africa. *Accounting, Organizations and Society*, 31 (8), 763–781.

DiMaggio, P. and Powell, W., 1983. The Iron Cage revisited: institutional isomorphism and collective rationality in organizational fields. *American Sociology Review*, 48 (2), 147–160.

Dube, S. and Maroun, W., 2017. Corporate social responsibility reporting by South African mining companies: evidence of legitimacy theory. *South African Journal of Business Management*, 48 (1), 23–34.

Dumay, J., Guthrie, J. and Farneti, F., 2010. Gri sustainability reporting guidelines for public and third sector organizations. *Public Management Review*, 12 (4), 531–548.

Eccles, R., Ioannou, I. and Serafeim, G., 2012. The impact of corporate sustainability on organisational processes and performance. *NBER WORKING PAPER SERIES* [Online]. Available: www.nber.org/papers/w17950.pdf.

Farneti, F. and Guthrie, J., 2009. Sustainability reporting by Australian public sector organisations: why they report. *Accounting Forum*, 33 (2), 89–98.

Frost, G. R. and Seamer, M., 2002. Adoption of environmental reporting and management practices: an analysis of New South Wales public sector entities. *Financial Accountability & Management*, 18 (2), 103–127.

Glennie, M. and Lodhia, S., 2013. The influence of internal organisational factors on corporate – community partnership agendas: an Australian case study. *Meditari Accountancy Research*, 21 (1), 52–67.

Goddard, A. and Juma Assad, M., 2006. Accounting and navigating legitimacy in Tanzanian NGOs. *Accounting, Auditing & Accountability Journal*, 19 (3), 377–404.

Gondor, D. and Morimoto, H., 2011. Role of World Wildlife Fund (WWF) and Marine Stewardship Council (MSC) in seafood eco-labelling policy in Japan. *Sustainability Accounting, Management and Policy Journal*, 2 (2), 214–230.

Goswami, K. and Lodhia, S., 2014. Sustainability disclosure patterns of South Australian local councils: a case study. *Public Money & Management*, 34, 273–280.

Gray, R., 2006. Social, environmental and sustainability reporting and organisational value creation? Whose value? Whose creation? *Accounting, Auditing & Accountability Journal*, 19 (6), 793–819.

Greenlee, J. S. and Tuckman, H., 2007. Financial health. *In:* D. R. Young, ed. *Financing nonprofits*. New York: AltaMira Press, 315–335.

GRI, 2005. *Sector supplement for public agencies (Amsterdam).* Out of circulation

GRI, 2010. *GRI reporting in government agencies.* Available: www.globalreporting.org/resource library/GRI-Reporting-in-Government-Agencies.pdf [Accessed 10 February 2017].

GRI, 2012. *Public sector sustainability reporting: remove the clutter, reduce the burden.* Available: www. globalreporting.org/resourcelibrary/Public-sector-sustainability-reporting-remove-the-clutter%20reduce-the-burden.pdf [Accessed 10 February 2017].

GRI, 2013. *GRI-G4 NGO sector disclosure.* Available: www.globalreporting.org/resource library/GRI-G4-NGO-Sector-Disclosures.pdf [Accessed 10 February 2017].

GRI, 2016. *Consolidated set of GRI sustainability reporting standards (2016)*. Available: www.globalreporting.org/standards/gri-standards-download-center/?g=ae2e23b8-4958-455c-a9df-ac372d6ed9a8 [Accessed 10 February 2017].

Guthrie, J., Ball, A. and Farneti, F., 2010. Advancing sustainable management of public and not for profit organizations. *Public Management Review*, 12 (4), 449–459.

Guthrie, J. and Farneti, F., 2008. GRI sustainability reporting by Australian public sector organizations. *Public Money & Management*, 28 (6), 361–366.

Hopwood, A., 2009. Accounting and the environment. *Accounting, Organizations and Society*, 34 (3–4), 433–439.

Hopwood, A. G., Unerman, J. and Fries, J. (eds.), 2010. *Accounting for sustainability: practical insights*. London: Earthscan.

Institute of Chartered Accountants in Australia (ICAA), 2011. *Integrating sustainability into business practices: a case study approach*. ICAA.

Institute of Directors in Southern African (IOD), 2016. *King IV report on corporate governance in South Africa*. Johannesburg, South Africa: Lexis Nexus South Africa.

International Integrated Reporting Council (IIRC), 2013. *The international framework: integrated reporting*. Available: www.theiirc.org/wp-content/uploads/2013/12/13-12-08-THE-INTERNATIONAL-IR-FRAMEWORK-2-1.pdf [Accessed 1 October 2013].

Jones, C. L. and Roberts, A. A., 2006. Management of financial information in charitable organizations: the case of joint-cost allocations. *The Accounting Review*, 81 (1), 159–178.

Kaur, A. and Lodhia, S., 2016. Institutional Influences on stakeholder engagement in sustainability accounting and reporting. *In:* D. Crowther and S. Shalfi, eds. *Corporate responsibility and stakeholding*.

Kaur, A. and Lodhia, S. Forthcoming. Stakeholder engagement in sustainability accounting and reporting: a study of Australian local councils" *Accounting, Auditing and Accountability Journal*.

Kaur, A. and Lodhia, S. K., 2014. The state of disclosures on stakeholder engagement in sustainability reporting in Australian local councils. *Pacific Accounting Review*, (1/2), 54–74.

King, M., 2016. Comments on: *Integrated reporting, GARI Conference*, Henley on Thames, UK, 23 October.

Kolk, A. and Lenfant, F., 2013. Multinationals, CSR and partnerships in Central African conflict countries. *Corporate Social Responsibility and Environmental Management*, 20 (1), 43–54.

Lauwo, S. G., Otusanya, O. J. and Bakre, O., 2016. Corporate social responsibility reporting in the mining sector of Tanzania: (Lack of) government regulatory controls and NGO activism. *Accounting, Auditing & Accountability Journal*, 29 (6), 1038–1074.

Lodhia, S. K. and Burritt, R. L., 2004. Public sector accountability failure in an emerging economy: the case of the National Bank of Fiji. *International Journal of Public Sector Management*, 17 (4), 345–359.

Lodhia, S. K. and Jacobs, K., 2013. The practice turn in environmental reporting: a study into current practices in two Australian commonwealth departments. *Accounting, Auditing & Accountability Journal*, 26 (4), 595–615.

Lodhia, S. K., Jacobs, K. and Park, Y. J., 2012. Driving public sector environmental reporting. *Public Management Review*, 14 (5), 631–647.

Lodhia, S. K. and Martin, N., 2011. Stakeholder responses to the National Greenhouse and Energy Reporting Act: an agenda setting perspective. *Accounting, Auditing & Accountability Journal*, 25 (1), 126–145.

Lynch, B., 2010. An examination of environmental reporting by Australian state government departments. *Accounting Forum*, 34 (1), 32–45.

Mahomed, N., 2015. The risky business of state-owned companies: how they report on their risks. *Accounting Perspectives in Southern Africa*, 3 (1), 18–25.

Maroun, W., 2017. Assuring the integrated report: insights and recommendations from auditors and preparers. *British Accounting Review*, 49 (3), 329–346.

Merkl-Davies, D. M., Brennan, N. M. and McLeay, S. J., 2011. Impression management and retrospective sense-making in corporate narratives: a social psychology perspective. *Accounting, Auditing & Accountability Journal*, 24 (3), 315–344.

Milne, M. J. and Gray, R. H., 2013. W(h)ither ecology? The triple bottom line, the global reporting initiative, and corporate sustainability reporting. *Journal of Business Ethics*, 118 (1), 13–29.

Milne, M., Tregidga, H. and Walton, S., 2009. Words not actions! The ideological role of sustainable development reporting. *Accounting, Auditing and Accountability Journal*, 22 (8), 1211–1257.

Moneva, J. M., Archel, P. and Correa, C., 2006. GRI and the camouflaging of corporate unsustainability. *Accounting Forum*, 30 (2), 121–137.

O'Dwyer, B., 2005. The construction of a social account: a case study in an overseas aid agency. *Accounting, Organizations and Society*, 30 (3), 279–296.

O'Dwyer, B., Unerman, J. and Bradley, J., 2005. Perceptions on the emergence and future development of corporate social disclosure in Ireland: engaging the voices of non-governmental organisations. *Accounting, Auditing & Accountability Journal*, 18 (1), 14–43.

Patten, D. M., 2002. The relation between environmental performance and environmental disclosure: a research note. *Accounting, Organizations and Society*, 27 (8), 763–773.

Power, M. K., 1994. *The audit explosion*. London: Demos.

Ryan, C. and Irvine, H., 2012a. Accountability beyond the headlines: why not-for-profit organisations need to communicate their own expenditure stories. *Australian Accounting Review*, 22 (4), 353–370.

Ryan, C. and Irvine, H., 2012b. Not-for-profit ratios for financial resilience and internal accountability: a study of Australian International Aid Organisations. *Australian Accounting Review*, 22 (2), 177–194.

Sargeant, A., Lee, S. and Jay, E., 2009. Communicating the "Realities" of charity costs: an institute of fundraising initiative. *Nonprofit and Voluntary Sector Quarterly*, 38 (2), 333–342.

Skouloudis, A., Evangelinos, K. and Malesios, C., 2015. Priorities and perceptions for corporate social responsibility: an NGO perspective. *Corporate Social Responsibility and Environmental Management*, 22 (2), 95–112.

Solomon, J. and Maroun, W., 2012. *Integrated reporting: the new face of social, ethical and environmental reporting in South Africa?* London: The Association of Chartered Certified Accountants.

Solomon, J. F., Solomon, A., Joseph, N. L. and Norton, S. D., 2013. Impression management, myth creation and fabrication in private social and environmental reporting: insights from Erving Goffman. *Accounting, Organizations and Society*, 38 (3), 195–213.

Stubbs, W. and Higgins, C., 2014. Integrated reporting and internal mechanisms of change. *Accounting, Auditing & Accountability Journal*, 27 (7), 1068–1089.

Suchman, M. C., 1995. Managing legitimacy: strategic and institutional approaches. *The Academy of Management Review*, 20 (3), 571–610.

Toh, D. and Frost, G., 1998. Environmental accounting practices and management attitudes: an investigation of New South Wales public sector entities. *Accountability and Performance*, 4 (3), 51–67.

Unerman, J. and O'Dwyer, B., 2006. On James Bond and the importance of NGO accountability. *Accounting, Auditing & Accountability Journal*, 19 (3), 305–318.

Yetman, M. and Yetman, R. J., 2012. Do donors discount misleading accounting information? *Social Science Research Network*. Available: http://papers.ssrn.com/sol3/papers cfm?abstract_id=126858 [Accessed 7 December 2011].

11 Management control systems to support sustainability and integrated reporting

Binh BUI
Victoria University Wellington

Charl DE VILLIERS
The University of Auckland, and University of Pretoria

Abstract

This chapter reviews the current literature to examine the role played by sustainability management control systems (MCSs) in supporting sustainability reporting and a sustainability strategy, proposing a sustainability MCS framework that categorizes sustainability MCSs into informal and formal controls. These controls interact in different operational and strategic uses to either achieve compliance or improve performance. Quality of sustainability information and language of control are also important drivers of control effectiveness. Combining controls enhances their effectiveness.

Introduction

This chapter illustrates the role played by sustainability management control systems (MCSs) in supporting sustainability strategy and sustainability reporting. Prior research into sustainability MCSs has examined aspects, such as eco-control (Henri and Journeault 2010) and the sustainability balanced scorecard (Burritt and Schaltegger 2010). However, few studies have examined sustainability MCSs using a comprehensive MCS framework. Most researchers have investigated one or two sustainability controls or tools in isolation and almost without exception have limited their enquiry to the types and uses of sustainability controls, ignoring other potentially important issues such as interaction between controls, quality of control and perception of controls. Overall, our understanding of how companies design and use MCSs to drive sustainability strategy remains limited (Crutzen and Herzig 2013). As MCSs have the capacity to guide and shape organizational practices and actors' behaviour and support strategy (Ahrens and Chapman 2007; Kober et al. 2007; Langfield-Smith 1997, 2005), they can promote sustainability (Gond et al. 2012).

This chapter provides a review of the literature on sustainability MCSs, organizing findings in the extant literature using a MCS framework, thereby providing a richer, multi-dimensional picture of the complexity and variety of sustainability MCSs in practice.

Consistent with Ferreira and Otley (2009), we adopt a wider definition of MCSs which involves

> formal and informal mechanisms, processes, systems, and networks used by organizations for conveying the key *sustainability* objectives and goals elicited by management, for assisting the strategic process and on-going management through analysis, planning, measurement, control, rewarding, and broadly managing *sustainability* performance, and for supporting and facilitating organizational learning and change.
>
> (italics added by the authors)

This chapter first examines the relationship between sustainability reporting and MCSs, followed by the development of a sustainability-focused MCS framework. The next two sections discuss different types of formal and informal controls, before interactions between controls are examined. Then, the use and objectives of controls, the quality of MCS information and the language of control are discussed. Finally, a critique of the extant literature is presented along with opportunities for future research.

The relationship between sustainability reporting and MCSs

Examining how sustainability data are used in internal processes to generate improvement is of theoretical and practical importance (Adams and Larrinaga-González 2007). Passetti et al. (2014) suggest that future research needs to pay attention to sustainability management and measurement and how they are linked to external sustainability disclosure. Durden (2008) argues that a broader conceptual basis is needed to align both external disclosure and MCS perspectives to enable the design of accounting systems oriented towards sustainability issues. It is illogical for an organization to produce extensive sustainability reporting in order to claim accountability, without designing an MCS to reflect this position. Furthermore, it is interesting if an organization has an MCS that integrates sustainability reporting in decision making but has no desire to disclose such information externally.

Some studies have started to investigate the linkages between sustainability reporting and the internal use of sustainability information. Norris and O'Dwyer (2004) examined a UK firm that published social reports for five years and found that the firm undertook a social, informal, clan-based approach to addressing social issues. Adams and McNicholas (2007) demonstrated that the adoption of a sustainability report increases the internal use of sustainability information. Reporting was seen as introducing and reinforcing sustainability principles, motivating the integration of sustainability issues into strategy planning and enhancing the visibility of sustainability performance indicators. The Italian multinational studied by Contrafatto and Burns (2013) adopted social and environmental reporting practices and as a result of reporting, had to develop sustainability rules and routines, and incorporated sustainability information in corporate strategies and practices. Bouten and Hoozée's (2013) study of four Belgian companies revealed that environmental reporting drives environment-related management accounting (EMA) as disclosing information leads to the realization that supporting data are required. The dynamic interplay between external disclosure and EMA was found to have the potential to hinder or facilitate organizational change towards sustainability.

Kerr et al's (2015) case study of three New Zealand organizations revealed that the integration of sustainability reporting into MCSs helps operationalize sustainability objectives, increase stakeholder accountability, formalize organizational beliefs and improve internal sustainability communication. While a balanced scorecard (BSC) can facilitate sustainability reporting, some organizations choose to fully integrate sustainability reporting into their MCSs. De Villiers et al. (2016) developed a model to capture the relationship between BSC measures, sustainability reports and management focus (Figure 11.1). They found that stakeholders influence the choice of BSC measures, sustainability report measures and management focus. MCSs containing these three central constructs increase individual accountabilities by sharpening employees' focus

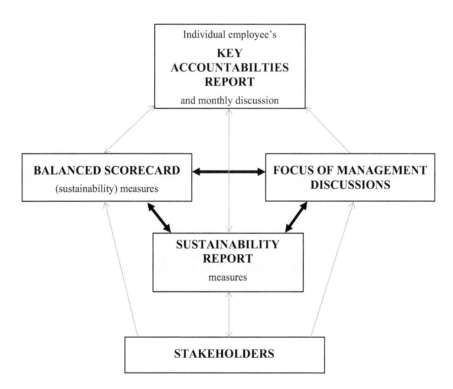

Figure 11.1 Model of key influences driving corporate sustainability

Source: De Villiers et al. 2016

on sustainability measures. In turn, these individual accountabilities reinforce the drive towards sustainability.

In contrast, some studies have found little relationship between sustainability reporting and internal MCSs. Larrinaga-González et al. (2001) examined nine Spanish organizations and found that they primarily used environmental reporting to negotiate and influence national environmental agenda; when reporting was used to serve this purpose, it had little impact on internal processes and organizational change. Adams and Frost (2008) presented an interesting case illustrating that multinationals had started to use sustainability indicators in strategic planning, risk management and performance measurement practices, but did not consider external disclosure important.

Overall, prior studies have not produced a simple conclusion on the nature of the relationship between sustainability reporting and sustainability MCSs. It seems that this relationship depends on a number of organizational factors, among which are top management commitment and organizational resource availability. Moreover, the objective at which the reporting is aimed is important. When reporting aims towards compliance or influencing an external agenda, it seems decoupled from MCSs. However, when reporting is motivated by performance improvement, a change in the MCS to enable integration of sustainability issues into formal control systems and decision making is essential.

Towards a sustainability-focused MCS framework

The extant literature has examined sustainability MCSs in an isolated manner. Most papers focus on one or more specific management controls, such as sustainability performance measurement systems (Bonacchi and Rinaldi 2007; De Villiers et al. 2016), organizational structure and complexity (Epstein and Roy 2007), strategic planning (Galbreath 2010), culture and leadership (Van Velsor et al. 2009).

We need to adopt a broader view of management control and examine sustainability controls as a package to gain a more comprehensive understanding (Norris and O'Dwyer 2004; Otley 1999). Effective implementation of sustainability strategy requires a comprehensive MCS to ensure the integration of sustainability into core businesses and push the organization towards a sustainable future (Epstein 1996; Epstein and Wisner 2005; Gond et al. 2012).

Some studies have examined sustainability controls from a management control systems perspective. Martinov-Bennie (2012) pointed out that a carbon management system needs to include the design of measurement systems and the process of data capturing, calculation, compilation and reporting, each underpinned by specific key controls. Gond et al. (2012) argued that the integration of sustainability control systems into an organization's traditional MCS is essential to the delivery of sustainability policies. Arjaliès and Mundy (2013) showed that companies manage sustainability strategy through a variety of MCSs, including internal and external communication processes. Tang and Luo (2014) developed a framework that encapsulates carbon governance, emission tracking and reporting and engagement and disclosure. Bui (2011) grouped sustainability-oriented management control systems into: internally oriented strategy MCS, externally oriented strategy MCS and pressure-related MCSs. However, due to the differences in the types and components of controls, the insights from these studies are not comparable.

We develop a sustainability MCS framework based on that of Tessier and Otley (2012) (hereafter referred to as T&O). The T&O framework incorporates Simons' (1995) levers of control (diagnostic controls, interactive controls, belief systems and boundary controls). Belief systems are used to communicate values throughout the organization. Boundary systems elaborate on the limits to practices and the areas to be avoided. Diagnostic systems are used to monitor the performance of the organization against set targets and to undertake corrective actions. Interactive systems are selected and used by top managers to regularly and personally involve themselves in the decision-making of subordinates, and generate dialogue and learning about strategic uncertainties to identify new strategies to obtain competitive advantage.

Consistent with T&O, we classify sustainability controls into formal and informal controls. Formal controls are further categorized into four types. Sustainability strategic performance controls (SPC) ensure that the sustainability strategy in place is appropriate, while sustainability strategic boundaries (SBC) impose sustainability limits on strategic opportunity searches (e.g., only

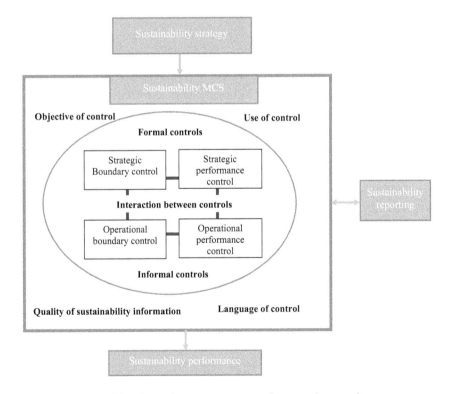

Figure 11.2 Sustainability-focused management control systems framework

searching for environmentally friendly or low-impact investments or technologies). Sustainability operational performance controls (OPC) involve performance indicators needed for day-to-day operations, and operational boundary controls (OBC) prescribe unacceptable behaviour, procedures and rules. These types of control interact with each other in affecting sustainability performance.

Based on T&O, our framework incorporates objectives of control: i) compliance with internal or external environmental regulations and rules; or ii) managing environmental or economic performance. Our framework also captures the different uses of sustainability controls in decision-making processes and other organizational practices, such as facilitating decision making, stakeholder engagement or external reporting (Tang and Luo 2014; Schaltegger and Csutora 2012; Burritt et al. 2011; Henri and Journeault 2010; Etzion 2007). We also add quality of control and language of control as prior sustainability-related studies have identified these two aspects as important influences on sustainability management effectiveness. Our framework is presented in Figure 11.2.

Formal controls

Sustainability operational performance controls

Sustainability operational performance controls involve critical performance indicators and hence includes controls that enable the measurement, monitoring and management of sustainability performance against a predetermined sustainability policy, plan or strategy. The sustainability controls examined in the extant literature include sustainability measurement and monitoring systems, sustainability indicators and performance measurement systems, targets and budgetary controls, environmental management accounting and other tools. This type of control is the most extensively examined in the prior literature, compared to other types.

Sustainability goals and targets

Formulating sustainability goals can be seen as the first step in managing sustainability performance. Lee (2012) argues that in developing and implementing a sustainability plan, an organization needs to first know its sustainability goals and objectives. Goal setting can be at a general level (e.g., a general reduction in the organization's total carbon emissions) or a detailed level (e.g., reducing emissions by 5 percent at an operational site or plant) (Lee 2012). A reliable and reasonable target needs to help allocate resources efficiently and coordinate across departments so that an organization's strategic objectives are achieved (Kumarasiri and Jubb 2016). The target can also be used for benchmarking and performance evaluation across departments, firms and industries (Tang and Luo 2014). The linking of targets to reward and bonus systems can also help align managerial and staff behaviour with sustainability goals. More difficult targets are more likely to lead to higher performance when these targets are flexible (Rouse and Putterill 2003).

Empirically, Passetti et al. (2014) found that most firms adopt a conservative approach to sustainability management, and few recognize the importance of setting targets or plans for sustainability. Papers focusing on carbon issues have provided similar insights. Durden (2008) found that for leading companies, having a systematic approach to carbon management, including strategic planning, target setting, carbon measurement and performance evaluation, is essential. Lee's (2012) case study of a Korean automobile manufacturer also shows that setting targets facilitates emission reduction. In contrast, Schaltegger and Csutora (2012) and Perego and Kolk (2012) found that regulation that influences firms' economic interests rather than merely requiring disclosure is an important driver of firms' engagement with setting reduction targets. Ioannou et al. (2016) noted that firms that report to the Carbon Disclosure Project achieve a higher percentage of their targets when these targets are difficult. A field study of Netherlands firms participating in a certification scheme that required target setting (Rietbergen et al. 2015) revealed that the process of target setting does not lead to more ambitious targets, suggesting that other approaches to target setting, such as specifying minimum performance levels, are more effective in encouraging green procurement.

Sustainability measures and performance management system

To achieve a sustainability strategy or plan, organizations need to determine the extent of achievement or deviation in performance from that strategy or plan. Burritt et al. (2002) proposed a five-dimensional framework for environmental information, including its intended users (internal vs. external), the nature of the information (physical vs. monetary), the time frame (past vs. current or future), the length of the time frame (short-term vs. long-term) and the level of routineness of information (routine vs. ad hoc). In contrast, Rouse and Putterill (2003) argue that a sustainability performance management system needs to cater to stakeholder interests and expectations. Schaltegger and Csutora (2012) suggested two types of sustainability measures: corporate accounts for sustainability improvement and accounts for unsustainability. Accounts for sustainability improvement are indicators that support or facilitate an improvement in sustainability performance, such as budgets for carbon mitigation or the number of carbon emissions avoided in a project. In contrast, accounts for unsustainability demonstrate the current status of sustainability or unsustainability performance, such as total emissions levels or carbon liability or costs. Lee (2012) suggested that effective carbon management requires data collection on both monetary and physical levels, such as savings from emission reductions and investment in carbon reduction, or the amount of reduction and the level of energy efficiency.

Empirically, Comoglio and Botta (2012) found that Italian automotive firms used a large number of environmental performance indicators to monitor a range of environmental aspects. These indicators were useful not only in monitoring past performance but also in evaluating risk, developing plans and determining performance-based rewards. Bonacchi and Rinaldi's (2007) study of Procter and Gamble suggested that sustainability principles are internalized into an organization through the integration of sustainability strategies into the traditional performance measurement system. This integration enables a progressive integration of sustainability into organizational actions and culture rather than a radical change. Perego and Hartmann's (2009) survey of Netherlands manufacturing firms found that a proactive environmental strategy leads to increased use of environmental information in decision making when an environmental performance management system is focused on financially quantifiable information. However, the use of environmental information in evaluation and reward schemes is limited, potentially due to the lack of controllability. Passetti et al. (2014) found that organizations have developed environmental and social performance indicators but have not used them to track or monitor sustainability performance. This has led to a primary use of sustainability information for legal compliance rather than decision making aimed at improving sustainability performance. Focusing on carbon information, Tang and Luo (2014) found that Australian firms have calculated carbon footprints and inventories, and such carbon information enables comparisons across periods, companies and industries, independent review and assurance, and benchmarking. Lisi's (2015) survey of Italian firms revealed that the more environmental performance measures are used in decision making and control processes, the more likely those measures are to drive better environmental performance.

Sustainability measurement and monitoring system

Developing performance measures is not enough to drive performance without an underlying system that measures, collects, and monitors sustainability information. With only a few exceptions, the extant literature pays little attention to the importance of this system. Lee (2012) argues that to make decisions regarding the organization's carbon management strategy, managers require the collection of systematically organized data. This is achieved through the development of relevant systems and controls throughout the process of data capturing and measurement. This involves two steps: first, setting the goals, and second, mapping the process and scope, and then collecting data. Similarly, Martinov-Bennie (2012) notes that a carbon management system needs to include a formal process for data capturing, measurement, compilation and reporting. This process needs to be supported by other carbon-related controls (Martinov-Bennie 2012). Generally, the literature provides very limited insights into the process and nature of the underlying sustainability data measurement and monitoring system.

Environmental Management Accounting (EMA)

Environmental management accounting (EMA) is the control that has probably received the most extensive research coverage. Bartolomeo et al. (2000) defined environmental management accounting as: "The generation, analysis and use of financial and related non-financial information, in order to support management within a company or business, in integrating corporate environmental and economic policies and building sustainable business" (p. 31). We distinguish EMA from the previously discussed performance management system by limiting our review to the techniques of generating and analyzing information to support environment-related activities or business objectives. Environmental cost accounting measures direct and indirect environmental costs to help calculate production costs for products or services (Parker 2000). Environmental life cycle assessment measures the environmental impacts of a product during its life-cycle and can help forecast environmental consequences and undertake early preventive actions (Gray and Bebbington 2001). Other techniques include the identification, classification and allocation of environment-related costs, development and use of environmental indicators and various product-related environmental analyses (Ferreira et al. 2010). These EMA techniques are useful in evaluating the "whole-of-life" environmental impacts and costs of products and services, facilitating different business decisions and strategies (Ratnatunga and Balachandran 2009).

Empirically, Bartolomeo et al. (2000) found limited application of EMA among European firms: application was piecemeal and only applied to experimental projects rather than integrated systematically in internal processes. Deegan's (2003) study of Australian firms revealed that EMA adoption leads to a number of environmental and economic benefits, but this depends on firm size and industry. Focusing on the antecedents of EMA, Qian and Burritt (2007), using the survey responses from 77 Australian manufacturing managers, revealed that the adoption of EMA is contingent upon an organization's environmental strategies, its size and the industry it is a part of. Adams and Frost (2008) noted that EMA information is only used in internal processes when environmental issues are considered important by management. Ferreira et al. (2010) surveyed the use of twelve EMA techniques by Australian firms and found that the adoption of EMA is associated with the identification of new opportunities such as production improvement. Furthermore, EMA adoption varies across industries, but is not driven by environmental strategy. In contrast, Burritt et al. (2011) asserted that social structures such as regulatory pressure and community expectation also motivate the use of EMA in internal strategic management.

Incentive systems

A reward and incentive system is an indispensable element of sustainability OPC as it ensures the congruence of managerial and employee behaviour with sustainability goals and plans (Tang and Luo 2014). However, the relationship between incentive systems and performance is not straightforward. Top management effort is constrained as it has to be balanced against the profit enhancement and environmental compliance objectives of the organization. When top management effort is not constrained, managerial incentive is an essential mechanism for motivating sustainability behaviour. However, when managers are bound by profit enhancement objectives, linking managerial effort on environmental performance to incentive systems may become inefficient. Further, managers have an incentive to favour managerial activities providing immediate results over activities bringing remote and unquantifiable benefits, such as those associated with sustainability strategies (Eccles et al. 2014). Employee perceptions of the significance of sustainability issues also matter. When employees perceive sustainability as strategically important to the organization, monetary incentives may encourage efforts and lead to environmental performance enhancement. However, when environmental mitigation is seen to lead to societal benefits rather than private ones, monetary incentives will crowd out employees' efforts (Eccles et al. 2014).

Empirically, focusing on Australian firms, Tang and Luo (2014) found that incentives for carbon issues were not linked to carbon mitigation, attributing this to poor design of incentive systems. Using time series data for firms reporting to CDP, Eccles et al. (2012) found that the use of monetary (non-monetary) incentives was associated with higher (lower) carbon emissions. Furthermore, the negative impact of monetary incentives on performance is mitigated when incentives were provided to employees with formally assigned environmental responsibility. Using the CDP database, Ioannou et al. (2016) found that monetary incentives reduce the positive impact of difficult carbon reduction targets on target achievement; in other words, monetary incentives make it less likely that difficult reduction targets will be achieved.

Budgets

Budgeting and budgetary control are important management controls as they allow the allocation of resources and monitoring of performance against targets in achieving organizations' objectives (Johansson and Siverbo 2014). An environmental (social) budget is a future-oriented planning tool which determines the funds available for environmental (social) issues for the coming period (Gray and Bebbington 2001; Figge et al. 2002). Without a sustainability budget, managers and employees lack sufficient resources and motivation to undertake sustainability initiatives, especially when those initiatives are beyond the traditional responsibilities of their core roles. It is difficult to achieve challenging sustainability targets when these are not accompanied by appropriate supporting budgets.

Empirically, Bui (2011) found that New Zealand electricity generators assign separate sustainability budgets for the implementation of energy efficiency, carbon reduction and carbon-offsetting programmes. Bui and De Villiers' (2017) New Zealand study found that reduction targets and carbon budgets are features of carbon management accounting systems when firms pursue proactive and creative strategies with regard to climate change–related risks. However, when they revert to reactive strategies, carbon budgets are either discarded or merged into operational budgets, making sustainability initiatives contestable or secondary to economic ones. Passetti et al. (2014) found that carbon and environmental budgets are among the least frequently used controls in Italian firms. Hence, despite a potentially important role, sustainability budgets are rarely used as controls by organizations.

Communication systems

While an extensive body of literature has examined sustainability disclosure, little attention has been paid to the channels through which sustainability information is disseminated within an organization. Communication platforms can facilitate the exchange of ideas and perceptions, interactions and dialogue between people with different viewpoints about sustainability (Heidmann et al. 2008).This dialogue helps overcome cognitive boundaries, allow a shared understanding and promoting goal congruence in implementing sustainability initiatives. Properly communicated across the organization, sustainability information can motivate knowledge sharing and enable organizational learning.

Most prior studies have not considered the role played by formal or informal sustainability communication systems. Gupta (1995) discussed the need for a formal channel through which corporate environmental groups can contribute to the environment-related strategic planning process. Judge and Douglas (1998) found empirical evidence that coordination between environmental functions and other functions is positively associated with the level of involvement of environmental personnel in the strategic process. Bui (2011) found that New Zealand generators use cross-functional communication systems extensively to promote staff awareness of sustainability issues and promote cooperation between units during strategy implementation. Further, internal communication systems were used both formally (e.g., strategy meetings) and informally (e.g., internal newsletters and networking) to promote staff morale and encourage employees' goal congruence.

Sustainability operational boundary controls

Sustainability operational boundary controls (OBCs) define the limits, practices and risks for companies when carrying out their operations. Prior studies suggest OBCs are often operationalized through formal sustainability rules, plans, policies and job descriptions.

Environmental plan and policy

Having an environmental policy or plan is normally the first prerequisite of a formal environmental management system.A formal sustainability policy or plan shows an organization's commitment to sustainability issues, and hence, to some extent, reflects its willingness to undertake initiatives and allocate resources to address those issues and improve sustainability performance. Some studies show empirical evidence of the impacts of a formal plan on behaviour or firm performance. Dasgupta et al. (2000) reported higher environmental performance in plants with a formal environmental plan. Ramus and Steger (2000) found that having a published environmental plan significantly increases the likelihood of employees being involved in organizational environmental initiatives. Other studies have examined the drivers for environmental plan adoption. Henriques and Sadorsky (1996) noted that environmental plan formulation is positively influenced by customer, shareholder, government regulatory, neighbourhood and community group pressures, but is negatively influenced by other lobby group pressures. Álvarez Gil et al. (2001) found that larger organizations have more resource availability and can afford a formal environmental plan, giving them a basis for more extensive environmental management.

Faulkner et al. (2005) caution that there is a gap between environmental plan formulation and implementation as organizations are still primarily motivated by short-term rather than long-term imperatives and tend to undertake a reactive position with regard to environmental issues. Epstein and Wisner (2005) explain that environmental plans can vary signficantly across organizations, from merely a mission statement, to detailed plans and procedures, and even the incorporation of measures and goals into decision-making and strategic processes. Bui (2011) found that firms with higher emissions profiles use environmental/sustainability policies more extensively and at times integrate such policies in their strategic planning process. This is due to an increased emphasis by these firms on carbon credit and emissions management strategies in preparation for an emissions trading scheme (Bui 2011).

Formal assignment of duties (job description)

Assignment of duties related to sustainability management works as a boundary control as it highlights expectations that certain tasks will be carried out by specific people. It reduces opportunism by avoiding the risk of one person being in charge of too many or potentially conflicting roles (Bui 2011). The allocation can vary between organizations. Some choose to have dedicated roles with environmental management responsibilities, while other organizations find it more efficient to add such responsibilities on to existing operational or support roles. Epstein and Wisner (2005) argued that environmental strategy is successfully implemented when environmental responsibility is integrated to employees in operational and support functions. Burritt and Schaltegger (2010) suggested data collection and processing is not solely the function of accountants but is normally shared across several departments. Lee (2012) argued that carbon information should be collected by production managers and then reported to senior managers for consolidation and onward reporting to top management. In contrast, Bui (2011) found a clear separation of responsibilities between the management, measurement and reporting of carbon-related information in case study organizations, with each of these responsibilities assigned to a separate department or team.

Other boundary controls

Other boundary controls can also be used to define the risks to be avoided or to prescribe acceptable behaviour with regard to sustainability issues, but these have rarely been examined in the literature. Bui (2011) reported that a required rate of return on investment is a popular boundary control, ensuring that investment projects pursued will provide a sufficient return to the shareholders. Interestingly, Almihoub et al. (2013) found that the net present value and internal rate of return are considered the biggest hurdles to enhancing sustainability performance. Bui (2011) also noted the presence of carbon-related spending limits, which help avoid undertaking sustainability and carbon-focused projects whose costs exceed an organization's risk appetite. Furthermore, in relation to energy generation and consumption, sustainable procurement policies and energy efficiency guides are mechanisms that help an organization's members change their procurement practices and resource consumption behaviour to ensure consistency with the generators' internal energy efficiency strategies.

Sustainability strategic performance controls

Sustainability strategic performance controls (SPCs) ensure the appropriateness of a current sustainability strategy or policy. The literature suggests three controls in this context: i) risk monitoring systems; ii) strategic planning processes; and iii) interactive controls.

Risk assessment and risk monitoring systems

It is now widely recognized that sustainability issues bring significant risks and opportunities to organizations (Bromiley et al. 2015; Ireland and Hitt 1992; Solomon et al. 2011; Kim et al. 2015). Having a formal environmental plan or policy does not guarantee appropriateness; in fact, the external environment has to be frequently monitored for changes and feedback provided to top management to assist in strategic review. Risk management can change lines of accountability and responsibility within organizations by representing a particular way of organizing (Soin and Collier 2013). Risk management frameworks can help link risk management to business strategy and objective setting, making risk management more akin to a management control function (Arena et al. 2010). Given this potential, it is surprising that little research has examined the role played by risk assessment and risk management in sustainability MCSs.

Busch and Hoffmann (2007) suggested that corporate risk assessment should include sustainability aspects and key natural resources used within an organization's value chain. They also cautioned that different organizations may have different risk exposures depending on the level of dependence on carbon-based materials and energy. Tang and Luo (2014) also found that among Australian firms, risk assessment involving a formal procedure to identify carbon-related risks and opportunities is a key element of an effective carbon management system. Such assessment should include regular examination of the impacts of climate change science, government policies and public expectations about the organization's assets and operations. Examining New Zealand electricity generators, Bui (2011) also found that risk monitoring is a key element of their MCSs used to respond to climate change issues. They monitor changes in government policies and regulations, consumer and societal pressures and use the information to assess the changing risk exposure of their organization over time.

Strategic planning

The integration of sustainability issues into the strategic planning process means sustainability becomes the driver or a key pillar of business strategy. Strategic planning allows the risks and opportunities associated with sustainability issues to be considered and assessed, based on which business strategy will be formulated, or evaluated and revised to ensure the appropriate organizational response and a balance between sustainability objectives and other organizational objectives. This ensures that sustainability issues are not regarded as secondary to profit maximization, or unnecessary inconveniences to the organization's everyday activities and operations. Prior studies provide ample evidence that the integration of sustainability into strategic planning influences behaviour and performance. Judge and Douglas (1998) and Sharma (2000) found that such integration is positively associated with organizational financial performance and the level of resources allocated to environmental issues. Jansson et al. (2000) noted that the detachment of environmental management systems from traditional control systems, in particular the strategic planning process, explains why environmental issues have not become a natural part of corporate business development. Pérez et al. (2007) argued that integration into strategic planning is one of the intangible assets that determine the level of embeddedness of environmental management systems in an organization. Adams and Frost (2008) noted that multinationals are increasingly using environmental and social indicators in strategic planning; however, the nature of the issues and the management operations that they impact vary considerably. Galbreath (2010) found that formal strategic planning creates awareness of and formulates strategies to respond to stakeholder sustainability-focused demands. Bui (2011) found that firms used environmental policy and information about carbon risks in their strategic planning to review and revise organizational responses during periods of government policy change.

Interactive control systems/ top management engagement

Prior studies suggest that the engagement and commitment of top management in sustainability issues are crucial to improving sustainability performance and environmental performance (Pérez et al. 2007). Top management commitment and the presence of an environmental champion help to explain the relationship between environmental disclosure and environmental management systems (Bouten and Hoozée 2013). In management control literature, interactive control systems are widely accepted as the main mechanism through which top managers monitor strategic uncertainties and engage with lower management decision-making processes to facilitate organizational learning and strategic renewal (Bisbe and Otley 2004; Simons 1991; Tuomela 2005). However, insights into how sustainability control systems are used interactively to deal with strategic uncertainties arising from sustainability issues are limited.

Bui (2011) found that when climate change issues are considered to create strategic uncertainties, top management uses interactive control systems extensively during the strategic planning process to gain insights into climate change risks and opportunities and review and formulate appropriate responses. Gond et al. (2012) used diagnostic and interactive uses of sustainability control systems and traditional management control systems to derive different patterns of integration of sustainability issues into organizational strategy and operations. Rodrigue et al. (2013) found that top management uses environmental performance indicators interactively, creating an opportunity for learning via the focus on threats and opportunities that challenge the existing strategy. Through the recognition of stakeholder pressures and other external factors, interactive use of environmental indicators leads to the emergence of new strategic indicatives and new indicators and promotes interaction between internal players and external parties. This leads to richer understanding and dialogue, and facilitates strategic renewal.

Sustainability strategic boundary controls

In order to unlock employees' potential and motivate optimal environmentally oriented behaviour, organizations need strong signals regarding their commitment to environmental protection (Brammer and Pavelin 2006; Tang and Luo 2014). Sustainability strategic boundaries (SBCs) provide such signals by highlighting the sustainability limits on strategic opportunity searches. Rather than affecting individual departments or activities, these controls have wide-ranging impacts on all organizational members by highlighting the desirable sustainability characteristics for investments, technologies or products. Two SBCs are considered below: mission statements and belief systems.

Mission/vision statements

Firms increasingly rely on mission statements to communicate strategy-related information to their stakeholders (Bartkus et al. 2002). Mission statements publicly declare the purpose, goals, product/markets, and philosophical views of the organization (Ireland and Hitt 1992). Many organizations have embraced sustainability rhetoric in their mission statements (Gond et al. 2012). Mission statements visualize an attractive, even idealistic future to help organizational members envision, prepare for and commit to the strategic changes required to achieve the desired outcome (Gioia and Thomas 1996). Mission statements can also help managers communicate their values and expectations to subordinates, thus indirectly guiding their behaviour towards sustainability. However, very few studies have examined the use of mission statements by management. Ramus and Steger (2000) argued that a strong sense of the company's mission increases employees' commitment to the organization and reduces uncertainty about the appropriate courses of action to take. Bartkus et al. (2002) found that mission-type statements can be found in a large proportion of European, Japanese and US firms, but they are rarely targeted or linked to specific stakeholder groups, such as customers, employees, investors or suppliers. Bui (2011) found some firms with a proactive environmental strategy formalized sustainability and carbon issues into their mission statement and communicated and discussed this statement frequently at operational and strategic levels to support their sustainability-led investment strategy. Lee et al. (2013) found that while many Australian universities publicly endorsed sustainability-related goals and values, this commitment was not reflected in their vision and mission statements. This questions the commitment of universities in pursuing sustainable development and enacting it at the strategic and operational levels.

Belief systems

A belief system reflects an organization's core values and motivates managers and employees to commit to organizational objectives (Ferreira and Otley 2009; Simons et al. 2000). Belief systems are often designed to be broad enough to appeal to a range of stakeholders and can become powerful controls when linked to the mission statement. Having a shared belief system or a common set of core values enables employees to align their behaviours with the firm's mission (Merchant 1985). When employees perceive that their values and belief systems are reflected in the company's goals via the mission statement, they are more motivated, particularly in undertaking environmental initiatives (Ramus and Steger 2000). Tuomela (2005) found that belief systems stimulate the integration of environmental information into the strategic performance measurement system. Epstein and Wisner (2005) found evidence for a positive association between belief systems and environmental compliance. Rodrigue et al. (2013) also observed that core values inspire organizational members to commit to the organization's objectives. This lever of control also embraces the notion of shared responsibility, where different parties help each other to achieve common goals. Furthermore, by promoting environmental awareness and protection, an organization creates an environmental mind-set which leads to the integration of environmental values into performance measurement systems and the mission statement.

Informal controls

While formal MCSs are the focus of many prior studies, informal controls have received much less academic attention. An informal system, in contrast to a formal system, does not control behaviour through explicit, verifiable measures. Instead, it comprises shared values, beliefs and traditions guiding the behaviour of groups or individuals (Falkenberg and Herremans 1995). Norris and O'Dwyer's (2004) case study firm used a highly informal approach to enable "socially responsive decision making", which can be characterized as social, self and clan-based. This informal control promotes high awareness of social responsibility goals but simultaneously creates conflicts and tensions for managers when these goals are not reflected in formal control systems. A study by Van Velsor et al. (2009) suggested that managers may nurture a culture of sustainability through cultural dynamics and processes. Via employee surveys and various cultural tools, leaders influence how employees perceive, feel and respond to corporate strategic uncertainties. These informal controls are seen as powerful components of successful management of sustainability.

Epstein and Roy (2007) indicated that having a formal MCS is essential but not sufficient for implementing environmental strategy. Formal and informal controls should be consistent to motivate decision makers to behave in a sustainable way. The two elements of MCS should be consistent, working together to motivate the decision-maker to operate in a sustainable way. Similarly, Riccaboni and Leone (2010) argued that a formal MCS has to be consistent, and supported by informal controls to ensure that the MCS leads to the achievement of sustainability goals. Though not referring to explicit and quantifiable measures, informal controls influence behaviour through a shared belief system, values and understandings. While a formal MCS is a fundamental lever for integrating sustainability into core operations, the key facilitator for the integration process is the inclusion of sustainability values into the organizational culture.

Interaction between controls

Sustainability controls do not act in isolation but interact and are related to each other, strengthening or weakening the overall impact of sustainability MCSs on organizational activities and performance. Ferreira and Otley (2009) suggested that the links between controls influence the strength and coherence of the overall MCS package, and Tessier and Otley (2012) implied the existence of synergies between controls, but neither emphasized these links. Simons et al. (2000) suggested two-way relationships between interactive and belief systems, and between boundary and diagnostic systems. Widener (2007) suggested that belief systems influence the other three systems: diagnostic, interactive and boundary. Hence, interaction between controls should be an important element of a sustainability-focused MCS framework.

These interactions can be between controls of the same category, or across different categories. Within sustainability SBCs, a mission statement may crystallize the implicit values in the belief system, further increasing goal congruence with sustainability objectives. However, a belief system that prioritizes competition or profit maximization may defeat the purpose of a sustainability-oriented mission statement. An organization may monitor sustainability-related risks and opportunities closely; however, if this information is not used in the strategic planning process, data generated by the risk monitoring system will be considered irrelevant by management. Within sustainability OBCs, an organization may have a formal sustainability-oriented environmental plan, but if there is no formal segregation of duties or assignment of responsibilities, it is unlikely that the plan will be implemented effectively or efficiently. Within sustainability OPCs, the integration of carbon-related indicators into the financial incentive system can mitigate the impact of targets and budgets (Ioannou et al. 2016).

Interaction across different control categories is also likely. For example, managers may intend interactive controls to reinforce belief systems, whereas belief systems could hinder or reduce the need for interactive controls, because a belief system that incorporates sustainability values already motivates subordinates' sustainability-oriented behaviour without needing top management intervention. Furthermore, formal and informal controls also have a close relationship. Both forms of control system need to support each other if they are to motivate socially responsive decision-making by management (Norris and O'Dwyer 2004). In their study, careful staff selection and employee socialization efforts motivated socially responsive decision-making. These formal controls were supported by the perceived congruence between managers' values and those promoted by the organization in its mission statement and belief system, and the overwhelming organizational culture (Norris and O'Dwyer 2004). Frow et al. (2005) found that managers drew upon formal management control procedures and combined them with informal social interaction to resolve the tensions at the interface between accountability and controllability. This suggests that the interaction between formal and informal controls can address the quality problems perceived in sustainability information (e.g., lack of controllability).

Use of MCSs

Sustainability MCSs can be used for different purposes. Burritt et al. (2011) argued that the appropriate accounting tool depends on varying decision settings, including the short- or long-term nature of the decision, managerial need for physical or monetary data, and whether the decision relates to past or future activities. Sustainability MCSs are considered to play important roles in many organizational functions such as production, distribution, procurement, supply chain management, communication and marketing (Schaltegger and Csutora 2012). Sustainability MCSs can also help monitor legal compliance, enabling environmental improvement and product innovation, and ensuring efficiency and cost savings (Henri and Journeault 2010; Schaltegger and Csutora 2012). Sustainability controls can help evaluate "whole of life" costs of products and services and enable organizations to determine appropriate pricing (Ratnatunga and Balachandran 2009)

Passetti et al. (2014) confirmed that monitoring compliance and efficiency are the two dominating uses of sustainability MCSs, and only a small number of firms use sustainability MCS in internal decision making. In contrast, Masanet-Llodra (2006) found a larger amount of environmental accounting information being used for internal purposes than for external purposes. They argued that the successful implementation of environmental management systems depends on whether environmental accounting is perceived to provide useful information for decision making by managers.

Sustainability information is recommended to be used in employee and external stakeholder engagement, and integrated in a training and communication strategy to ensure the success of a sustainability-oriented strategy (Etzion 2007; Tang and Luo 2014). Finally, providing data for external reporting is considered a key purpose of a carbon MCS (Bebbington and Larrinaga-Gonzalez 2008; Henri and Journeault 2010; Hopwood 2009; Rankin et al. 2011). Carbon controls can thus serve different objectives, achieving a competitive advantage and creating value; complying with regulations and maintaining value; or ensuring social legitimacy (Rankin et al. 2011; Schaltegger and Csutora 2012).

Objectives of controls

In examining sustainability, it is important not only to consider its types and uses, but also what managers intend its use to achieve. A sustainability control can be used to achieve either compliance or performance (Tessier and Otley 2012). It is these objectives that determine which types of sustainability control will be used, and for which purposes.

A beyond-compliance/proactive carbon strategy aims at improving internal efficiency and gaining a competitive advantage (Burritt et al. 2011; Rankin et al. 2011), while a compliance-focused/reactive strategy aims at the minimum for compliance (Schaltegger and Csutora 2012; Tang and Luo 2014). A beyond-compliance sustainability strategy would focus on SBCs so that risks and opportunities are identified and strategies continuously reviewed and revised to maintain and improve performance (Henri and Journeault 2010). Sustainability-focused belief systems and mission statements can motivate employees and increase their commitment to organizations' sustainability goals (Mundy 2010; Simons 1995). Further, interactive processes (SPCs) should be combined with rules (OBCs) to regulate internal relationships while leaving room for flexibility and learning (Berry et al. 2009; Van der Meer-Kooistra and Scapens 2008). Similarly, advanced sustainability monitoring and reporting systems (OPCs) are required to provide timely and accurate information for decision making, and to identify improvement and business opportunities (Burritt et al. 2011). It is likely that sustainability information will be used in a variety of decision settings, such as staff training and performance evaluation, product and process innovation, strategy formulation and review. Sustainability information will also be used to provide information to regulators and external stakeholders to fulfil the organization's reporting obligations and signal its strong environmental performance.

In contrast, a compliance-focused sustainability strategy is likely to use fewer types of sustainability controls, most likely OPCs and OBCs. As the focus is on meeting regulated environmental performance standards and external reporting requirements, organizations only need systems that measure, monitor and report sustainability information (OPCs). Diagnostic processes that monitor sustainability performance against regulated environmental standards help avoid non-compliance incidents. An environmental plan (OBC) is also important to publicly demonstrate the organization's commitment to environmental issues. Assignment of duties (OBC) is also required to ensure the accuracy and timeliness of sustainability information reported to external parties. However, the use of strategic controls such as SPCs will be limited as top management is not interested in engaging with sustainability information for strategic planning or risk assessment processes. Mission statements and belief systems (SBCs) are also likely to decouple from sustainability goals. In contrast to a beyond-compliance strategy, a compliance-focused strategy will mean sustainability MCSs primarily influence production, environmental and accounting functions that have direct responsibility for collecting and reporting sustainability information. Use of sustainability information will be limited to external reporting to fulfil external regulatory requirements.

Prior studies have highlighted the potential benefits of sustainability MCSs for organizational environmental performance, ranging from quality enhancement to cost savings, more accurate product pricing and retention of skilled personnel by creating an environmentally conscious culture (Dunk 2007; Sands et al. 2015). Indirectly, through the enhancement of eco-learning, continuous innovation, stakeholder integration and shared vision capabilities, sustainability MCSs can foster corporate environmental performance (Journeault 2016). In addition, sustainability MCSs can give firms an advantage over their competitors by ensuring that environmental issues are dealt with through a continuous process. However, Henri and Journeault's (2008) survey of Canadian manufacturing firms found no association between the integration of eco-controls in organizational MCSs and firms' financial performance. Given these inconclusive results, more research is needed to examine how the objective of a sustainability MCS drives its design and use, and affects organizational performance.

Quality of MCS information

The effectiveness of sustainability MCSs in facilitating decision making and other uses depends to a large extent on the quality of the sustainability information generated by these systems. Prior sustainability-related studies identify informational quality as a key driver of control effectiveness (Bowen and Wittneben 2011; Martinov-Bennie 2012). Without accurate and objective data, sustainability controls are unlikely to be perceived positively by managers and employees, reducing their potential to be integrated into decision making (Martinov-Bennie 2012).

Perego and Hartmann (2009) argued that in examining sustainability MCSs and their use, it is important to pay attention to both the different configurations of controls and the quality of information embedded in these systems (Perego and Hartmann 2009). Bowen and Wittneben (2011) posited that a fully functioning carbon accounting system must rely on measurement that is materially accurate, is consistent over space and time and incorporates data uncertainty. However, their study reveals significant tension between these characteristics in carbon accounting information used within and across organizational fields. Cooper and Pearce (2011) found that climate change indicators developed by English local authorities are questioned by organizations with regard to their appropriateness, accuracy, timeliness and controllability. The quality of the information creates doubts about whether local authorities should be held accountable for such indicators.

A study of German firms by Burritt et al. (2011) found that many firms face a significant challenge in organizing the amount of carbon-related information collected. The lack of feasible technical solutions results in a large volume of ad hoc data being collected, leading to poor data assurance and process inefficiency. This causes difficulty in managing carbon performance and prevents the development of an integrated carbon-focused MCS. Schaltegger and Csutora (2012) noted that ambiguity and uncertainty related to emissions data are caused by a lack of organizational understanding of primary production processes, especially when contractors are involved; the multiple ways of calculating emissions; and the need to rely on third-party expert options.

Overall, the literature suggests that it is not sufficient to have sophisticated control systems that embed sustainability issues. A key facilitator for the use of such systems by managers and employees is the quality of information being generated. Only with both high-quality information and strong sustainability-focused control systems do managers have the assurance and incentive to rely on sustainability information in decision making and internal functions, and thus improve organizational performance.

Language of control

Tessier and Otley (2012) suggested that the way that control is presented can have a significant impact on employee perceptions. Tessier and Otley (2012) suggested that language use can be one of the factors that drives the presentation of control but did not fully explain how, and did not consider language to be of much significance on its own. A careful choice of language can be a rhetorical tool that blurs boundaries between different patterns of thinking and promotes the development of a shared understanding (cognitive agreement) regarding the objective and use of sustainability MCSs (Gond et al. 2012). Achieving cognitive consistency is seen as crucial for the integration of sustainability in organizations (Heidmann et al. 2008; Hoffman and Bazerman 2007). As discussed above, sustainability accounts can be challenged due to the uncertainties and complexities surrounding measurements. Presenting sustainability issues in a way that is understandable and relatable to organizational members can help to overcome these challenges. Choosing a presentation style that is consistent with the organization's mission statement or belief system can also help to achieve goal congruence. For example, if an organization's core values are continuous improvement or the pursuit of efficiency, presenting carbon information in efficiency terms will help operational managers understand its relevance and motivate them to act to improve carbon performance. Lack of controllability can significantly inhibit action (Frow et al. 2005). Separating emissions levels into different scopes will make them more controllable by highlighting which parts are under the organization's direct control (e.g., Scope 1 and Scope 2) and which parts are less controllable (e.g., Scope 3). Increased perceived controllability is likely to facilitate action. We argue that the complexity surrounding the language of control and its consequences on organizational behaviour deserve more academic attention.

Discussion and conclusion

The literature review highlights several gaps, which offer significant opportunities for future research to understand sustainability controls in more depth and breadth. Studies have examined single a MCS, or small subsets of MCSs. Generally, prior studies have not examined carbon controls in a comprehensive MCS framework, resulting in only partial understanding of how management uses MCSs to mobilize sustainability strategy, because other important controls or characteristics of controls have been excluded from the picture.

Prior studies have tended to examine one or two controls but have not distinguished between them in terms of organizational level (strategic versus operational levels) and nature of control (e.g., prescribing limits and boundaries versus monitoring against critical performance indicators). Our MCS framework classifies sustainability controls based on these two dimensions and can help future research to better operationalize sustainability controls.

Within each category of formal controls, there are significant variations in the level of academic attention paid across different controls. Sustainability performance measures and EMA have been extensively researched, but our understanding of other sustainability OPCs, such as targets, incentive systems, and communication systems, is very limited. Environmental plans and policy have been most frequently studied, while formal assignment of duties and other operational boundary controls have been largely ignored. Strategic planning, as a key driver of the integration of sustainability into organizations, has been researched extensively, but little attention has been paid to other strategic performance controls, such as risk monitoring systems and interactive controls. The extant research has begun to recognize the importance of sustainability SBCs, including mission statements and belief systems, but significant scope remains for exploring how management uses these controls to mobilize sustainability-oriented behaviour within their organization.

The sustainability literature suggests an increasingly important role for informal controls in sustainability management. However, these informal controls are often considered under the umbrella of "organizational culture" without separating them into elements or components that may affect behaviour differently. Informal controls include shared values or understandings among a group (e.g., clan-based); individually applied principles (self-control); and socialization mechanisms. Trust as an informal control is of increasing interest in management accounting literature (Busco et al. 2006; Johansson and Baldvinsdottir 2003) but has not been explored in the sustainability control literature.

With a few exceptions, the interaction between controls has been largely ignored in the extant literature. This is partly due to the focus on one or two isolated control mechanisms rather than control as a package. Our review points out that the interaction between different controls has important consequences for the effectiveness of sustainability MCSs as a whole in affecting behaviour and organizational performance. Hence it is important that future research examining the impact of or association between sustainability controls and performance pays attention to the presence of other controls, which may reinforce or mitigate the relationship under study.

Finally, the quality of MCS information and the language of control are two important issues that deserve more investigation. We have argued that even when multiple sustainability controls are formulated and used, their effectiveness can be significantly influenced by the quality of sustainability information provided or embedded in those controls and the way such information is communicated to organizational participants. High-quality information will determine the likelihood or extent to which the information is used in managers' decision making. An appropriate language of control will increase the perceived match between sustainability objectives and organizational values, managers' beliefs and perceived responsibilities, promoting goal congruence. Sophisticated sustainability controls without appropriate presentation or communication can lead to tensions and conflicts that may have significant consequences for managerial behaviour.

In conclusion, much can be gained from examining sustainability controls as a package with due consideration of characteristics such as type of control, use, objectives, language and quality of control, and the interactions between them. Using an MCS framework such as the one developed in this chapter can go some way towards unpacking the complexity in internal sustainability controls and explaining the relationships and gaps between sustainability strategy, sustainability disclosure and firm performance.

References

Adams, C. A. and Frost, G. R., 2008. Integrating sustainability reporting into management practices. *Accounting Forum*, 32 (4), 288–302.

Adams, C. A. and Larrinaga-González, C., 2007. Engaging with organisations in pursuit of improved sustainability accounting and performance. *Accounting, Auditing & Accountability Journal*, 20 (3), 333–355.

Adams, C. A. and McNicholas, P., 2007. Making a difference: sustainability reporting, accountability and organisational change. *Accounting, Auditing & Accountability Journal*, 20 (3), 382–402.

Ahrens, T. and Chapman, C. S., 2007. Management accounting as practice. *Accounting, Organizations and Society*, 32 (1), 1–27.

Almihoub, A. A. A., Mula, J. M. and Rahman, M. M., 2013. Are there effective accounting ways to determining accurate accounting tools and methods to reporting emissions reduction? *Journal of Sustainable Development*, 6 (4), 118–129.

Álvarez Gil, M. J., Burgos Jiménez, J. and Céspedes Lorente, J. J., 2001. An analysis of environmental management, organizational context and performance of Spanish hotels. *Omega*, 29, 457–471.

Arena, M., Arnaboldi, M. and Azzone, G., 2010. The organizational dynamics of Enterprise Risk Management. *Accounting, Organizations and Society*, 35 (7), 659–675.

Arjaliès, D.-L., and Mundy, J., 2013. The use of management control systems to manage CSR strategy: a levers of control perspective. *Management Accounting Research*, 24 (4), 284–300.

Bartkus, B., Glassman, M. and Mcafee, B., 2002. Do large European, US and Japanese firms use their web sites to communicate their mission? *European Management Journal*, 20 (4), 423–429.

Bartolomeo, M., Bennett, M., Bouma, J. J., Heydkamp, P., James, P. and Wolters, T., 2000. Environmental management accounting in Europe: current practice and future potential. *European Accounting Review*, 9 (1), 31–52.

Bebbington, J. and Larrinaga-Gonzalez, C., 2008. Carbon trading: accounting and reporting issues. *European Accounting Review*, 17 (4), 697–717.

Berry, A. J., Coad, A. F., Harris, E. P., Otley, D. T. and Stringer, C., 2009. Emerging themes in management control: a review of recent literature. *The British Accounting Review*, 41 (1), 2–20.

Bisbe, J. and Otley, D., 2004. The effects of the interactive use of management control systems on product innovation. *Accounting, Organizations and Society*, 29 (8), 709–737.

Bonacchi, M. and Rinaldi, L., 2007. DartBoards and Clovers as new tools in sustainability planning and control. *Business Strategy and the Environment*, 16 (7), 461–473.

Bouten, L. and Hoozée, S., 2013. On the interplay between environmental reporting and management accounting change. *Management Accounting Research*, 24 (4), 333–348.

Bowen, F. and Wittneben, B., 2011. Carbon accounting: negotiating accuracy, consistency and certainty across organisational fields. *Accounting, Auditing & Accountability Journal*, 24 (8), 1022–1036.

Brammer, S. and Pavelin, S., 2006. Voluntary environmental disclosures by large UK companies. *Journal of Business Finance and Accounting*, 33 (7–8), 1168–1188.

Bromiley, P., Mcshane, M., Nair, A. and Rustambekov, E., 2015. Enterprise risk management: review, critique, and research directions. *Long Range Planning*, 48 (4), 265–276.

Bui, B., 2011. *Strategy-driven implications for the management control systems of electricity generators due to government climate change policies.* Thesis (PhD). Victoria University of Wellington.

Bui, B. and De Villiers, C., 2017. Business strategies and management accounting in response to climate change risk exposure and regulatory uncertainty. *The British Accounting Review*, 49 (1), 4–24.

Burritt, R. L., Hahn, T. and Schaltegger, S., 2002. Towards a comprehensive framework for environmental management accounting – links between business actors and environmental management accounting tools. *Australian Accounting Review*, 12 (27), 39–50.

Burritt, R. and Schaltegger, S., 2010. Sustainability accounting and reporting: fad or trend? *Accounting, Auditing & Accountability Journal*, 23 (7), 829–846.

Burritt, R., Schaltegger, S. and Zvezdov, D., 2011. Carbon management accounting: explaining practice in leading German companies. *Australian Accounting Review*, 21 (1), 80–98.

Busch, T. and Hoffmann, V., 2007. Emerging carbon constraints for corporate risk management. *Ecological Economics*, 62, 518–528.

Busco, C., Riccaboni, A. and Scapens, R. W., 2006. Trust for accounting and accounting for trust. *Management Accounting Research*, 17 (1), 11–41.

Comoglio, C. and Botta, S., 2012. The use of indicators and the role of environmental management systems for environmental performances improvement: a survey on ISO 14001 certified companies in the automotive sector. *Journal of Cleaner Production*, 20 (1), 92–102.

Contrafatto, M. and Burns, J., 2013. Social and environmental accounting, organisational change and management accounting: a processual view. *Management Accounting Research*, 24 (4), 349–365.

Cooper, S. and Pearce, G., 2011. Climate change performance measurement, control and accountability in English local authority areas. *Accounting, Auditing & Accountability Journal*, 24 (8), 1097–1118.

Crutzen, N. and Herzig, C., 2013. A review of the empirical research in management control, strategy and sustainability. *In*: L. Songini, A. Pistoni and C. Herzog, eds. *Accounting and control for sustainability*. Bingley, UK: Emerald Group, 165–195.

Dasgupta, S., Hettige, H. and Wheeler, D., 2000. What improves environmental compliance? Evidence from Mexican industry. *Journal of Environmental Economics and Management*, 39 (1), 39–66.

De Villiers, C., Rouse, P. and Kerr, J., 2016. A new conceptual model of influences driving sustainability based on case evidence of the integration of corporate sustainability management control and reporting. *Journal of Cleaner Production*, 136, 78–85.

Deegan, C., 2003. *Environmental management accounting: an introduction and case studies for Australia*. Sydney, Australia: Institute of Chartered Accountants in Australia.

Dunk, A. S., 2007. Assessing the effects of product quality and environmental management accounting on the competitive advantage of firms. *Australasian Accounting Business and Finance Journal*, 1 (1), 28–38.

Durden, C., 2008. Towards a socially responsible management control system. *Accounting, Auditing & Accountability Journal*, 21 (5), 671–694.

Eccles, R. G., Ioannou, I., Li, S. X. and Serafeim, G., 2012. *Pay for environmental performance: the effect of incentive provision on carbon emissions*. Cambridge, MA: Harvard Business School Working Paper, 13–043.

Eccles, R. G., Ioannou, I. and Serafeim, G., 2014. The impact of corporate sustainability on organizational processes and performance. *Management Science*, 60 (11), 2835–2857.

Epstein, M. J., 1996. You've got a great environmental strategy – now what? *Business Horizons*, 39 (5), 53–59.

Epstein, M. J. and Roy, M.-J., 2007. Implementing a corporate environmental strategy: establishing coordination and control within multinational companies. *Business Strategy and the Environment*, 16 (6), 389–403.

Epstein, M. J. and Wisner, P. S., 2005. Managing and controlling environmental performance: evidence from Mexico. *Advances in Management Accounting*, 14, 115–137.

Etzion, D., 2007. Research on organizations and the natural environment, 1992-present: a review. *Journal of Management*, 33 (4), 637–664.

Falkenberg, L. and Herremans, I., 1995. Ethical behaviours in organizations: directed by the formal or informal systems? *Journal of Business Ethics*, 14 (2), 133–143.

Faulkner, D., Carlisle, Y. M. and Viney, H. P., 2005. Changing corporate attitudes towards environmental policy. *Management of Environmental Quality*, 16 (5), 476–489.

Ferreira, A., Moulang, C. and Hendro, B., 2010. Environmental management accounting and innovation: an exploratory analysis. *Accounting, Auditing & Accountability Journal*, 23 (7), 920–948.

Ferreira, A. and Otley, D., 2009. The design and use of performance management systems: an extended framework for analysis. *Management Accounting Research*, 20 (4), 263–282.

Figge, F., Hahn, T., Schaltegger, S. and Wagner, M., 2002. The sustainability balanced scorecard – linking sustainability management to business strategy. *Business Strategy and the Environment*, 11 (5), 269–284.

Frow, N., Marginson, D. E. W. and Ogden, S., 2005. Encouraging strategic behaviour while maintaining management control: multi-functional project teams, budgets, and the negotiation of shared accountabilities in contemporary enterprises. *Management Accounting Research*, 16 (3), 269–292.

Galbreath, J., 2010. Drivers of corporate social responsibility: the role of formal strategic planning and firm culture. *British Journal of Management*, 21 (2), 511–525.

Gioia, D. A. and Thomas, J. B., 1996. Identity, image, and issue interpretation: sensemaking during strategic change in academia. *Administrative Science Quarterly*, 41, 442–476.

Gond, J.-P., Grubnic, S., Herzig, C. and Moon, J., 2012. Configuring management control systems: theorizing the integration of strategy and sustainability. *Management Accounting Research*, 23 (3), 205–223.

Gray, R. and Bebbington, J., 2001. *Accounting for the environment*. London, UK: Sage.

Gupta, M. C., 1995. Environmental management and its impact on the operations function. *International Journal of Operations and Production Management*, 15 (8), 34–51.

Heidmann, M., Schäffer, U. and Strahringer, S., 2008. Exploring the role of management accounting systems in strategic sensemaking. *Information Systems Management*, 25 (3), 244–257.

Henri, J.-F. and Journeault, M., 2008. Environmental performance indicators: an empirical study of Canadian manufacturing firms. *Journal of Environmental Management*, 87 (1), 165–176.

Henri, J.-F. and Journeault, M., 2010. Eco-control: the influence of management control systems on environmental and economic performance. *Accounting, Organizations and Society*, 35 (1), 63–80.

Henriques, I. and Sadorsky, P., 1996. The determinants of an environmentally responsive firm: an empirical approach. *Journal of Environmental Economics and Management*, 30 (3), 381–395.

Hoffman, A. J. and Bazerman, M. H., 2007. Changing practice on sustainability: understanding and overcoming the organizational and psychological barriers to action. *In:* S. Sharma, M. Starik, and B. Husted, eds. *Organizations and the sustainability mosaic: crafting long-term ecological and societal solutions*. Northampton, MA: Edward Elgar, 84–105.

Hopwood, A., 2009. Accounting and the environment. *Accounting, Organizations and Society*, 34 (3–4), 433–439.

Ioannou, I., Xin Li, S. and Serafeim, G., 2016. The effect of target difficulty on target completion: the case of reducing carbon emissions. *The Accounting Review*, 91 (5), 1467–1492.

Ireland, R. D. and Hitt, M. A., 1992. Mission statements: importance, challenge, and recommendations for development. *Business Horizons*, 35 (3), 34–42.

Jansson, Å., Nilsson, F. and Rapp, B., 2000. Environmentally driven mode of business development: a management control perspective. *Scandinavian Journal of Management*, 16 (3), 305–333.

Johansson, I.-L. and Baldvinsdottir, G., 2003. Accounting for trust: some empirical evidence. *Management Accounting Research*, 14 (3), 219–234.

Johansson, T. and Siverbo, S., 2014. The appropriateness of tight budget control in public sector organizations facing budget turbulence. *Management Accounting Research*, 25 (4), 271–283.

Journeault, M., 2016. The influence of the eco-control package on environmental and economic performance: a natural resource-based approach. *Journal of Management Accounting Research*, 28 (2), 149–178.

Judge, W. Q. and Douglas, T. J., 1998. Performance implications of incorporating natural environmental issues into the strategic planning process: an empirical assessment. *Journal of Management Studies*, 35 (2), 241–262.

Kerr, J., Rouse, P. and De Villiers, C., 2015. Sustainability reporting integrated into management control systems. *Pacific Accounting Review*, 27 (2), 189–207.

Kim, Y.-B., An, H. T. and Kim, J. D., 2015. The effect of carbon risk on the cost of equity capital. *Journal of Cleaner Production*, 93, 279–287.

Kober, R., Ng, J. and Paul, B. J., 2007. The interrelationship between management control mechanisms and strategy. *Management Accounting Research*, 18 (4), 425–452.

Kumarasiri, J. and Jubb, C., 2016. Carbon emission risks and management accounting: Australian evidence. *Accounting Research Journal*, 29 (2), 137–153.

Langfield-Smith, K., 1997. Management control systems and strategy: a critical review. *Accounting, Organizations and Society*, 22 (2), 207–232.

Langfield-Smith, K., 2005. What do you we know about management control systems and strategy. *In:* C. S. Chapman, ed. *Controlling strategy: management, accounting and performance measurements*. Oxford: Oxford University Press, 62–85.

Larrinaga-González, C., Carrasco-Fenech, F., Caro-González, F. J., Correa-Ruiz, C. and Páez-Sandubete, M. J., 2001. The role of environmental accounting in organizational change-an exploration of Spanish companies. *Accounting, Auditing & Accountability Journal*, 14 (2), 213–239.

Lee, K.-H., Barker, M. and Mouasher, A., 2013. Is it even espoused? An exploratory study of commitment to sustainability as evidenced in vision, mission, and graduate attribute statements in Australian universities. *Journal of Cleaner Production*, 48, 20–28.

Lee, S.-Y., 2012. Corporate carbon strategies in responding to climate change. *Business Strategy and the Environment*, 21 (1), 33–48.

Lisi, I. E., 2015. Translating environmental motivations into performance: the role of environmental performance measurement systems. *Management Accounting Research*, 29, 27–44.

Martinov-Bennie, N., 2012. Greenhouse gas emissions reporting and assurance: reflections on the current state. *Sustainability Accounting, Management and Policy Journal*, 3 (2), 244–251.

Masanet-Llodra, M. J., 2006. Environmental management accounting: a case study research on innovative strategy. *Journal of Business Ethics*, 68 (4), 393–408.

Merchant, K. A., 1985. *Control in business organizations*. Marshfield, MA: Financial Times/ Prentice Hall.

Mundy, J., 2010. Creating dynamic tensions through a balanced use of management control systems. *Accounting, Organizations and Society*, 35 (5), 499–523.

Norris, G. and O'Dwyer, B., 2004. Motivating socially responsive decision making: the operation of management controls in a socially responsive organisation. *The British Accounting Review*, 36 (2), 173–196.

Otley, D., 1999. Performance management: a framework for management control systems research. *Management Accounting Research*, 10 (4), 363–382.

Parker, L. D., 2000. Environmental costing: a path to implementation. *Australian Accounting Review*, 10 (22), 43–51.

Passetti, E., Cinquini, L., Marelli, A. and Tenucci, A., 2014. Sustainability accounting in action: lights and shadows in the Italian context. *The British Accounting Review*, 46 (3), 295–308.

Perego, P. and Hartmann, F., 2009. Aligning performance measurement systems with strategy: the case of environmental strategy. *Abacus*, 45 (4), 397–428.

Perego, P. and Kolk, A., 2012. Multinationals' accountability on sustainability: the evolution of third-party assurance of sustainability reports. *Journal of Business Ethics*, 110 (2), 173–190.

Pérez, E. A., Ruiz, C. C. and Fenech, F. C., 2007. Environmental management systems as an embedding mechanism: a research note. *Accounting, Auditing & Accountability Journal*, 20 (3), 403–422.

Qian, W. and Burritt, R., 2007. Environmental accounting for waste management: a study of local governments in Australia. *The Environmentalist*, 27 (1), 143–154.

Ramus, C. A. and Steger, U., 2000a. The roles of supervisory support behaviors and environmental policy in employee "ecoinitiatives" at leading-edge European companies. *Academy of Management Journal*, 43 (4), 605–626.

Rankin, M., Windsor, C. and Wahyuni, D., 2011. An investigation of voluntary corporate greenhouse gas emissions reporting in a market governance system: Australian evidence. *Accounting, Auditing & Accountability Journal*, 24 (8), 1037–1070.

Ratnatunga, J. and Balachandran, K. R., 2009. Carbon business accounting: the impact of global warming on the cost and management accounting profession. *Journal of Accounting, Auditing & Finance*, 24 (2), 333–355.

Riccaboni, A. and Leone, E. L., 2010. Implementing strategies through management control systems: the case of sustainability. *International Journal of Productivity and Performance Management*, 59 (2), 130–144.

Rietbergen, M. G., Van Rheede, A. and Blok, K., 2015. The target-setting process in the CO2 Performance Ladder: does it lead to ambitious goals for carbon dioxide emission reduction? *Journal of Cleaner Production*, 103, 549–561.

Rodrigue, M., Magnan, M. and Boulianne, E., 2013. Stakeholders' influence on environmental strategy and performance indicators: a managerial perspective. *Management Accounting Research*, 24 (4), 301–316.

Rouse, P. and Putterill, M., 2003. An integral framework for performance measurement. *Management Decision*, 41 (8), 791–805.

Sands, J., Lee, K.-H., Gunarathne, N. and Lee, K.-H., 2015. Environmental Management Accounting (EMA) for environmental management and organizational change: an eco-control approach. *Journal of Accounting and Organizational Change*, 11 (3), 362–383.

Schaltegger, S. and Csutora, M., 2012. Carbon accounting for sustainability and management. Status quo and challenges. *Journal of Cleaner Production*, 36, 1–16.

Sharma, S., 2000. Managerial interpretations and organizational context as predictors of corporate choice of environmental strategy. *Academy of Management Journal*, 43 (4), 681–697.

Simons, R., 1991. Strategic orientation and top management attention to control systems. *Journal of Financial Economics*, 12 (1), 49–62.

Simons, R., 1995. *Levers of control: how managers use innovative control systems to drive strategic renewal*, Boston, MA: Harvard Business School Press.

Simons, R., Davila, A. and Kaplan, R. S., 2000. *Performance measurement and control systems for implementing strategy: text and cases*. Upper Saddle River, NJ: Prentice Hall.

Soin, K. and Collier, P., 2013. Risk and risk management in management accounting and control. *Management Accounting Research*, 24 (2), 82–87.

Solomon, J. F., Solomon, A., Norton, S. D., and Joseph, N. L., 2011. Private climate change reporting: an emerging discourse of risk and opportunity? *Accounting, Auditing & Accountability Journal*, 24 (8), 1119–1148.

Tang, Q. and Luo, L., 2014. Carbon management systems and carbon mitigation. *Australian Accounting Review*, 24 (1), 84–98.

Tessier, S. and Otley, D., 2012. A conceptual development of Simons' Levers of Control framework. *Management Accounting Research*, 23 (3), 171–185.

Tuomela, T.-S., 2005. The interplay of different levers of control: a case study of introducing a new performance measurement system. *Management Accounting Research*, 16 (3), 293–320.

Van Der Meer-Kooistra, J. and Scapens, R. W., 2008. The governance of lateral relations between and within organisations. *Management Accounting Research*, 19 (4), 365–384.

Van Velsor, E., Morsing, M. and Oswald, D., 2009. Sustainable leadership: management control systems and organizational culture in Novo Nordisk A/S. *Corporate Governance: The International Journal of Business in Society*, 9 (1), 83–99.

Widener, S. K., 2007. An empirical analysis of the levers of control framework. *Accounting, Organizations and Society*, 32 (7–8), 757–788.

12 Assurance of sustainability and integrated reports

Muhammad Bilal FAROOQ
Auckland University of Technology

Charl DE VILLIERS
The University of Auckland, and University of Pretoria

Abstract

Sustainability reporting aims to communicate an organization's sustainability performance to stakeholders. Integrated reporting is designed to provide information on how well the organization has managed its financial and non-financial capital to the providers of that capital. However, the credibility of these documents is often questioned by stakeholders; i.e., are the claims made within these reports reliable, and do they provide a balanced account of the reporter's performance? Responding to stakeholder scepticism, organizations have begun to secure external assurance over their sustainability reports and integrated reports. This chapter explores these new forms of assurance, looking first at the demand and supply side of the sustainability assurance market and subsequently exploring issues relating to the assurance of integrated reports.

Introduction

In recent years, there has been a significant increase in the number of organizations publishing sustainability reports[1] (KPMG 2015). However, the credibility (i.e., reliability and balance) of sustainability reports is often debated. Consequently, reporters are using a variety of mechanisms to build stakeholder confidence in their disclosures and to address this credibility gap. These mechanisms include participating in (and winning) national international sustainability reporting awards (e.g., the ACCA sustainability reporting awards), securing certification (e.g., International Organizations for Standardization [ISO] certification) and internal review by the audit department (although this raises questions over the independence of the review process and is only effective where there is a high level of trust between stakeholders and the reporting organization) and getting high-profile experts of good public standing to comment on the sustainability reports (Dando and Swift 2003).

An alternative approach, similar to a financial statements audit, is to undertake sustainability assurance. The International Audit and Assurance Standards Board (IAASB)[2] defines assurance as "an engagement in which a practitioner aims to obtain sufficient appropriate evidence in order to express a conclusion designed to enhance the degree of confidence of the intended users other than the responsible party about the subject matter information" (IAASB 2013, p. 7). Farooq and De Villiers (2017, p. 82) defined sustainability assurance as "an engagement in which an external SA provider (SAP) undertakes assurance over a sustainability report". KPMG (2013, 2015) surveys show that in 2015 approximately 63 percent (up from 59 percent in 2013) of the world's largest 250 companies that published a sustainability report chose to have their reports subject to sustainability assurance (Junior et al. 2014). Thus sustainability assurance is no longer an optional extra but rather is considered a part of established organizational practice.

The next two sections of this chapter explore sustainability assurance engagements, examining first the demand side and then subsequently the supply side of the sustainability assurance market. The following section discusses assurance of integrated reports. Integrated reports are different from sustainability reports in that they attempt to provide information, in an integrated manner, on how an organization is managing its financial and non-financial capital (IIRC 2013). As this new form of reporting gains prominence, regulators and stakeholders are asking whether these reports should also be subject to assurance.

Factors driving the demand for sustainability assurance services

In a review of the literature, Farooq and De Villiers (2017) identified a range of external and internal factors driving the demand for voluntary sustainability assurance[3] as well as factors which inhibit or discourage organizations from undertaking sustainability assurance:

External factors

Studies have noted that the inclusion of sustainability assurance statements alongside published sustainability reports positively influence stakeholders' perceptions of sustainability report credibility (Cheng et al. 2015; Coram et al. 2009; Hodge et al. 2009; Romero et al. 2014; Wong and Millington 2014). For example, Hodge et al. (2009) surveyed Australian MBA students and found that sustainability assurance statements positively influenced perceptions of sustainability report credibility. Thus, reporters secure sustainability assurance as it allows them to enhance the credibility of their disclosures.

The size of the reporting entity and its industry membership also influence the demand for sustainability assurance (KPMG 2013, 2015; Sierra et al. 2013; Simnett et al. 2009; Zorio et al. 2013). The KPMG (2013, 2015) reports show that sustainability assurance rates increased from 59 percent in 2013 to 63 percent in 2015 amongst the world's largest 250 companies. Similarly, studies have found that reporters based in high social and environmental impact industries are more prone to securing sustainability assurance (Cho et al. 2014; Zorio et al. 2013). Such organizations are more visible, receive greater media coverage/criticisms and thus need to demonstrate credibility in their disclosures. For example, Gillet-Monjarret (2015) explored sustainability assurance in French listed companies and found that companies facing high levels of negative media coverage are more likely to secure sustainability assurance. However, as the practice gains greater recognition amongst the Fortune 250 companies, the role of industry membership is diminishing (Perego and Kolk 2012).

In terms of country-level indicators, sustainability assurance adoption rates have been highest amongst reporters based in Europe and Japan, while US companies have been slow on the uptake (Kolk and Perego 2010; Perego and Kolk 2012). The US is characterized by a highly litigious culture, where legal compliance is stressed, and where companies have not been willing to secure voluntary sustainability assurance. Other scholars have noted that organizations operating in stakeholder-orientated countries (i.e., those where organizations emphasize a stakeholder perspective over a shareholder perspective) (Simnett et al. 2009) and countries with weak regulatory environments are more prone to adopting sustainability assurance to enhance disclosure credibility (Kolk and Perego 2010; Perego and Kolk 2012; Perego 2009). Additionally, Herda et al. (2014) found that organizations in countries with weaker shareholder protection mechanisms are more likely to secure sustainability assurance. External assurance appears to act as a substitute for the weaker investor protection mechanisms in these countries and assists in enhancing disclosure credibility. However, Simnett et al. (2009) found the opposite and argued that reporters based in stronger legal environments are more prone to securing sustainability assurance.[4]

Internal factors

Internal factors discussed in the literature include financial indicators and the potential value-added nature of sustainability assurance. However, there are no conclusive results in these areas. For example, Simnett et al. (2009) found that financial indicators such as profitability or financial risk/leverage (i.e., how much debt an organization has accumulated) do not influence the decision to secure sustainability assurance. Sierra et al. (2013) similarly found no evidence to support a link between a reporter's profitability and the demand for sustainability assurance, but found that highly leveraged reporters are less likely to demand external assurance over their sustainability reports.

In terms of value addition, O'Dwyer et al. (2011) found that sustainability assurance providers are marketing their services as value added (i.e., offering benefits in addition to enhanced disclosure credibility) to potential clients. In their review of the literature on sustainability assurance, Farooq and De Villiers (2017) identified a number of different sources of value addition arising from sustainability assurance. For example, Park and Brorson (2005) noted that managers demanded external assurance over their sustainability reports as this provided them with confidence in the disclosures they were making. These managers were afraid of reporting incorrect or misleading information and the potential legal and reputational risks that arise from misreporting (Darnall et al. 2009; Sawani et al. 2010). Sustainability assurance providers also guide inexperienced reporters on weaknesses in their underlying systems and how these can be addressed (Gray 2000; Jones et al. 2014; O'Dwyer at al. 2011). Similarly, sustainability assurance practitioners assist reporters in improving the quality of their sustainability reporting (Moroney et al. 2012) and also help reporters align sustainability policies, programmes and strategies with key issues identified in the sustainability reporting process (Gillet 2012).

Factors inhibiting demand

In addition to factors driving the demand for sustainability assurance, the literature also identifies several factors that inhibit the demand for sustainability assurance. First and foremost, reporters complain of the time and cost involved in securing external assurance, which can be significant for large multinational entities (De Moor and De Beelde 2005; Jones and Solomon 2010; Park and Brorson 2005; Sawani et al. 2010). For example, Park and Brorson (2005) noted that one manager complained that the sustainability assurance fee was approximately one-third of the budget their company had set aside for sustainability reporting.

Other managers argue that sustainability assurance adds little if any value (Park and Brorson 2005). These managers were confident in their underlying sustainability reporting systems and final reports and felt that sustainability assurance did little to enhance stakeholders' perceptions of disclosure credibility.

Some managers perceived sustainability assurance as a challenging and difficult undertaking (Park and Brorson 2005). These managers believed that their systems were not robust enough and were thus incapable of withstanding the demands of external independent assurance (Dillard 2011; Jones and Solomon 2010; Sawani et al. 2010). As a result, sustainability assurance providers will often need to address weaknesses in clients' underlying systems. Perego and Kolk (2012), using the resource based view (RBV) of the organization, argued that only those organizations that have the required resources and capabilities (i.e., financial resources and systems) will demand sustainability assurance. This explains why few organizations choose to secure assurance over their first sustainability report (CorporateRegister.com Limited 2008).

The lack of regulation over sustainability reporting and sustainability assurance is also identified as one of the factors inhibiting the demand for sustainability assurance (Park and Brorson 2005; Sawani et al. 2010). As long as corporate governance codes focus on shareholders (as opposed to a broader range of stakeholders), organizations will have little incentive to improve the credibility of the disclosures they make to external stakeholders (Deegan et al. 2006a, Owen et al. 2000). Indeed, without regulation over sustainability reporting and sustainability assurance, scholars fear that these tools will be subject to managerial (i.e., reporters/managers) and professional (i.e., practitioners) capture, leading to the promotion of personal interests that frustrate attempts to promote organizational accountability (Ball et al. 2000; Smith et al. 2011).

De Moor and De Beelde (2005) point out that issues, such as breach of environmental legislation, raised by the sustainability assurance provider at the conclusion of an environmental audit raise possibilities of legal and reputational risks for organizations. If these issues remain unaddressed, subsequent incidents can lead to managers being investigated because they did not take action on the sustainability assurance provider's recommendations. Finally, as discussed in the introduction, sustainability assurance represents only one potential option or tool that a reporter can use to improve stakeholders' perceptions of disclosure credibility. Alternative options are often easier and cheaper to adopt, and thus organizations question the benefit of undertaking costly sustainability assurance.

Sustainability assurance providers and sustainability standards

Sustainability assurance, unlike sustainability reporting, is a relatively new practice. In most countries, sustainability assurance is voluntary,[5] and as a result, there is no consensus on how such engagements should be undertaken. There is a range of providers operating in the sustainability assurance market. These practitioners can be grouped into two categories: accounting and non-accounting sustainability assurance providers (CorporateRegister.com Limited 2008; Edgley et al. 2015; Manetti and Toccafondi 2012). Accountants are the 'Big Four' accounting firms (Deloitte, KPMG, E&Y International and PwC). These firms represent big global operators that are developing new assurance markets to supplement their core source of revenue, which is from traditional financial audit services (Ackers 2009; Elliott 1998; Wallage 2000). However, sustainability assurance is unregulated, and accountants do not enjoy a monopoly as they do in the market for financial statements audits (Elliott 1998).

Non-accounting sustainability assurance providers are diverse, including multinational engineering consultancies and certification providers, sustainability/corporate social responsibility consultancies, universities, non-governmental organizations, individual assurance providers, social and environmental experts and public opinion leaders[6] (CorporateRegister.com Limited 2008; Perego and Kolk 2012). However, KPMG (2015) notes that accountants dominate the sustainability assurance market among the global 250 companies. Similarly, Junior et al. (2014) analysed the sustainability reporting and assurance practices of the Fortune 500 companies. They found that accountants held the majority share of the sustainability assurance market in Europe, South America and Russia, while non-accountants held a more dominant position in Australasia, Asia and North America. Interestingly, they found that a small minority have opted to assure their sustainability reports using a combination of accountants and non-accountants. However, it is interesting that accounting firms have employed non-accountants in their sustainability assurance teams (O'Dwyer 2011).

Reviewing the literature in the field, Farooq and DeVilliers (2017) identified six areas of difference between accounting and non-accounting sustainability assurance providers (see table 12.1). First, there is a debate regarding which group of practitioners has the required expertise and knowledge to perform the engagement (Adams and Evans 2004). Some scholars argue that accountants, with their experience in financial audits, have the competencies necessary to undertake financial statement audits (Gray 2000). Some studies have found that managers prefer to recruit accountants as they are perceived to have a better understanding of the organization, having undertaken the financial statements audits (Gillet 2012). However, others argue that non-accountants are more qualified for the role of sustainability assurance providers as they have a better understanding of sustainability (the subject matter of sustainability assurance): physicists, sociologists and ethicists have a better understanding of social and environmental issues than accountants (Gray 2000).

Commentators argue that accounting firms, given their size, are more suitable for the role of sustainability assurance provider (Perego and Kolk 2012). The size of large accounting firms allows them to achieve economies of scale and thus offer services at a lower fee (Mock et al. 2013; Simnett et al. 2009). Additionally, accountants have the resources required to invest in improving audit and assurance technologies. Finally, only large practices have the resources necessary to audit the sustainability reports of large multinational companies. However, these arguments are less relevant when comparing accountants with larger non-accounting sustainability assurance providers (such as the global engineering consultancies and certification providers).

Sustainability assurance providers must be perceived to be independent and objective by stakeholders (Adams and Evans 2004). The literature argues that accountants, with their experience in providing financial statement audit services, understand the need for an assurance provider to maintain independence more than non-accountants (Gray 2000). Furthermore, the larger accounting firms are less dependent on one organization (Perego and Kolk 2012; Simnett et al. 2009). Finally, accountants are members of professional accounting bodies and thus must adhere to the requirements of ethical codes, which lay down strict requirements for maintaining independence and objectivity. However, others counter this by arguing that recent corporate scandals and collapses have involved financial auditors, thus tarnishing the image of the accounting profession as independent and objective (Dando and Swift 2003).

Researchers have investigated stakeholder preferences for sustainability assurance providers. For example, Jones and Solomon (2010) conducted semi-structured interviews with managers (i.e., internal stakeholders) in the UK. These managers preferred to choose an accounting firm as they believed that sustainability assurance was essentially an extension of the financial statements audit and therefore better suited to an accountant. Furthermore, these managers believed that recruiting one assurance provider would lead to a reduction in cost and time (Huggins et al. 2011). In comparison, Wong and Millington (2014) found that external stakeholders (such as investors and procurement officers) leaned more towards non-accountants, who were seen to be experts in the subject matter of assurance and more independent than accountants.

Studies have also investigated the potential impact of sustainability assurance on the quality of an organization's disclosure. For example, Moroney et al. (2012) analysed environmental reports of Australian listed companies and found that the quality of assured environmental reports was better. However, they

Table 12.1 Summary of differences between ASAPs and NASAPs

Factor	ASAP	NASAP
Expertise and knowledge	ASAPs have expertise in audit and assurance. As financial statements auditors ASAPs have a better understanding of the organization and its industry	NASAPs have expertise in knowledge of sustainability
Size	ASAPs (especially the big 4) can leverage their size advantage to offer services to larger organizations, offer reduced fees, invest in audit and assurance technologies and maintain quality of assurance services	Some NASAPs (especially global certification firms) also have size advantages similar to the big 4 ASAPs. However, other NASAPs are small entities and find it difficult to compete against larger ASAPs.
Perceived independence of the SAP	ASAPs through their experience with financial audits have a better understanding of independence. The size advantage of ASAPs also means that they are not dependent on any one client. ASAPs are bound by the requirements of professional code of ethics.	Corporate collapses and scandals involving financial auditors, e.g., Enron and Arthur Anderson, have dented the image of independence and objectivity associated with accountants. Furthermore, large NASAPs similar to ASAPs are not dependent on a single source of revenue and have in place quality control measures
Stakeholders preference for SAP type	Sustainability reporting managers based in the UK prefer ASAPs as they believe that SA is an extension of a financial audit and thus the domain of accountants.	External stakeholders prefer NASAPs because they value subject matter expertise and because they do not perceive ASAPs being independent.
Impact on quality of disclosure	No difference on the quality of the sustainability report. However, ASAPs more comfortable assuring hard quantitative data.	NASAPs comfortable in providing assurance over soft qualitative data.
Differences in approach	ASAPs adopt ISAE3000 and thus follow the same approach as adopted in financial audits. They adopt a more cautionary approach focusing on verifying the accuracy/reliability of data and information contained within the sustainability report and restricting their assurance opinion to limited assurance.	NASAPs are not bound by any standard however most prefer AA1000AS. They are more willing to innovate and adopt creative assurance methodologies to achieve their objectives. They view SA as a tool that can drive sustainability in organizations and thus promote accountability and improve society. They are more willing to provide assurance over accuracy/ reliability and balance/relevance.

ASAPs – accounting sustainability assurance providers; NASAPs – non-accounting SAPs

Source: Farooq and De Villiers (2017, p. 87)

could find no significant difference in the quality of environmental reports assured by accountants versus non-accountants. They did find that environmental reports assured by non-accountants contained more qualitative disclosures (or soft disclosures).These findings highlight accountants' preferences for assuring hard/quantifiable data.

Numerous studies have examined published sustainability assurance statements to assess the differences in approach between accountants and non-accountants (Ball et al. 2000; Belal 2002; Cooper and Owen 2007; Deegan et al. 2006a, 2006b; Gray 2000; Manetti and Becatti 2009; O'Dwyer and Owen 2005, 2007; Segui-Mas et al. 2015), finding that accountants focus more on providing assurance over the reliability of sustainability report content (i.e., whether content is verifiable/supported by evidence) while non-accountants provide assurance over the reliability and balance (i.e., whether the reporter provides disclosure of both good and bad news) of the report.The studies noted that the detailed procedures performed by accountants and non-accountants are similar; however, accountants use ISAE3000 while non-accountants use AA1000AS when undertaking sustainability assurance engagements.

ISAE3000 (International Standard on Assurance Engagements 3000 – developed by the IAASB)[7] categorizes engagements into those in which the practitioner offers a reasonable/high level of assurance and those in which a limited/low level of assurance is provided (Hasan et al. 2003). ISAE3000 allows assurance providers to offer a mix of reasonable and limited levels of assurance to cover different content within a single sustainability report (Wallage 2000). However, ISAE3000 is not a specialist sustainability assurance standard and is designed

Table 12.2 Summary of the findings of studies analyzing sustainability assurance statements

Area	Observation
Addressee	Many SA statements do not identify an addressee. Of those that do most are issued by ASAPs. However, ASAPs are more likely to address their assurance statements to internal stakeholders, while NASAPs are more willing to address their assurance statements to the sustainability report readers.
Objectives of SA	There is a lack of uniformity in the stated objectives of SA engagements.The most common objective is to review/verify the accuracy of information contained within the sustainability report.This objective is more popular amongst ASAPs while NASAPs will aim to evaluate the reporter's sustainability performance against the AA1000 principles.
Scope of SA engagements	In some engagements ASAPs provide assurance over the entire contents of the sustainability report while in other engagements assurance over only some sections of the sustainability report. NASAPs appear more willing to provide assurance over the entire sustainability report.

Area	*Observation*
Nature, timing and extent of procedures	Description of the work done varied from a brief one-paragraph to on-epage descriptions. The detailed procedures adopted by ASAPs and NASAPs were similar. NASAPs adopt a more consultative approach and are often involved from the start of the sustainability reporting process rather than coming in at the end stages to verify data as is the case with ASAPs.
Materiality assessment	Few engagements aimed to verify materiality (including stakeholder engagement mechanisms) and relevance of information. Instead most engagements focused on verifying the accuracy of data and information contained in the sustainability report. Thus SA follows the approach of traditional financial audits. However, this was more common amongst ASAPs than NASAPs.
SA standard	Some statements made no reference to a SA standard (these are attributed to NASAPs). A number of statements used more than one standard in combination. ASAPs prefer ISAE3000 and thus adopt traditional auditing techniques focusing primarily on verifying the accuracy of data and information. NASAPs, however, prefer AA1000AS, are more innovative and are more willing to review materiality and relevance.
Assurance opinion	NASAPs appear more willing than ASAPs to provide detailed statements addressing accuracy, reliability and completeness of the sustainability report. Overall NASAPs statements offer a more detailed discussion of the level of assurance provided. In comparison, ASAPs appeared more cautious, focusing on assuring accuracy and reliability and less on performance. This leads O'Dwyer and Owen, (2007) to identify two main categories of SA engagements, including those that focused on verifying data and information accuracy and those that had a broader focus aimed at verifying data and information relevance/materiality (and stakeholder engagement).
SAP recommendations	Providing recommendations are common practice and indicates the consultancy nature of SA. NASAPs are more likely to provide recommendations than ASAPs. Recommendations are very broad, generalized and brief. In some cases, these recommendations are of a strategic nature however in most cases they focus on weaknesses were in underlying systems, sustainability report content and sustainability reporting process.

Source: Farooq and De Villiers (2017, p. 90)

for a broad range of engagements (IAASB 2013; Manetti and Becatti 2009; O'Dwyer et al. 2011; Smith et al. 2011).

In comparison, AA1000AS (AA1000 Assurance standards, developed by AccountAbility)[8] is a specialist sustainability assurance standard (AccountAbility 2015; Manetti and Becatti 2009; Perego and Kolk 2012). The standard classifies sustainability assurance engagements into two types labelled as Type 1 and Type 2 engagements (AccountAbility 2008a). The scope of these two engagements differs, with Type 1 engagements focusing on assessing the reporter's implementation of the AA1000APS sustainability principles.[9] Type 2 engagements are broader in scope than type 1 engagements and the practitioner provides assurance over both the AccountAbility principles and sustainability disclosure/information.

The studies mentioned earlier also highlight several other characteristics of published sustainability assurance statements. The findings from these studies are summarized in Table 12.2.

Assurance of integrated reports

More recently, organizations have started publishing what are referred to as integrated reports. An integrated report is different from a sustainability report; nor is it an aggregation of an annual report and a sustainability report. Instead the integrated report is designed to provide a concise portrayal of the interconnection between material financial and non-financial performance measures (IIRC 2013). As with sustainability reporting, the assurance of integrated reports is also gaining international attention. Similar to sustainability assurance, the aim of assurance of integrated reports is to improve the reliability of the data and information in an integrated report (IIRC 2013). However, given the nature of an integrated report, assurance represents a significant challenge to assurance providers.

Maroun and Atkins (2015) examined assurance over integrated reports in a South African context, where integrated reporting has been mandated for listed companies. Maroun (2017) similarly examined the assurance of integrated reports in South Africa, with both studies reporting similar results. The more comprehensive Maroun (2017) involved interviews with 20 assurance providers and 20 integrated report preparers. These participants described the challenge of assuring prospective data and information that includes a combination of qualitative and quantitative data. Practitioners noted that assurance of integrated reports would involve a high degree of subjectivity and would be difficult to undertake. The study identified three possible approaches to assurance of integrated reports. As with sustainability assurance, there is considerable diversity in the scope, objectives and methodologies used to undertake this new form of assurance.

The first approach, called a restricted assurance model, is to simply assure the financial statements part of an integrated report. An external auditor would audit the financial statements (as is current practice) and would provide an opinion on the reliability of the financial statements, following a traditional financial statement audit with the scope and objectives determined by auditing standards. This opinion may be supported by additional assurance opinions on other information (of a non-financial nature) contained within the integrated report; however, the assurance provider would not provide any assurance over the interconnection (or otherwise) between the two (or more) assurance reports. The second approach, referred to as an integrated assurance model, involves using different sources of assurance to collectively assure the reliability of the information contained within the integrated report. The scope of this engagement is determined by those charged with governance (i.e., the board of directors of a company). The assurance provider would attempt to highlight (if applicable) areas within the integrated report in which no information (or insufficient information) is provided regarding how an organization is managing the different capitals it controls in order to achieve long-term value. The final approach, referred to as a Delphi-inspired assurance model, involves an external assurance provider using a panel of experts who comment on the process used to prepare the integrated report. However, assurance of integrated reports is still in its early years and therefore it will take time before practitioners can identify the best way to undertake this new form of assurance.

Conclusion

In conclusion, sustainability assurance and assurance of integrated reports provide examples of new accounting tools developed by practitioners to hold organizations accountable for the claims made in their sustainability reports and integrated reports. In most jurisdictions, these new forms of assurance are voluntary, and therefore the scope and objective of engagements is determined by the free market forces of demand and supply. Thus there is little consensus on what the scope and objective of these engagements should be, who should undertake them and how they should be undertaken.

Notes

1 The term 'sustainability' report refers to both a stand-alone sustainability report and sustainability information contained within a single annual report containing traditional financial and non-financial/sustainability information).
2 The IAASB is a sub body of the International Federation of Accountants or IFAC.
3 In most jurisdictions, sustainability assurance, like sustainability reporting, is a voluntary undertaking. However, as stock exchanges across the world begin to introduce listing requirements on sustainability reporting, it is likely that sustainability assurance will also follow suit.
4 See also Branco et al. (2014) for a country specific study of sustainability assurance in a Portuguese context.
5 Exceptions include countries such as France where the "Grenelle 2 Law" encourages organizations to undertake sustainability reporting and to secure third-party assurance over their sustainability reports (Gillet-Monjarret 2015).
6 Consequently, NASAPs consist of both large MNCs and smaller local firms operating at a national level (Simnett et al. 2009).
7 The IAASB refers to the International Audit and Assurance Standards Board.
8 AccountAbility is a London-based consultancy that specializes in developing sustainability standards.
9 These principles include inclusivity, materiality and responsiveness (AccountAbility 2008b).

References

AccountAbility, 2008a. *AA1000 assurance standard 2008* [online]. Available: www.accountabil ity.org/wp-content/uploads/2016/10/AA1000AS_english.pdf [Accessed 19 June 2017].
AccountAbility, 2008b. *AA1000 accountAbility principles standard 2008* [online]. Available: www.mas-business.com/docs/AA1000APS%202008%20Final.pdf [Accessed 19 June 2017].

Ackers, B., 2009. Corporate social responsibility assurance: how do South African publicly listed companies compare? *Meditari Accountancy Research*, 17 (2), 1–17.

Adams, C.A. and Evans, R., 2004. Accountability, completeness, credibility and the audit expectations gap. *Journal of Corporate Citizenship*, 14 (Summer), 97–115.

Ball, A., Owen, D.L. and Gray, R., 2000. External transparency or internal capture? The role of third-party statements in adding value to corporate environmental reports. *Business Strategy and the Environment*, 9 (1), 1–23.

Belal, A.R., 2002. Stakeholder accountability or stakeholder management? A review of UK firms' social and ethical accounting, auditing and reporting practices. *Corporate Social Responsibility and Environmental Management*, 9 (1), 8–25.

Branco, M.C., Delgado, C., Gomes, S.F. and Pereira Eugeno, T.C., 2014. Factors influencing the assurance of sustainability reports in the context of the economic crisis in Portugal. *Managerial Auditing Journal*, 29 (3), 237–252.

Cheng, M.M., Green, W.J. and Ko, J.C.W., 2015. The impact of strategic relevance and assurance of sustainability indicators on investors decisions. *Auditing: A Journal of Theory and Practice*, 34 (1), 131–162.

Cho, C.H., Michelon, G., Patten, D.M. and Roberts, R.W., 2014. CSR report assurance in the USA: an empirical investigation of determinants and effects. *Sustainability Accounting, Management and Policy Journal*, 5 (2), 130–148.

Cooper, S.M. and Owen, D.L., 2007. Corporate social reporting and stakeholder accountability: the missing link. *Accounting, Organizations and Society*, 32 (7), 649–667.

Coram, P.J., Monroe, G.S. and Woodliff, D.R., 2009. The value of assurance on voluntary nonfinancial disclosure: an experimental evaluation. *Auditing: A Journal of Practice and Theory*, 28 (1), 137–151.

CorporateRegister.com Limited, 2008. *Assure view: the CSR assurance statement report*. London: CorporateRegister.com Limited.

Dando, N. and Swift, T., 2003. Transparency and assurance: minding the credibility gap. *Journal of Business Ethics*, 44 (2), 195–200.

Darnall, N., Seol, I. and Joseph, S., 2009. Perceived stakeholder influences and organizations' use of environmental audits. *Accounting, Organizations and Society*, 34 (2), 170–187.

De Moor, P. and De Beelde, I., 2005. Environmental auditing and the role of the accountancy profession: a literature review. *Environmental Management*, 36 (2), 205–219.

Deegan, C., Cooper, B. J. and Shelly, M., 2006a. An investigation of TBL report assurance statements: Australian evidence. *Australian Accounting Review*, 16 (39), 2–18.

Deegan, C., Cooper, B. J. and Shelly, M., 2006b. An investigation of TBL report assurance statements: UK and European evidence. *Managerial Auditing Journal*, 21 (4), 329–371.

Dillard, J., 2011. Double loop learning; or, just another service to sell: a comment on 'The case of sustainability assurance: constructing a new assurance service'. *Contemporary Accounting Research*, 28, 1266–1276.

Edgley, C., Jones, M. J. and Atkins, J., 2015. The adoption of the materiality concept in social and environmental reporting assurance: a field study approach. *The British Accounting Review*, 47 (1), 1–18.

Elliott, R. K., 1998. Assurance services and the audit heritage. *Auditing: A Journal of Theory and Practice*, 17, 1–7.

Farooq, M. B. and De Villiers, C., 2017. The market for sustainability assurance services: a comprehensive literature review and future avenues for research. *Pacific Accounting Review*, 29 (1), 79–106.

Gillet, C., 2012. A study of sustainability verification practices: the French case. *Journal of Accounting and Organizational Change*, 8 (1), 62–84.

Gillet-Monjarret, C., 2015. Assurance of sustainability information: a study of media pressure. *Accounting in Europe*, 12 (1), 87–105.

Gray, R., 2000. Current developments and trends in social and environmental auditing, reporting and attestation: a review and comment. *International Journal of Auditing*, 4 (3), 247–268.

Hasan, M., Roebuck, P. J. and Simnett, R., 2003. An investigation of alternative report formats for communicating moderate levels of assurance. *Auditing: A Journal of Theory and Practice*, 22 (2), 171–187.

Herda, D.N., Taylor, M.E. and Winterbotham, G., 2014. The effect of country-level investor protection on the voluntary assurance of sustainability reports. *Journal of International Financial Management and Accounting*, 25 (2), 209–236.

Hodge, K., Subramaniam, N. and Stewart, J., 2009. Assurance of sustainability reports: impact on report users' confidence and perceptions of information credibility. *Australian Accounting Review*, 19 (3), 178–194.

Huggins, A., Green, W.J. and Simnett, R., 2011. The competitive market for assurance engagements on greenhouse gas statements: is there a role for assurers from the accounting profession?. *Current Issues in Auditing*, 5 (2), 1–12.

IAASB, 2013. *International standard on assurance engagements 3000 (revised): assurance engagements other than audits or reviews of historical financial Information*. New York: International Federation of Accountants.

IIRC, 2013. *The international framework* [online]. Available: http://integratedreporting.org/resource/international-ir-framework/ [Accessed 19 June 2017].

Jones, M. and Solomon, J., 2010. Social and environmental report assurance: some interview evidence. *Accounting Forum*, 34 (1), 20–31.

Jones, P., Hillier, D. and Comfort, D., 2014. Assurance of the leading UK food retailers' corporate social responsibility/sustainability reports. *Corporate Governance*, 14 (1), 130–138.

Junior, R. M., Best, P. J. and Cotter, J., 2014. Sustainability reporting and assurance: a historical analysis on a world-wide phenomenon. *Journal of Business Ethics*, 120 (1), 1–11.

Kolk, A. and Perego, P., 2010. Determinants of the adoption of sustainability assurance statements: an international investigation. *Business Strategy and the Environment*, 19 (3), 182–198.

KPMG, 2013. *The KPMG survey of corporate responsibility reporting 2013*. Netherlands: KPMG.

KPMG, 2015. *The KPMG survey of corporate responsibility reporting 2013*. Available: https://assets.kpmg.com/content/dam/kpmg/pdf/2016/02/kpmg-international-survey-of-corporate-responsibility-reporting-2015.pdf [Accessed 1 June 2015].

Manetti, G. and Becatti, L., 2009. Assurance services for sustainability reports: standards and empirical evidence. *Journal of Business Ethics*, 87, 289–298.

Manetti, G. and Toccafondi, S., 2012. The role of stakeholder in sustainability reporting assurance. *Journal of Business Ethics*, 107 (3), 363–377.

Maroun, W., 2017. Assuring the integrated report: insights and recommendations from auditors and preparers. *The British Accounting Review*, 49 (3), 329–346.

Maroun, W. and Atkins, J., 2015. *The challenges of assuring integrated reports: views from the South African auditing community*. London: The Association of Chartered Certified Accountants.

Mock, T.J., Rao, S.S. and Srivastava, R.P., 2013. The development of worldwide sustainability reporting assurance. *Australian Accounting Review*, 23 (4), 280–294.

Moroney, R., Windsor, C. and Aw, Y.T., 2012. Evidence of assurance enhancing the quality of voluntary environmental disclosures: an empirical analysis. *Accounting and Finance*, 52 (3), 903–939.

O'Dwyer, B., 2011. The case of sustainability assurance: constructing a new assurance service. *Contemporary Accounting Research*, 28 (4), 1230–1266.

O'Dwyer, B. and Owen, D.L., 2005. Assurance statement practice in environmental, social and sustainability reporting: a critical perspective. *British Accounting Review*, 37 (2), 205–229.

O'Dwyer, B. and Owen, D. L., 2007. Seeking stakeholder-centric sustainability assurance: an examination of recent sustainability assurance practice. *Journal of Corporate Citizenship*, 25 (Spring), 77–94.

O'Dwyer, B., Owen, D. and Unerman, J., 2011. Seeking legitimacy for new assurance forms: the case of assurance on sustainability reporting. *Accounting, Organizations and Society*, 36 (1), 31–52.

Owen, D. L., Swift, T. A., Humphrey, C. and Bowerman, M., 2000. The new social audits: accountability, managerial capture or the agenda of social champions? *European Accounting Review*, 9 (1), 81–98.

Park, J. and Brorson, T., 2005. Experiences of and views on third-party assurance of corporate environmental and sustainability reports. *Journal of Cleaner Production*, 13 (10), 1095–1106.

Perego, P., 2009. Causes and consequences of choosing different assurance providers: an international study of study of sustainability reporting. *International Journal of Management*, 26 (3), 412–425.

Perego, P. and Kolk, A., 2012. Multinationals' accountability on sustainability: the evolution of third-party assurance of sustainability reports. *Journal of Business Ethics*, 110 (2), 173–190.

Romero, S., Fernandez-Feijoo, B. and Ruiz, S., 2014. Perceptions of quality of assurance statements for sustainability reports. *Social Responsibility Journal*, 10 (3), 480–499.

Sawani, Y., Zain, M. M. and Darus, F., 2010. Preliminary insights on sustainability reporting and assurance practices in Malaysia. *Social Responsibility Journal*, 6 (4), 627–645.

Segui-Mas, E., Bollas-Araya, H.-M. and Polo-Garrido, F., 2015. Sustainability assurance on the biggest cooperatives of the world: an analysis of their adoption and quality. *Annals of Public and Cooperative Economics*, 86 (2), 363–383.

Sierra, L., Zorio, A. and Garcia-Benau, M. A., 2013. Sustainable development and assurance of corporate social responsibility reports published by Ibex-35 companies. *Corporate Social Responsibility and Environmental Management*, 20 (6), 359–370.

Simnett, R., Vanstraelen, A. and Chua, W. F., 2009. Assurance on sustainability reports: an international comparison. *The Accounting Review*, 84 (3), 937–967.

Smith, J., Haniffa, R. and Fairbrass, J., 2011. A conceptual framework for investigating 'capture' in corporate sustainability reporting assurance. *Journal of Business Ethics*, 99 (3), 425–439.

Wallage, P., 2000. Assurance on sustainability reporting: an auditor's view. *Auditing: A Journal of Practice and Theory*, 19, 53–65.

Wong, R. and Millington, A., 2014. Corporate social disclosures: a user perspective on assurance. *Accounting, Auditing and Accountability Journal*, 27 (5), 863–887.

Zorio, A., Garcia-Benau, M. A. and Sierra, L., 2013. Sustainable development and the quality of assurance reports: empirical evidence. *Business Strategy and the Environment*, 22 (7), 484–500.

13 The future of sustainability accounting and integrated reporting

Charl DE VILLIERS
The University of Auckland, and University of Pretoria

Warren MAROUN
University of the Witwatersrand

Abstract

This chapter provides a brief overview of the book and discusses the likely future of the practice of and research on sustainability accounting and integrated reporting. Sustainability accounting includes reporting, the management control systems to support reporting and the assurance of external reporting. The rapid mainstreaming of sustainability issues, corporate social responsibility, and reporting on these matters has also reinvigorated research interest in these areas. These trends are bound to be maintained and a future where these matters are not seen as important can hardly be contemplated. A future where the integration of sustainability and social and environmental responsible action are taken for granted as prerequisites for any successful organization is a much more likely scenario.

Introduction

This book has provided an overview of the practice and theory of sustainability accounting and integrated reporting. This includes its history; what we can learn from different theoretical perspectives which have been applied to this practice, especially concerning why organizations choose to disclose environmental, social or governance issues in their sustainability or integrated reports; the information stakeholders require; what happens to reporting after a crisis; broad determinants of disclosure; the consequences of disclosure; disclosures by public sector and not-for-profit organizations; the management control systems that underpin reporting; and the assurance of sustainability and integrated reporting.

The practice of sustainability and integrated reporting evolved because of society's need for information. Stakeholders have pressured organizations to disclose more social and environmental information. Organizations felt the need to explain their activities and to explain the reasons for negative events and how they dealt with the events; for example, major oil and chemical spills, or mining accidents (Deegan et al. 2002; De Villiers and Van Staden 2010). Disclosure frameworks evolved to enable organizations to claim that their disclosure complied with best practice. The Global Reporting Initiative has emerged as the most important framework provider (Dumay et al. 2010).

Integrated reporting centres on the understanding and communication of organizations' future value-creation plans, while paying particular attention to providing non-financial information, such as social and environmental disclosures, in an integrated way. The International Integrated Reporting Council (IIRC) promotes the evolving practice of integrated reporting (IIRC 2013).

Legitimacy theory explains organizations' voluntary sustainability and integrated reporting as a method to maintain and repair legitimacy to ensure continued access to resources. Organizations can use disclosures in an attempt to alter values and expectations, manage perceptions, or explain how they have adapted and conformed (Deegan 2002; De Villiers and Van Staden 2006).

Institutional theory posits that organizations react to the pressures they encounter by adopting rules and procedures, which are likely to converge for different organizations that occupy a similar position (Suchman 1995). Decoupling is where organizations do one thing and disclose another. By contrast, institutional work acknowledges that individuals (especially professionals) have the capacity to create, maintain and change institutions through various mechanisms (Meyer and Rowan 1977).

Managers know more about a company's operations than the owners (shareholders), a phenomenon known as information asymmetry, which is a key concept in agency theory (Jensen and Meckling 1976). Managers would generally be reluctant to reveal bad news voluntarily, as this could lead to loss of employment and/or reduced career prospects. Managers on share-based incentives are likely to disclose good news voluntarily to maximize their income. Managers are also likely to voluntarily disclose the reasons for bad news that is already known to the market (De Villiers and Van Staden 2011).

Investors need sustainability information in order to fully understand companies' future prospects, including future cash flows and the associated risks. Apart from private and institutional investors, investment professionals, such as analysts and financial advisors, also use the information (De Villiers and Van Staden 2010; De Klerk and De Villiers 2012; De Klerk et al. 2015). Managers, employees, auditors, customers, pressure groups (for example, environmental groups) and the media have all been shown to demand sustainability information. Stakeholders tend to rely on corporate sustainability and integrated reports for periodic assessments, referring to organizational websites for current information as important matters, such as an environmental crisis, unfold (Zhou et al. 2017).

Environmental and social challenges give rise to threats to legitimacy and prompt companies to adopt different reporting strategies to either maintain or repair legitimacy. The intention is not necessarily to mislead stakeholders but to reassure them that a company is managing an identified problem in the best interests of the relevant social group (Atkins et al. 2015).

There are several other determinants of sustainability and integrated reporting, including: company-specific features such as size, strategic attitude, organizational culture and financial performance; external forces (including industry characteristics and geographical location); and stakeholder pressures (Alrazi et al. 2015; McNally et al. 2017).

Better sustainability or integrated reporting provide more accountability; enhance legitimacy; improve profitability/performance; reduce information asymmetry; and enhance governance.

The public and not-for-profit sector form an important part of the global economy. As a result, many of the determinants of sustainability and integrated reporting discussed in the context of private sector are equally applicable to the public and not-for-profit sector (Farneti and Guthrie 2009; Dumay et al. 2010). This book has discussed the drivers of sustainability and integrated reporting in these sectors in more detail and dealt with the challenges involved (Kaur and Lodhia 2014).

The book examined the role played by sustainability management control systems (MCSs) in supporting sustainability reporting and sustainability strategy, proposing a sustainability MCS framework for both formal and informal controls. Different controls support each other and are used for operational and strategic purposes.

Finally, given that organizations use sustainability and integrated reports to legitimize themselves, stakeholders question the credibility of the reports. One of the ways to enhance credibility is to publish an external assurance report. This demand for assurance represents a business opportunity for the accounting profession (Maroun and Atkins 2015; Farooq and De Villiers 2017).

A discussion of the likely future of the practice of and research around sustainability accounting and integrated reporting follows.

The future of the practice of sustainability accounting and integrated reporting

Reporting

It is likely that sustainability reporting will increasingly be taken for granted as a necessity. Ever more companies and other organizations are providing sustainability disclosures, including smaller companies and organizations. For example, KPMG (2015) report that 92 percent of the 250 largest global companies, and 73 percent of the 100 largest companies in 45 countries, now report corporate responsibility information in their annual reports. The GRI guidelines are used by 60 percent of all companies that report corporate responsibility information, and in 72 percent of all stand-alone reports (since changed to standards) (KPMG 2015). KPMG (2015) also report that companies in emerging economies have played catch-up and have in many cases surpassed companies in the developed world in terms of corporate responsibility reporting; for example, the top reporting countries measured on the basis of the 100 largest companies in each country, were India (100 percent), Indonesia (99 percent), Malaysia (99 percent) and South Africa (99 percent), ahead of countries like the UK, France, Japan, Denmark, Norway and Sweden.

This mainstreaming of reporting is driven by the realization that sustainability matters for the identification and evaluation of risks and opportunities, which increases the demand for information from investors. The increased availability of information, which is driven by information technology and social media, is leading to a better-informed public, who is more aware of the fact that society is organized in different ways in different parts of the world, leading to growing expectations (King 2016). The democratization of information is also leading to increased knowledge about abuses in societies that expect better behaviour from organizations. This leads to increased social and environmental regulation, which in turn leads to increased costs of compliance and increased penalties for non-compliance. This makes it more likely that compliance/violation-related issues will have cost implications and affect future cash flows and risk. Given that normal accounting rules require the disclosure of material matters, because sustainability-related matters are now more likely to have cash flow implications, sustainability-related matters are more likely to find their way into reports through normal criteria (De Villiers and Van Staden 2011; Atkins et al. 2016). In addition, organizations try to portray themselves as responsible and use disclosure for this purpose. In several jurisdictions, direct disclosure regulations have followed changes in social norms, compelling social and environmental disclosure. For example, an EU directive that came into force in 2017 will affect all companies with more than 500 employees, and potentially the SME suppliers of such companies.

There is a demand for more social and environmental information, which is increasingly formalized in disclosure regulations. From organizations' point of view, there is a need to use disclosure to explain their responsible nature, the fact that their risks are being appropriately managed, and that they have sustainability opportunities that is being pursued. From the accounting profession's point of view, sustainability and integrated report implementation and improvement represent business opportunities. Therefore, it is probably safe to predict that sustainability and integrated reporting will increase in future and that the accounting profession will play a major role in assisting organizations to commence, improve and institutionalize reporting. This could be labelled a professionalization of the field of sustainability and integrated reporting (Dumay and Dai 2017).

Management control systems

As reporting is mainstreamed, the realization is bound to grow that reporting cannot be based on periodic procedures and a last-minute scramble for information to be included in reports. This will lead to more companies and organizations incorporating sustainability objectives into their management control systems. These systems will be used not only for the purpose of supporting the sustainability and integrated reporting but also to encourage behaviour that is consistent with the organization's sustainability objectives. The accounting profession is also likely to play a role in the promotion and implementation of sustainability and integrated reporting-related management control systems through their assurance practice. Sustainability assurance providers demand that evidence of reported matters be gathered, maintained, and controlled in similar fashion to accounting information. These demands for auditable evidence are likely to result in more institutionalization of sustainability and integrated reporting related management control systems.

Assurance

Organizations use sustainability and integrated reporting to influence public perceptions and portray themselves in the best possible light (Cho 2009). However, users of these reports are aware of the fact that organizations try to emphasize the positive and play down or explain away the negative; hence they do not always find reports credible. In turn, organizations respond with assurance to enhance the credibility of the reports (Cho et al. 2014). As reporting increases in prevalence and public knowledge about organizations' disclosure biases increases, the market for sustainability and integrated report assurance is bound to expand. KPMG (2015) reports that 63 percent of the 250 largest companies in the world, and 42 percent of the top 100 companies in 45 countries (i.e., 4,500 companies in total) now have their corporate responsibility reporting assured. These percentages have been increasing over time. About two-thirds of assurance services, both among the top 250 global and the top 100 companies in each country, are provided by major accounting firms (KPMG 2015).

Assurance is bound to become more institutionalized and standardized, and assurance providers are likely to increasingly offer an array of different assurance and management consulting services in the form of standardized packages (Maroun 2017).

The future of research into sustainability accounting and integrated reporting

Reporting

More interest in sustainability and integrated approaches is likely to lead to more research opportunities. Theory will be developed to provide more nuanced understandings of increasingly complex and non-standard settings. As the reporting practices become more established, research may begin to focus more on actual changes and processes than on speculative analysis pointing to impression management, reporting capture, and symbolic displays of compliance.

Management control systems

The increased prevalence of sustainability and integrated reporting-based management control systems will increase interest in the reasons for adoption, the benefits of adoption and what exactly constitutes best practice. The increased prevalence will ensure that there are appropriate case cites and will enable more case-based research.

Assurance

The increased practice of assurance will enable more case-based research, both from the point of view of the reporting organization and the assurance provider. The increased prevalence of assurance will also increase interest in the reasons for managers/companies to choose to have their reports assured, the different levels or types of assurance, the costs and benefits of different levels/ types of assurance, what exactly constitutes best assurance practice and how professional accountants and the accounting profession manage to shape the market for assurance to suit the profession.

Specific research opportunities

Even though it is impossible to foresee the many research opportunities that will present themselves, the following ideas and themes may be used as a starting point.

- The development of reporting bodies, such as the Global Reporting Initiative and the International Integrated Reporting Council.
- The influence of different groups in society on the reporting bodies.
- The influence of the reporting bodies on different groups in society.
- The development of the standards and frameworks of these reporting bodies, including a focus on who influences the agenda.
- Which aspects of reporting, control systems and assurance become taken for granted and why?
- How are sustainability accounting control systems different from (or similar to) control systems in general?
- How do capital markets react to different sustainability events, different sustainability disclosures, different formats of sustainability disclosures, the provision of an assurance statement and different kinds of assurance statements?
- Which capital market-related events lead to which kinds of changes in sustainability and integrated reporting?
- The difficulties involved in sustainability and integrated reporting implementation and improvement.
- What leads companies to stop (certain aspects of) sustainability and integrated reporting?

Conclusion

Sustainability accounting and integrated reporting practice and research have rapidly increased in prevalence and in perceived value. There is no indication of a slowing down in these trends. Now is a good time for organizations and individuals to get involved in all aspects of this dynamic field. Organizations which do not embrace social and environmental reporting, the control systems to support it and appropriate levels of assurance of these reports, are likely to find that they are viewed with suspicion in a world where these practices become taken for granted as an essential part of being granted a 'licence to operate'. In addition, companies preparing high-quality sustainability and integrated reports are likely to benefit through reduced cost of financing, with both shareholders and lenders adjusting their required returns. Individual managers could champion sustainability and integrated reporting as a 'safe' self-promotion strategy. The accounting profession can develop their practice by taking advantage of the new business opportunities that present themselves with the increased professionalization of this field. Finally, given these trends, researchers will be able to find more relevant questions, gain access to more data, and find a ready audience for sustainability accounting and integrated reporting research.

References

Alrazi, B., De Villiers, C. and Van Staden, C. J., 2015. A comprehensive literature review on, and the construction of a framework for, environmental legitimacy, accountability and proactivity. *Journal of Cleaner Production*, 102, 44–57.

Atkins, J. F., Barone, E., Maroun, W. and Atkins, B., 2016. Bee accounting and accountability in the UK. *In:* K. Atkins and B. Atkins, eds. *The business of bees: an integrated approach to bee decline and corporate responsibility.* Sheffield, UK: Greenleaf Publishers.

Atkins, J. F., Solomon, A., Norton, S. and Joseph, N. L., 2015. The emergence of integrated private reporting. *Meditari Accountancy Research*, 23 (1), 28–61.

Cho, C. H., 2009. Legitimation strategies used in response to environmental disaster: a French case study of total SA's Erika and AZF incidents. *European Accounting Review*, 18 (1), 33–62.

Cho, C. H., Michelon, G., Patten, D. M. and Roberts, R. W., 2014. CSR report assurance in the USA: an empirical investigation of determinants and effects. *Sustainability Accounting, Management and Policy Journal*, 5 (2), 130–148.

Deegan, C., 2002. Introduction: the legitimising effect of social and environmental disclosures – a theoretical foundation. *Accounting, Auditing & Accountability Journal*, 15 (3), 282–311.

Deegan, C., Rankin, M. and Tobin, J., 2002. An examination of the corporate social and environmental disclosures of BHP from 1983–1997. *Accounting, Auditing & Accountability Journal*, 15 (3), 312–343.

De Klerk, M. and De Villiers, C., 2012. The value relevance of corporate responsibility reporting: South African evidence. *Meditari Accountancy Research*, 20 (1), 21–38.

De Klerk, M., De Villiers, C. and van Staden, C., 2015. The influence of corporate social responsibility disclosure on share prices: evidence from the United Kingdom. *Pacific Accounting Review*, 27 (2), 208–228.

De Villiers, C. and Van Staden, C. J., 2006. Can less environmental disclosure have a legitimising effect? Evidence from Africa. *Accounting, Organizations and Society*, 31 (8), 763–781.

De Villiers, C. and Van Staden, C. J., 2010. Shareholders' requirements for corporate environmental disclosures: a cross country comparison. *The British Accounting Review*, 42 (4), 227–240.

De Villiers, C. and Van Staden, C. J., 2011. Where firms choose to disclose voluntary environmental information. *Journal of Accounting and Public Policy*, 30 (6), 504–525.

Dumay, J. and Dai, T., 2017. Integrated thinking as a cultural control? *Meditari Accountancy Research*, 25 (4).

Dumay, J., Guthrie, J. and Farneti, F., 2010. Gri sustainability reporting guidelines for public and third sector organizations. *Public Management Review*, 12 (4), 531–548.

Farneti, F. and Guthrie, J., 2009. Sustainability reporting by Australian public sector organisations: why they report. *Accounting Forum*, 33 (2), 89–98.

Farooq, M. B. and De Villiers, C., 2017. The market for sustainability assurance services: a comprehensive literature review and future avenues for research. *Pacific Accounting Review*, 29 (1), 79–106.

IIRC, 2013. *The international framework: integrated reporting*. Available: www.theiirc.org/wp-content/uploads/2013/12/13-12-08-THE-INTERNATIONAL-IR-FRAMEWORK-2-1.pdf [Accessed 1 October 2013].

Jensen, M. C. and Meckling, W. H., 1976. Theory of the firm: managerial behavior, agency costs and ownership structure. *Journal of Financial Economics*, 3 (4), 305–360.

Kaur, A. and Lodhia, S. K., 2014. The state of disclosures on stakeholder engagement in sustainability reporting in Australian local councils. *Pacific Accounting Review*, 26 (1/2), 54–74.

King, M., 2016. Comments on: *integrated reporting, GARI Conference*, Henley on Thames, UK, 23 October.

KPMG, 2015. *The KPMG survey of corporate responsibility reporting 2015*. Available: https://home.kpmg.com/xx/en/home/insights/2015/11/kpmg-international-survey-of-corporate-responsibility-reporting-2015.html [Accessed 17 May 2017].

Maroun, W., 2017. Assuring the integrated report: insights and recommendations from auditors and preparers. *The British Accounting Review*, 49 (3), 329–346.

Maroun, W. and Atkins, J., 2015. *The challenges of assuring integrated reports: views from the South African auditing community*. London: The Association of Chartered Certified Accountants.

McNally, M.-A., Cerbone, D. and Maroun, W., 2017. Exploring the challenges of preparing an integrated report. *Meditari Accountancy Research*, 25 (4).

Meyer, J. W. and Rowan, B., 1977. Institutionalized organizations: formal structure as myth and ceremony. *American Journal of Sociology*, 83 (2), 340–363.

Suchman, M. C., 1995. Managing legitimacy: strategic and institutional approaches. *The Academy of Management Review*, 20 (3), 571–610.

Zhou, S., Simnett, R. and Green, W., 2017. Does integrated reporting matter to the capital market? *Abacus*, 53 (1), 94–132.